praise for magic of the otherworld

"*The Magic of the Otherworld* is a delight to read. In clear prose with skillful use of language, Morpheus Ravenna has written a valuable handbook for the practitioner and scholar alike. Her writing is rich with imagery and grounded in thorough research as well as in her own experiences. Of particular note is the range of history, lore, and culture upon which she draws… Each chapter contains examples of the techniques and methods she describes, illuminated by personal stories that demonstrate how to apply them. Throughout, Morpheus addresses the context for and above all the ethics of using these magics, with insight and clarity. This is a solid volume and a valuable addition to any library."

—Barbara Cormack, MA, MLS, Coru Cathubodua Priesthood

"From lead curse tablets at the bottom of chthonic hot springs to king-deposing rites chanted from the hilltops, Morpheus offers grounded guidance for the beginning practitioner and new insights for the experienced sorcerer alike. Firmly rooted in research, tested through extensive experience, and ever situated within an animist and relational worldview, *The Magic of the Other-world* is a potent and much-needed contribution to the spiritual arsenal of collective liberation."

—Heathen Chinese, writer

"This might truly be one of the best and most thorough books on magic and animistic polytheism in recent years, especially from a Celtic perspective. Morpheus Ravenna has managed to create a massive treasure trove of practice replete with a spirit-work oriented mindset that will enrich both beginners and experienced practitioners. Wholeheartedly recommended!"

—Stefanos Chelydoreus, writer and creator of the
Greek Witch and the Equine Serpent

"Another invaluable resource on the shelves of many pagans and polytheists. And what witch has not longed for a book on effective, accessible sorcery with precedents for its contents set in the textual history and lore of Proto-Indo-European (PIE) cultures in which our gods were venerated? Morpheus continues to build bridges from ancient animists to present-day practitioners who want effective magic that is enveloped in a spirit of reciprocity and right relationship … It is as close to in-person teaching and mentorship as one can acquire in a book. For new practitioners, it is a map complete with guideposts, tips, and essential protections. For those who have been around a while, it is a road to deepening our work and finding a rhythm again."

—Chris Hippe, cofounder of Coinnle Bodba and priest of the Morrigan

"*The Magic of the Otherworld* effectively weaves a diverse range of source materials with practical experience into a compelling, practical work. Morpheus synthesizes this complex and at times contradictory body of material into a coherent, easy to follow guide that will inspire new and experienced practitioners for years to come."

—Ryan Smith, author of *The Way of Fire & Ice*

"A beautiful text which provides a solid educational framework for the modern practitioner of magic based on the Celtic traditions. It is very well researched and evidences each area of practice through a close reading of historical source material. The author then also gives some compelling personal anecdotes of her practice which also illustrate her own deep experiential explorations of the subject … A very welcome addition to a growing body of literature that serves to reawaken the practical living of indigenous Celtic spirituality for the times we live in today."

—John-Paul Patton, author of *The Poet's Ogam*

THE MAGIC OF THE
Otherworld

THE MAGIC OF THE
OTHERWORLD

MODERN SORCERY
from the
WELLSPRING
of
CELTIC
TRADITIONS

MORPHEUS RAVENNA

Llewellyn Publications • Woodbury, Minnesota

FIRST EDITION
First Printing, 2023

Book design by M. Brasington
Cover art by Morpheus Ravenna
Cover design by Shannon McKuhen
Editing by Marjorie Otto
Interior art by Morpheus Ravenna

Llewellyn Publications is a registered trademark of Llewellyn Worldwide Ltd.

Library of Congress Cataloging-in-Publication Data (Pending)
ISBN: 978-0-7387-7280-6

Llewellyn Publications
A Division of Llewellyn Worldwide Ltd.
2143 Wooddale Drive
Woodbury, MN 55125-2989
www.llewellyn.com

Printed in the United States of America

© Matthew Wong

About the Author

Morpheus Ravenna is a genderfluid sorcerer, artist, Celtic polytheist spirit worker, and writer. Sí is a dedicant of the Morrígan, with a practice rooted in animism, folk magic, and Celtic polytheism. Sí has a love of monsters, Otherworldly creatures, haunted places, and hidden lore. A lifelong polytheist, hir childhood spiritual experiences were in a yogic tradition rooted in Hinduism. Sí found hir home in European witchcraft traditions, beginning with training and initiation in the Anderson Feri tradition, and has practiced devotional Celtic polytheism and the magical arts for over twenty-five years. Sí co-founded and serves as a priest in the Coru Cathubodua Priesthood.

Morpheus is the author of *The Book of the Great Queen: The Many Faces of the Morrígan from Ancient Legends to Modern Devotions*, and the Shield-maiden blog. Sí has also published pieces in journals and anthologies, including *Harp, Club, and Cauldron*; *By Blood, Bone, and Blade*; and *Walking the Worlds* journal.

With hir spouse, a haunted cat, and an adorable Corgi, Morpheus resides in the East Bay area of California, where sí makes hir living as a tattoo artist, with a passion for ritual tattoos and design inspired by ancient art. Sí also creates devotional artworks and sorcerous crafts in a variety of media. When sí is not creating, sí also practices medieval armored combat and is very fond of spears. Sí strives to bring a queer, feminist, anti-racist, and decolonizing ethos to everything sí does. Morpheus can be reached through hir website at bansheearts.com.

To all those who have taught me—
the living, the ancestors, and the Others.

contents

Rituals and Workings

Figures and Tables

acknowledgments

First and always, thanks to my beloved spouse, Brennos, for unwavering gracious support and encouragement. Honor belongs also to the many co-conspirators who have joined me in exploring, experimenting, studying, lore-dorking, and taking risks in the study of magic and helped me to develop these techniques: John Medellín, Vyviane Armstrong, Barbara Cormack, Izzy Swanson, Caróg Liath, Marjorie Coffey, Vali Jenkins, Victoria Hendrix, Joe Perri, River Devora, Areïon, Devin Antheus, Segomâros Widugeni, Viducus Brigantici filius, among many other friends and teachers over the years. Gratitude to all the members of the Coru Cathubodua Priesthood, past and present, for creating a fellowship of learning and reverence within which my studies have flourished. And finally, to the many spirits, ancestors, and gods who have walked with me, for the guidance, protection, teaching, and humbling inspiration: with you goes my love, honor, and gratitude without end.

I am only ever a passionate student, and it has been my honor to learn with the very best of companions beside me. I hope to always continue learning.

Foreword

There has never been a time without magic. Humans have been enacting practices we could believably label "magical" since the dawn of our species. We live in a relational, shifting world—we impact and are impacted by our environment, we learn from those who came before, and we pass our knowing on to those who will continue past our time here. But what is magic? My quick and dirty definition of magic is it is the art of influencing probabilities, tipping the scales of luck and chance just enough to make it more likely for our desired outcomes to be achieved. Magic is not a guarantee, nor is it a replacement for practical, mundane work. But in an uncertain and unpredictable world, magic gives us a way to access the help of unseen forces, giving us a way to try and tip the odds in our favor.

In the modern Western world, many folks no longer have unbroken lineages of reciprocity and ancestral, traditional, community-tested protocols for interacting with the unseen forces in their current and local environments. And many folks are acutely feeling that absence. Some try to remedy this by seeking out magical or religious traditions that still maintain that wisdom. Some seek to recreate those ways through studying traditions of the past, or through trial and error experimentation. Some steal other people's practices and folkways. In the absence of a foundational magical framework and way of understanding the unseen world around us (or in the absence of the guidance of elders from living traditions with grounding in those foundations and knowledge of the protocols necessary to navigate and maintain respectful, reciprocal relationships with the unseen world), many folks find their experiments to be piecemeal at best, or not as effective as they feel they could be. And there can be real and sometimes lingering dangers for doing magic "wrong."

I have been an Oloricha, priest, and spirit worker for many years, holding traditional initiations in several magical and religious lineages. When I first began the Strong Roots and Wide Branches pan-polytheist learning community, my main focus was on getting polytheists more comfortably established in grounded, well fleshed-out religious practices and relationships. But magic and religion, while tightly related and sometimes overlapping to the point of being indistinguishable, are still two different disciplines, with distinct goals and intentions. While religion generally focuses on maintaining right relationships with the seen and unseen world around us, magic seeks to shape and change the world itself.

The techniques and frameworks presented here are powerful, placing power and responsibility into the hands of the practitioner while holding firmly to principles of reciprocity and respect with the Otherworlds and the denizens that dwell there. Magic requires both intent (knowing and taking responsibility for the changes you wish to see in the world) and power, which can be augmented, directed, and supported through consensual, respectful partnerships with gods, spirits, and the living world around us. This work is deeply embedded in the principles of right relationship, enabling practitioners to stand in their own power while respectfully sharing, borrowing, bartering, and earning power from the web in which our lives are woven.

The Magic of the Otherworld provides a practical, modern roadmap for effectively working real magic. It is shaped and inspired by traditional Celtic ways of understanding and navigating unseen forces, and keyed to modern practitioners embedded in the complex and shifting living world around us. This book is a treasure trove of practical and useful magical tools, along with a comprehensive foundation for understanding and building balanced, effective magical practices. Morpheus brings a deep reverence and respect to the study and practice of modern, Celtic-embedded and inspired sorcery. From the basics of purification practices (and why such practices are important) to the nuts and bolts of magical strategies to rolling your sleeves up and getting to work, this book provides a comprehensive and respectful approach to partnering with the potent unseen forces that know and shape our world, and to participate in that shaping.

I have known Morpheus for many years, sí is someone I feel blessed to have as a peer and friend. We have collaborated on projects, done shared community organizing, co-led community rituals, and supported one another's work in a variety of ways. Morpheus is a skilled magic worker and priest with a broad and varied knowledge base and decades of magical experience. I have watched hir grow and develop the foundations of this work over many years. But this work is not just theories on developing a practice; these are practical methods, best practices, and living protocols that Morpheus regularly uses in hir own practice. And as someone who has done magical workings alongside Morpheus and hir community, I can attest to the effectiveness of these techniques. I am so delighted to see this body of work being made available to our communities.

Blessings on the work,
River Devora

introduction

The Celtic worlds are endlessly compelling. From the sinuous, spiraling, and interlaced art forms that seem to move as if inspirited, to the richly told sagas peppered with curious lore of druid rituals and poetic incantations, to the mysterious artifacts deposited in liminal dark waters that hold records of secret spells and vengeful curses—it is a wellspring of magic that never runs dry. For the practitioner of sorcery, there is always something more to learn, a deeper layer of lore to tease out.

This book seeks to offer a point of entry for a Celtic approach to magical praxis. It presents an interconnected set of magical and spiritual techniques rooted in and inspired by Celtic cultural traditions. It is an animist system, which sees and seeks relationship with the spirits that dwell in and enliven all things. It is polytheistic, weaving relationship with the gods into its approach to ritual.

1

And it is built on a cosmology that centers the Otherworld, the hidden but ever-present spirit realm from which the forces that enliven the world flow. It is a magic of connection and relationship with the Otherworld.

The practices I write about here are not specifically drawn from any one of the Celtic culture hearths. My practice draws from multiple different cultural roots. It drinks from the wells of ancient Gallic and Gallo-Roman practices, from Celtic Britain and Ireland, from medieval Irish literary tradition and early modern Irish and Scottish folk practice, and more. This is not a reconstructionist approach to magical and spiritual practice—I make no claims that the practices I teach in these pages represent any given part of the past. This is a contemporary approach to sorcery that has emerged in my own work, inspired by Celtic traditions, but also informed by modern witchcraft and folk magic and the time and place in which I live.

My writing on this subject emerges from a lifelong fascination with Celtic magic and religion and their unfolding in my own polytheist magical practice. The foundations of my practice are twofold: witchcraft and Celtic polytheism. Early training in an initiatory witchcraft tradition led me to the Morrígan; my devotion to her became dedication and led me into Celtic polytheism. That devotion also taught me to drink deeply from the wellsprings of lore, a habit that intensified with the research I undertook for my first book, *The Book of the Great Queen*.

In my studies of history, literature, myth, and folklore, I find myself constantly drawn to the glimpses of ritual and magical practices that appear in these sources. I latch onto these fragments like a crow gathering shiny objects. To me, they are like pieces of a puzzle, and my mind turns them this way and that till a hidden picture emerges. I take an experimental approach in my magical practice: What if I tried it this way? Combined this bit of lore with this bit of folk custom? Do these fragments of ritual fit together? Over the years, this experimentation and play, often practiced together with friends and comrades, have nourished an adventurous and robust practice of sorcery. This book is the fruit of that practice.

Before diving into Celtic sorcery itself, we need to talk about what the term Celtic means—and what it doesn't.

тне celts–a very brief introduction

The word *Celtic* has been massively, and very casually, overused in popular culture to refer to everything from ethnicity and nationality to aesthetic, personal, religious, or spiritual identity. Properly, *Celtic* designates a family of cultures specifically linked based on shared language roots and similar material cultures. That is to say, where the term has concrete meaning is with reference to Celtic languages, both historical and living, and certain groups of historical artifacts displaying a recognizable artistic style. The groups of people thought to have produced these artifacts and to have spoken one of these Celtic languages are generally referred to as "Celtic peoples" or "the Celts."

The material culture now called Celtic flourished from the late Bronze Age through the Iron Age, apparently originating in the Danube basin regions around France, Austria, Switzerland, and parts of Germany.[01] From here, Celtic cultural influences spread across a large area of Europe. Areas of Celtic influence—as measured by the existence of Celtic-styled material culture—extended throughout France, Britain, Ireland, and into parts of the Iberian Peninsula, Germany, northern Italy, the Balkans, and Anatolia.[02] Its influence continued into the medieval period, as seen in the Celtic ornamental style found adorning many manuscripts and other medieval treasures. It can, however, be a mistake to identify an ethnicity just by material artifacts since these may be abundantly traded and transported. Also, social processes often lead to certain cultural motifs or artistic styles becoming fashionable as marks of status and exotic wealth and adopted outside the ethnic groups they originate from.

Language is a much more accurate marker of culture, and language analysis provides some additional detail and complexity to the picture of Celtic history. The Celtic languages are classified into several branches: the Goidelic branch (sometimes also called the Q-Celtic branch) includes Irish Gaelic, Scottish Gaelic, and Manx. The Brittonic branch (also called the P-Celtic branch) includes Welsh, Breton, and Cornish, as well as some now-extinct

---

01. Ó hÓgáin, *The Celts: A History,* 2–3.

02. Ó hÓgáin, *The Celts: A History,* 16.

ancient Brittonic languages such as Pictish. Both these branches are generally grouped as the Insular Celtic languages, meaning the Celtic languages of the western islands off mainland Europe—Ireland and Britain and the smaller islands around them. Historically, another group also existed, the Continental Celtic languages, spoken in Gaul and other Continental areas and now extinct as living languages.[03] Theories about the historical relationships between these languages and what is now identified as Celtic material culture are still contested and developing, but current findings lean toward the idea that early Celtic-speaking people brought their language from the Continent to the western islands in the Bronze or early Iron Age, language that developed into Irish and the other Goidelic languages. A second wave of influence from the Continent later brought what became the Brittonic languages into Britain. Alternately, some scholars have proposed that Celtic language and culture emerged in the Insular region not through population movement but through processes like cultural diffusion and exchange.[04]

What all this detail means is that Celtic cultural influences were conveyed through multiple channels—by the sharing of material culture as well as by the movement and mixing of peoples speaking different Celtic languages. To oversimplify by quite a bit, it means that the earliest recognizable Celtic cultures came from the Continent, took root at a very early stage in Ireland, and continued to spread through Britain as well as other areas of Continental Europe. In each of these regions, the presence and influence of Celtic-speaking peoples and their culture was interwoven with preexisting populations with their own languages and cultures.

An important lesson to take from this is that Celtic cultures are not interchangeable over time and geography. It is not very meaningful to talk about Celtic culture as if it were a single stream of culture and tradition. There has never been a singular Celtic identity or culture and certainly not a singular Celtic pantheon or unified Celtic mythology. These were tribally organized societies with localized traditions and customs, distinct languages, and dif-

---

03. Stifter, *Sendgoídelc: Old Irish for Beginners*, 2.

04. Waddell, "Celts, Celticisation, and the Irish Bronze Age," 164–166.

ferent regional influences. Most of the peoples now labeled as Celtic groups would likely not have identified as such—they would have identified as a member of their tribe or kingdom: the Ulaid, the Laigin, the Iceni, the Brigantes, the Aedui, etc. While trade, travel, and cultural exchange were significant between the various Celtic tribes and cultures and those surrounding them, these movements represent fractions of populations—textures woven into the traditions and experiences of a people—they do not mean that all these Celtic cultures were unitary or can be treated as one.

THE SOURCES

The sources available for studying Celtic pagan traditions present their own challenges. The pagan Celtic peoples of the ancient period were nonliterary— theirs were oral traditions. Writing was used in a limited way for inscriptions in some places, but poems, tales, myths, religious beliefs, and other core aspects of tradition were not written down. According to some historical sources, this was intentional: the Continental Celts were said to disdain the use of writing for sacred knowledge, believing it to be profane and preferring to maintain an oral tradition.[05] Thus, there is no native pre-Christian Celtic written literature extant in primary form.

Gaul and most of Britain were conquered by the Roman Empire and their cultures profoundly transformed starting in the last century BCE, prior to any widespread adoption of the custom of written literature. Some observations of Celtic cultures were written by Greek and Roman authors of the time, but this evidence is very fragmentary and problematic. All of these sources are secondary in nature, since they are not the product of the Celtic peoples themselves but written through the eyes of people from other cultures with their own agendas for what they recorded. Much of this material is also in the form of tertiary later works, copied or reinterpreted from the lost works of Posidonius, a Greek geographer and historian who traveled extensively and wrote ethnographic accounts of the Gauls based on direct observations.[06] Since his

---

05. Caesar, *The Gallic War*, 339.

06. Zeidler, "Cults of the 'Celts': A New Approach to the Interpretation of the Religion of Iron Age Cultures," 175.

original writings are lost, it remains impossible to say how much this ethnographic material was altered through this historical telephone game.

Some pre-Christian traditions of the Celtic peoples can be found in later literature. Ireland provides the richest source for this literature. As Ireland was not conquered by Rome, there was not significant Roman influence on the culture there. Ireland remained a pagan and strongly Celtic culture held until the arrival of Christianity in about the fifth century CE.[07] Christian conversion brought the custom of recording religious and cultural knowledge in books, and since there was no forced conquest, genocide, or major cultural destruction (as there had been in Gaul and Britain) between the pagan period and the advent of Christian literacy, the early Irish manuscripts represent the closest approach to documentation of a Celtic literature. They are, however, still heavily distanced secondary sources with respect to Celtic paganism.

The people writing these manuscripts were Irish, and in that sense still participants in a Celtic heritage, but they were not pagan; they were Christians and for the most part this work was done by scholars and monks operating within Christian religious orders and often in service to royal patrons. Much detail from the pre-Christian oral tradition appears to have been retained, but the material was also intentionally recontextualized for a Christian society and for the contemporary culture, politics, and interests of the time. Even the earliest Irish manuscripts in existence were written several centuries after conversion to Christianity. Conversion began in the fifth century CE, and while it took some time to spread throughout the island, by the time the earliest surviving literary manuscripts were produced in the ninth century, the island as a whole was converted at least in its ruling classes, even if elements of pagan custom may have been retained among the common folk.[08] Of these manuscripts, some of the contents can be earlier than manuscript date, with the earliest material dated to the seventh century based on linguistic analysis—still two centuries after the start of conversion. The Welsh medieval manuscript tradition also preserves some similar material from Celtic Britain,

---

07. Ó hÓgáin, *The Sacred Isle: Belief and Religion in Pre-Christian Ireland*, 184–186.

08. Williams, *Ireland's Immortals: A History of the Gods of Irish Myth*, 4–6.

though its sources are later and even more fragmentary due to the intervening influence of the Romans.

As I mentioned, there is also the survival of pagan elements of folk culture within and through the Christian period. Premodern and modern folklore collections and ethnographies of the living cultures that have inherited Celtic roots often reveal significant strands of tradition, custom, and beliefs that sometimes appear to be survivals of paganism. It may seem unlikely that any remnant of Celtic cultural elements could survive after a millennium and a half of Church dominance, waves of population movement, and absorption of new culture layers. It is not always easy or even possible to establish a line of connection between these early modern and modern sources and the pre-Christian past, but the parallels are often quite strong. Folk traditions are resilient and often quite conservative, even through the experience of being colonized.

Archaeology can fill out the picture with additional physical detail, providing a record of material culture and sometimes evidence of magical practices. The interpretation of cultural insight from physical remains is always tenuous but can also serve to confirm or detail things mentioned in textual sources. It is in the bringing together of these different forms of evidence that a study of Celtic beliefs and practices and magics becomes fully fleshed.

A final note about sources: Because this work draws on early material from a range of time and from historical periods before standardization of spelling, you will see variations in spelling of words and concepts from earlier languages. For example, the Irish manuscript corpus spans works from the Old Irish period, through Middle and Early Modern Irish. When I'm writing in my own words about a concept, I will typically stick with a single spelling, usually drawn from however it is most frequently represented in the sources. However, direct quotations from sources will retain their original spelling variations.

celtic cosmologies and worldviews

My approach to Celtic sorcery blends elements drawn from all these sources and across the breadth of Celtic cultures. I'm comfortable with this blending because I try to practice it with care and respect for the source cultures I'm drawing from. I don't believe cultural purity is a good value to strive for. In the first place, cultural purity is a fiction; the ancients adopted magical, ritual, and spiritual practices along with all kinds of other things from cultures they came into contact with and made them their own. The closer we look at any of the source cultures, the more we find that they were never a pure, unmixed cultural stream. Irish tradition as it exists today is layered with pre-Celtic, Celtic, Viking, and Anglo-Norman aspects. The ogham made their way across Ireland, Britain, the Hebrides, and Iceland. The Celtic magical inscriptions of Gaul were written in Lepontic and Greek as well as Latin, all scripts with Mediterranean roots. Cultural purity never existed, and there's no reason why practitioners of Celtic magic should strive for it now.

What does matter in a blended practice is to pay respect and honor to source, and to strive for right relationship to source. Every tradition and practice this work draws on emerged from a particular time and place, from the experience of a specific flowering of people, culture, and geography. The holy powers we engage with are rooted in these historical, cultural, and geographic realities as well. The goal here is to hold a way of working with these traditions that weaves them together in the way that folk cultures have always done, while acknowledging their individual roots and cultural identities, honoring where they come from and what makes them unique and distinctive.

With this understanding, let's look at some core themes that resurface again and again within Celtic sources that will inform this work. These can be thought of as themes emerging from commonalities of experience within Celtic cultures—varying in their details and textures but underpinned by some continuities in worldview and cultural frame.

The Inspirited Otherworld

Celtic magical paradigms are rooted in a cosmological understanding of the physical world as constantly in relationship with an inspirited Otherworld. The Otherworld is the source of animating forces that move in the world and is the home of unseen powers, such as gods, spirits, fairy folk, and the dead. Magic is accessed primarily through relationship with Otherworldly powers that may be personified differently in different contexts. This Otherworld is often framed as overlapping our own, accessible anywhere but most especially at liminal places where different spaces meet, such as the entrances to caves, earthen mounds, or tombs, or watery places such as rivers, lakes, bogs, and the sea. Looking closely at the Otherworld, particularly as described in the literary traditions of Ireland and Wales, it becomes clear that it is really more a case of Otherworlds—there are many spaces, landscapes, and worlds accessed within the Otherworld realms, and they are peopled with many different groups of Otherworldly beings.

The Three Realms

The architecture of the cosmos as understood by Celtic cultures tends toward a triune pattern—as do so many things. This is often described as the three worlds or three realms. Among the Continental Celts, it appears that the cosmology had a vertical architecture, with the three worlds comprising the living or physical world, the celestial Otherworld above, and the chthonic Otherworld below. The Irish seems to wrap this up a little differently, with the three worlds of land, sea, and sky being seen less in a vertical architecture and more as parts of a mutually interpenetrating, nested whole. Here there are still some parallels between the land as the realm of the living world, the sky as the celestial realm, and the sea as the deep realm—not an underworld in the Continental sense but an Otherworld accessed through the deep places.

This architecture—the living world and the Otherworld made up of bright celestial realms and deep chthonic realms—informs my approach to magical work. There are distinct, though sometimes overlapping, methods that apply to working with each of the realms. For example, from the living world we can work directly with physical, living substances: the plants, animals and products of animals, the land itself and all it offers us. Toward the sky and celestial realm, we can send prayer and petition to high gods, working with breath, voice, fire, and smoke to stir the weather, the sky, and the beings that dwell there. With the realms of the deep, we may call on the spirits of the dead, chthonic deities, and other subterranean powers, sending votive offerings into water or the darkness of cave and tomb.

The Three Worlds

Animism

Another important principle that moves through all aspects of this practice is animism. Animism is the recognition of life and intelligence in all things around us and the belief that it is possible to enter into relationship with the spirits that inhabit everything. It is an understanding that the world itself is alive and inspirited. Animism is implied in many aspects of the polytheistic Celtic cultures, from the naming of landforms and waters for beings of story, to the pervasive presence of gods, ancestors, fairies, and Otherworldly spirits of every kind. Celtic magics are thoroughly rooted in this animistic worldview and in cultivating spirit relationships. This practice seeks to leave behind the modern concept of the solitary magician working magic as a kind of technical achievement of the will, and instead enter into a way of life in which magic is a function of the powers we cultivate through relationship with the forces, beings, and spirits that animate all the worlds around us.

Ethical Considerations

When folks began asking me to publish Celtic sorcery material as a book, I was hesitant at first. In part, this is because the most often-requested topic was how to curse. I felt, and still feel, considerably conflicted about putting techniques for aggressive magic into a book for public consumption. I have directly experienced how impactful these magics can be; in a sense, in sharing them, I'm offering a suite of weapons. This brings a moral obligation to be mindful about how they are used. I can't control how you, the reader, may use this material, but it's my hope that I can encourage you to bring a deeply considered ethical framework to your practice, and to always try to be someone who punches up and not down.

Cóir and Justice

To begin, it is important to understand that this material arises from cultural frameworks that hold the concept of justice at their center. Celtic conceptions of justice arise from a cosmological worldview that sees the existence of a right order. Irish tradition expresses this sense of a right order in the concept of *cóir*, an Irish term that translates as "rightness, order, or justice."[09] It is the rightness of things, the sense of natural justice that should prevail, the set of conditions as they should be, where all beings have what is needful and prosperity is shared by all. An injustice represents a disruption to *cóir*, and this creates a spiritual imbalance in the world that wants to right itself. This is not to say that justice requires no action; *cóir* isn't assumed to right itself automatically. What it means is that when you act in the interests of justice and of restoring the rightness of things, *cóir* supports you. It represents a power that is accessible to the practitioner and functions as the motive force of magic.

An ethical approach to magic based on *cóir* requires finely honed discernment and moral sense. It's necessary to develop a keen eye for the difference between justice and vengeance, and between restitution and punishment. These differences matter because they determine to what extent a magical working is in alignment with *cóir*, and to what extent that working will be powered and upheld by it. These techniques are at their best and strongest when they are used in the service of justice. On the other hand, we can expect them to turn against us if we misappropriate them for unjust purposes.

How do you determine where you stand with respect to the principle of justice, and whether you are supported by *cóir* in your stance? There are two measures I would encourage everyone to consider when thinking about this: agency and power.

Agency and Consent

The principle of agency teaches that every being has agency that must be respected. This includes ourselves, and it also includes nonhuman and incorporeal beings. Agency is the ability to make one's own choices and the right not to have this ability stripped away. This is what is at work in the concept of consent. Most of us understand this intuitively when it comes to material action: people must have a right to consent to anything that is done to them, unless they have forfeited that right by causing harm or violating the consent of another. This

---

09. Royal Irish Academy, "EDIL 2019: An Electronic Dictionary of the Irish Language, Based on the Contributions to a Dictionary of the Irish Language, s.v. *cóir*." See also: Carmody and Thompson, "Some questions answered by the Story Archaeologists."

same logic applies to magic. It directs us to seek consent for any working we do that will directly impact another, unless it is in self-defense, or at the request of another in their defense.

Thinking about agency also brings up the question of standing. You might question whether you have standing that gives you a right to take action in a situation. It's my belief that the ethical considerations here aren't especially different from those that apply to nonmagical situations. As a bystander on the street, if you witnessed harm taking place, would you consider it your duty to intervene to the extent you could? To offer first aid and care to an injured person? To try to block, restrain, or disable an attacker? Similar ethics and principles of consent govern magical intervention.

This is not an invitation to appoint ourselves as knights in shining armor with a savior complex. When considering magical intervention, it's important to center the agency of those most directly impacted by the situation, just as you would not treat an injured person without their consent, unless it is to save a life where they are beyond ability to give consent. When a harm has been done, it's the harmed party whose voice should be heard. Sometimes, they may choose to refuse help.

Power and Solidarity

The principle of power provides a lens to help us identify who is in need of justice, and therefore where to direct action. Who has more power in a given situation or context? How is power flowing; is it shared, or is it being concentrated in certain hands? Who is being disempowered and is most in need of solidarity? In the worldview centered on *cóir*, justice is served by standing with those most in need or against whom there has been an injustice. When you take up the practice of magic, it should be focused on where power is needed most in order to move toward equality and liberation from oppression. This is in line with the general fact that witchcraft and magic have historically often been tools of the oppressed and marginalized to push back against the powerful. The powerful don't need our help.

Magical ethics are inherently political because politics is the flow of power among people. We can't insulate ourselves from the systems we live within.

Part of thinking about power is also considering our own social position, and the kinds of power and privilege we do and don't have access to based on that. How are we using our social position? What social and spiritual forces does it align us with and what do we want to do about that? In talking about magical action, people often worry over the consequences of taking action. But we need to also consider the consequences of *not* acting. Attempting to take an "apolitical" position is still political—it simply means choosing to remain in alignment with dominant systems that uphold the status quo. When we take up the tools of magical power, we take on a responsibility to direct our impact where it will bring greater justice into the world.

Action and Risk

Most anywhere aggressive magic comes up, someone will bring up beliefs that practicing baneful magic is worse for the practitioner than the target, that it inevitably leads to "backlash," or that curses will "rebound" on the caster. So, let's talk about risk. It's true that magical action entails risk, but I think popular beliefs often misunderstand how the risks actually apply.

To return to our *cóir* framework for thinking about magic, it teaches that injustice is a transgression of right order. This creates a tension in the fabric of things, and this tension wants to be set right. It is like a coiled spring that seeks a point of release of the tension created by injustice. If you are working in the service of justice—to right a wrong, restore agency, heal a harm, or equalize the flow of power—this tension spring-loads your magical work. If, on the other hand, you are working against justice and at the expense of others, then you're exacerbating that tension, and this can absolutely manifest in a painful backlash, as *cóir* seeks to right itself, and must do so at cross purposes to you.

Another kind of backlash can arise as a result of confrontation. Magical action that confronts or challenges other individuals, groups, or institutions will run into their magical protections or spirit systems. Even institutions that aren't overtly magical can have spiritual forces that protect them just by virtue of the collective power they wield. The same can be true of powerful individuals whether or not they actively practice magic. These protective forces can lash back when acted upon. If this happens to you, it doesn't mean that aggressive magic is inevitably dangerous to do. It just means that the person or group you went up against had stronger magics than you were prepared for, and it's time to up your game! Managing risk in magic is about considering what moral and spiritual authority you can call on for support, maintaining right relationship to *cóir*, being smart and intentional about protections, and choosing your battles with care.

It is also about working in collectives and leveraging solidarity. The riskier work you take on, the more important it becomes to deepen your support, both human and nonhuman, so that you are ready for the challenges you take on. And this brings me to another observation about risk: careful exposure to risk can enhance magic. Taking risks in the service of acting on an issue that matters to you demonstrates commitment, and this can result in greater commitment from spirits and divine powers in support of your work. You can think of it as showing them that you have skin in the game. For every issue that you might be doing magical work on, there exists a group of spirits whose stories and experiences relate to that issue or injustice—the ancestors and tutelary spirits of that particular struggle. Your willingness to face risk in order to take action on that issue invites the support and protection of that collective of spirits. Your work can become a votive act in which they have a vested interest in your success.

Sorcerer's Toolkit
ETHICS AND RISK ASSESSMENT

To help you in being prepared for magical work, I've organized these concepts into a set of questions. You can use this list when considering taking magical action, to help you assess where you stand ethically, and what kinds of risks and consequences you might need to be ready for.

Consider your situation with respect to *cóir* and the concept of natural justice. What is the cause for magical action? What need are you addressing? What impact are you seeking to achieve? Is the impact proportional to the need? What is the disruption to *cóir*, and will your work restore or exacerbate that rupture?

Consider the agency of each person in the situation. Whose need will be addressed by your action, and do you have their consent to engage? If they can't consent because they are unconscious, inaccessible, or not living, what gives you standing to engage on this? Who will be impacted or targeted by your work? If someone will be impacted without consent, what justifies your intervention in their agency? That is, have they earned this through their own actions?

Consider the power dynamics of the situation. Who or what holds the power in this situation? Think about different kinds of power: social, political, institutional, material, spiritual. How will your action intersect with existing power differentials? Who may be empowered or disempowered by your intervention? Is the action liberatory? Think about your own position. How will you be applying your own power here, and does that square with your values?

Consider any risks that may arise from your action. Will your work bring you into conflict with individuals or groups? Are there spiritual, social, or institutional forces that protect them? What powers or skills might you need to be ready to face? Are there spirits and powers related to the struggle you're engaged in who might be able to support you? If so, have you begun entering into relationship with them?

Consider this set of questions as a starting point. It's an important exercise to undertake as you contemplate situations in which you may want to take magical action. Going through such an assessment can help you identify angles of risk, or unintended impacts you might not have considered, which will give you the opportunity to plan for those issues. Sometimes, this type of exercise can help you see when you might be out of your depth and need to take a step back and do more preparation, or join up in support of others who have more direct connection to a cause. You may find other questions come up that I didn't include here, from which you can develop your own protocol for thinking about magical ethics. After some practice, you may find that you don't need to use a set list of questions, as you become used to thinking about all these angles organically as you consider any magical work.

using this book

Each of the chapters in this book delves into a major domain of Celtic magic and sorcery: spiritual hygiene, protection, spirit alliances, incantatory poetics, sigils and divination, necromancy, binding, justice magic and cursing, and war magic. You may be particularly drawn to certain subjects more than others and feel inclined to jump to those chapters. However, I strongly encourage the reader to take the material in sequence, or at least read all of it before using it in your practice, especially if you are newer to magical practice. This is because the practices are presented in the order they are needed as building blocks, to help construct a safe grounding for more intensive sorcery practices. Before it is advisable to delve into the more demanding and riskier practices in the later parts of the book, you will want to have a robust foundation in spiritual hygiene, protection, and spirit alliances to support you.

Along the way, you will meet some of the divinities and spirit collectives who have walked beside me and guided me in developing this blended Celtic sorcery practice. Each of these is introduced with a brief background along with an illustration depicting the spirits and the sigils that I use to connect with them. These sigils also can serve to help illustrate my approach to sigil-making, which is covered in chapter 5. These introductions are included to offer opportunities for connecting with some of the spirits who have been important in my experiences with these practices. However, it's up to you whether you wish to seek relationship with these particular divinities. You may have your own gods and spirits you are in relationship with who will better support your practice, and others may present themselves to you as you go forward in your path.

When it comes to interpreting material from lore into a living practice, there are an infinite variety of ways one can work with these tools. To help you get started, throughout the book I've included sections marked "Sorcerer's Tool Kit." These sections present practical approaches to begin working with these tools in your own practice. Since all these practices are adaptable, most of these Tool Kit sections are not simple ritual scripts or cookbook-style instructions, but instead present tools and exercises for building your own ritual practice.

I also wanted to show examples of the fluid and varied ways that these practices can be interpreted. For that reason, I've also included a few stories from my own practice, marked "Story." These narratives are based in real-life experiences I have had myself or with others. In some instances, I've combined experiences from more than one related event, but they are all rooted in real-life experiences. It is my hope that this approach encourages the reader to try novel approaches to bringing these practices together. Your experiences may not look like mine at all and that is as it should be.

CHAPTER 1

purification and spiritual hygiene

This practice begins with purification and spiritual hygiene, because the first thing you need to be able to enter magical practice safely is the ability to cleanse yourself, your tools, and your working spaces. The basis of spiritual hygiene is an understanding that people, places, and things can gather spiritual residue and need cleaning, just as they do physically.

purity and safety

It is important to state up front that when I talk about spiritual impurity, I am not talking about a moral condition. The idea of moral impurity is deeply ingrained in Western culture as a relic of Christianity and the relationship of impurity to sin. This practice works from an animist worldview where sin and moral impurity are simply not relevant. There is no inherent sense of moral wrong, fallenness, or sin in the concept of spiritual impurity here. This is why I like to use the language of hygiene, because in daily life most people already have a lived experience of cleanliness and dirtiness that they don't feel compelled to load with moral weight—we can just take a shower when we need to get clean.

Spiritual hygiene is similar. Throughout our days, we make contact with all kinds of beings, living and incorporeal. In an animist framework, everything is inspirited, so everything we see or experience also sees and experiences us. We are mutually affected by interactions with the living world around us. In particular, there is a stickiness to the life energies and emotions of living beings, as well as those of spirit beings, and the presences in a place. Things we make contact with brush up against our sensitive subtle bodies and leave effects: residues, reverberations, tendrils of feeling and spiritual force. Just as things we make physical contact with may leave residues on our skin and dust in our hair that we eventually want to wash off.

Continuing the analogy with physical health and cleanliness, we also create our own spiritual dirt. In addition to the ways that our experiences of others can linger or leave marks on us, our own feelings and responses can also form spiritual residues. Any feeling that we have difficulty shaking can function this way: stress, fear, anger, angst, trauma, grief, even what we may think of as positive emotions if we are gripped by them or return obsessively to them. It isn't that the emotions themselves are a problem or are anything to be washed away. It's that emotions take hold of parts of our life force, and when we are gripped by them, especially if there is an inability to process and release them, the life force held in them can become trapped, hardened, entangled, or otherwise altered in such a way that it isn't available to flow as it should. Spiritual hygiene practices can help release these residues and restore life force to a condition of flow and health.

Often, purification is also simply about separating one thing from another. This can mean separating the sacred from the mundane, but it can also simply be about drawing boundaries between one thing and another and ensuring that you don't mix or contaminate one kind of space or experience with the energies and presences of a different one. Many instances of religious purification practices in polytheist and animist traditions around the world are oriented around this function. You can think of it as analogous to the practice in many cultures of removing the shoes when entering a house to prevent the soil from the world outside from coming in on people's feet. Spiritual purification when crossing a sacred boundary is the spirit equivalent of this. It works both on a spiritual level—separating the energies and presences in a space from those outside—and on an emotional level—helping people to set aside the thoughts and feelings they've arrived with to focus on the purpose of the space they're entering.

Many folk traditions of purification and cleansing also focus on its protective function. These traditions operate from the insight that being in an uncleaned state can also make us vulnerable to harmful, predatory, and malevolent forces. Again, this extends from principles most people are already familiar with: that letting dirt and especially biological residues accumulate on us or in our environment makes us vulnerable to illness and infection, to the attack of harmful bacteria. That is to say, the world is full of living things, seen and unseen, and some of them can cause us harm, feed on us, or make us sick if we aren't paying attention. The spiritual ecology operates similarly; those accretions of uncleared emotion, energy, and life force may attract spiritual beings that can feed on us or take up residence in ways that are harmful.

Practices to cleanse spiritual contamination, purify the spiritual body, and rid us of harmful residues and forces can be broken down into three types based on function. These three types are *cleansing*, which removes contamination, *blessing*, which acts to realign or to restore a state of spiritual health, and *banishing*, which is used to turn unwanted spirits away.

These distinctions may seem theoretical, but from the perspective of considering the source of the unease or harm, they do matter. What should you do with a residue or spiritual accretion that arises from your own being, when it is essentially your own life force that has been entangled or hardened into something that can harm you? Animistic traditions teach that it is possible to tear off parts of our souls or to become separated from part of our life force, and that this in itself is a source of great illness and harm. When parts of our own being or life force have become entangled, hardened, or started to separate and take on a life of their own, that's exactly when we are at greater risk of soul loss or separation, and what we want to avoid at that point is cleansing away any parts of ourselves.

Thus, this distinction matters most when it comes to practices applied to our own bodies. For personal spiritual hygiene, you may sometimes need to use cleansing practices to wash away the residues of the world from yourself in the ritual equivalent of taking a shower and washing the dirt down the drain. In other instances, what you may need is a blessing practice that is designed to refresh, restore, or release trapped spiritual energies within your own being, without washing anything away. Similar distinctions can apply to the spiritual hygiene of a place or a space. In many cases of space clearing, it will be appropriate to use cleansing practices that wash or sweep away any forces or residues not wanted in that place. However, sometimes what's wanted is a blessing practice to restore harmony among the presences in the space, rather than washing anything away.

The third type is banishing, which refers specifically to practices designed to drive out spirit beings that are not wanted. It is keyed toward beings rather than residues, although there is a spectrum here since spiritual residues can and do accrue, strengthen, and take on a life of their own and become spirits or demons. Banishing practices tend to address the unwanted spirits as beings with agency, by attempting to command, frighten, or entrap and then push them out. When this kind of practice is applied to a person, it is also called an exorcism.

Distinctions are often less clear than the foregoing in folk customs. Often called *saining* in Scottish custom, these practices may be framed as blessing, cleansing, and protective all at once, or some combination of these, especially in the case of remedies practiced by everyday folk.[10] The distinctions of mechanism and function would tend to be the domain of the specialist.

---

10. Campbell, *Witchcraft & Second Sight in the Highlands & Islands of Scotland*, 73–76.

water rites and sacred waters

Water rites for cleansing and purification build on and intensify the natural cleaning and life-renewing properties of water. The waters of the landscape are inherently held sacred across Celtic cultures, as they tend to be in many animist societies. This is seen in the pervasive practice of identifying bodies of water with divinities, most typically goddesses. The very ancient origin of this practice survives in lore such as river names and is articulated in its later form through myths such as those of Sinann, Bóann, and others who become rivers.[11] There is also a belief implied through stories and folk practices that water enters the living world from the Otherworld, carrying its force and capacity for both magic and inspiration.

In their contemporary form, a great many water rites in folk practice are found embedded in Christian belief and symbolism. It is apparent, however, that some form of such water rites would have been native in Celtic cultures prior to conversion. For example, an Iron Age baptismal practice was documented among Continental tribes of the Rhine area around 200 BCE.[12] In a rite for the blessing of newborn children, the infant was carried on their father's shield to a river and bathed in its waters. This was believed to grant the child vitality. The Greek poet who recorded this ritual understood it as a test of the child's strength and constitution, although there is no direct testimony from the people who practiced this rite. Early hagiographies of the Irish conversion period note that pagans were already in the practice of venerating holy wells.[13]

Irish and Scottish folk practices recorded from the early modern to modern periods contain a rich vein of water rituals. While in most cases it would be difficult to document whether the practice is a survival of anything pre-Christian, many practitioners understand them in that way. Cleansing rituals are tied to seasonal customs in early Irish literature, such as this medieval

---

11. Beck, "Goddesses in Celtic Religion—Cult and Mythology: A Comparative Study of Ancient Ireland, Britain and Gaul," 403.

12. Koch, *The Celtic Heroic Age: Literary Sources for Ancient Celtic Europe and Early Ireland & Wales*, 8.

13. Royal Irish Academy, "Tírechán's Text in English (Transl. L. Bieler)."

poem about the Imbolc quarter day that suggests that special washing practices would be customary at this holy day:

> *Tasting every food in order,*
> *That is what behoves at Imbolc,*
> *Washing of hand and foot and head,*
> *It is thus I say.*[14]

Whatever the ritual forms may have been for such a tradition in pre-Christian times, it seems likely that they would center around similar features still seen in post-conversion water rites such as the sacredness of the water source, the rituals of gathering, and the mode of preserving or enhancing its sacredness in its use for cleansing. Whatever their origin, it is certain these folk practices align themselves well with an animistic worldview and fit perfectly into the weave of a pagan magical practice.

Gathering the Waters

A pervading theme in the engagement with the source of holy water is the making of the circuit around the well. Circuit rituals are mentioned in many sources, from the mythological to contemporary Catholic ritual. This circumnavigation practice, in the context of holy sites, is always made sunwise (*deiseal* in Irish; modern folk would understand this as clockwise).[15] Movement around the site in this way ritually reenacts the path of the sun, thus creating a microcosm of the cosmos itself within the physical space of the site, and in this way places it within a field of blessing and natural order.

Circuit rites may be elaborated on with a range of practices. Early nineteenth-century descriptions of Irish folk practice at holy wells note pilgrims traveling bareheaded and barefooted or walking on the knees. Such penitential practices may be Christian in nature, but many related elements of the practice seem more pagan in nature. The number of circuits made has significance, typically specified to odd numbers such as three, six, or nine times. These practices were

---

14. Meyer, *Hibernica Minora*. 48–49.

15. Armao, "Cathair Crobh Dearg: From Ancient Beliefs to the Rounds 2017," 22.

reported as ancestral customs held to guard against "the sorceries of the druids," to protect from disease, and to keep the fairies in goodwill.[16]

Practices of this type are also customary for the blessing of cattle, as for example in this account that combines the elements of sacred location, sacred day, and circumnavigation of the well:

> A pattern day occurred on May Day at the holy well in 'The City' [near Paps of Anu], when cattle were brought, some from great distances, and driven around it. This may have been an attempt to cure sick livestock, or to ensure their health and fertility. This tradition was recorded by O'Donovan in his Letters of the Ordnance Survey, written in the mid-nineteenth century, with the tradition persisting into living memory.[17]

The time of day as well as season is significant in many folk practices as well. In some traditions, the most sacred time to draw water is just after midnight on the eve of Bealtaine. Given that in the Celtic worldview the day begins in night, what this practice appears to indicate is that the power of the holy day was strongest in the waters at the darkest part of night on the eve. This first water drawn after midnight on the eve of Bealtaine was called "the purity of the well" and was considered especially powerful—local folk would compete to be the one to gather it.[18] It was kept all year for special protective blessings, including a ritual conducted to bless farms. After sunset, the blessed water was carried around the boundaries of the land, starting and finishing in the east. At cardinal points, the procession would stop for ceremonies conducted using seeds (for fertility, perhaps), and farming tools (perhaps for the protective qualities of

---

16. Wood-Martin, *Traces of the Elder Faiths of Ireland*, Vol. II, 86–87.

17. Coyne, *Islands in the Clouds: An Upland Archaeological Study on Mount Brandon and the Paps, County Kerry*, 21.

18. Wilde, *Ancient Legends Mystic Charms & Superstitions of Ireland*, 140.

iron).[19] This ritual combines the powers of season and hour, with the circum-navigation of the land being blessed using the holy water.

Another water ritual from Scottish tradition instantiates similar patterns, while highlighting the liminality of powers inherent in water. This is the tradition of gathering sacred water from "the living and the dead stream." The dead and living stream is a crossing point where the dead and the living both cross a body of water. In earlier times in rural areas, funeral processions traditionally used separate pathways to carry the dead to burial places, in order to minimize the likelihood of the dead haunting roads used by the living. Typically, the only points where these dead paths would cross living ones would be at crossroads, bridges, or shallow fords over streams and rivers. These crossing points where both the dead and living cross the same water held a special power and liminality.[20]

Ritual behaviors also attend the process of collection in order to preserve and enhance the sacredness and power of the water. These might include practices such as gathering it in silence, not looking back afterward until reaching the destination, and ritual prohibitions on who or what is allowed to touch the vessel of water. "At midnight and in silence the water was carried from a south-running stream near the house. Care was taken that the bearer did not look back, nor permit the vessel in which the water was carried to touch the ground."[21] It is easy to see how these practices contribute to maintaining the virtues of the water, which inhere in it the power of the place it is gathered from so that this power is not dispersed away before it is brought into use.

charging the waters

Many folkloric sources show that the blessing and cleansing powers of water can be enhanced by a variety of magical means. Descriptions of these practices to charge water with blessing power often appear in folklore collections, such as this example from folklorist John Gregorson Campbell:

---

19. Wood-Martin, *Traces of the Elder Faiths*, Vol. I, 281.

20. Black, *Scottish Charms and Amulets. Proceedings of the Society of Antiquaries of Scotland*, 454.

21. Polson, *Scottish Witchcraft Lore*, 179.

> The Eòlas (Knowledge), called also Teagasg (Teaching), was
> a charm for the cure of sickness in man or beast. It consisted
> of a rhyme, muttered over the sick person, and over water
> to be drunk by, or sprinkled over, the sick animal. To render
> it more impressive, its use was accompanied by trifling little
> ceremonies, such as making the sign of the cross, yawning,
> making up mysterious parti-coloured strings, getting par-
> ticular kinds of water on particular days, dipping stones of
> virtue in water, and similar mummeries.[22]

Commonly, objects and materials that bring their own virtues may be
placed in the waters, such as herbs, spirits, stones, crystals, and metals. It is
also not uncommon to hear of wine or spirits being sprinkled or added to
water that is used for blessing.[23] Whiskey tends to be more common as a form
of spirits used by common folk in Gaelic areas. Another theme is that words,
prayers, or rhymes are recited over the water.

This example from Scottish folklorist Alexander Carmichael's collection
mentions the use of precious metals: "The operator proceeds to a stream,
where the living and the dead alike pass, and lifts water, in name of the Holy
Trinity, into a wooden ladle…On returning, a wife's gold ring, a piece of
gold, of silver, and of copper, are put in the ladle. The sign of the holy cross
is then made, and this rhyme is repeated in a slow recitative manner."[24] Here
the water has been gathered from a liminal place, gathered with prayer. This
is enhanced by adding three kinds of precious metals, and these powers sealed
within the water through the use of the chanted rhyme. This belief that water
that has been in contact with gold or silver carried greater virtue appears in a
variety of folklore sources. It is not simply the economic value of these metals;
it seems to be related to their incorruptibility. Celtic scholar and folklorist
Ronald Black suggests that the belief in these powers of gold and silver to

---

22. Campbell, *Witchcraft & Second Sight in the Highlands & Islands of Scotland*, 57–58.

23. Campbell, *Witchcraft & Second Sight in the Highlands & Islands of Scotland*, 241–242.

24. Carmichael, *Carmina Gadelica*, Vol. II, 42.

transform water into a magically charged fluid may be an inheritance from alchemical traditions.[25]

Many sources also mention the use of amulets, stones, or crystals, which are similarly placed into the waters to confer blessings.[26] These stones include small objects of glass or rock crystal or holed stones, also called "hagstones," "elf-stones," "toad stones," or "adder stones," which may be a variety of types of stones or ancient artifacts around which folkloric beliefs have accrued.[27] Tradition seems to welcome a great variety here; the common element being an object that is felt to have an Otherworldly or mysterious origin, or an ancestral power of some kind, to be placed in the water to activate its blessing properties.

meeting brixta

Brixta is a Gallic goddess known from inscriptions found at the site of a Gallo-Roman bath and temple at Luxeuil-les-Bains in eastern France. She is connected with sacred springs, the cleansing and curative powers of water, and with magic.

Luxeuil-les-Bains was known from Gallic times for its curative mineral-rich hot springs and is still frequented for therapeutic baths. Votive dedications to Brixta and her consort god Luxovius were found there, along with dedications to another pair often associated with healing springs, Sirona and Apollo. *The Life of Saint Columbanus*, a seventh-century text about the monastery founded at Luxeuil, mentions its pagan past: "There hot baths had been built with considerable care; there a large number of stone images filled the neighbouring woodland: these, ancient pagan times had honoured with miserable ritual and profane rites, and for them they performed execrable ceremonies…"[28]

Excavations at the site of the baths and temple unearthed thousands of copper and silver coins, an ex-voto in the shape of a leg, and many oak figures

25. Black, *The Gaelic Otherworld*, 392, n. 451.

26. Black, *Scottish Charms and Amulets*, 437, 509.

27. Campbell, *Witchcraft & Second Sight in the Highlands & Islands of Scotland*, 85–87; Black, *Scottish Charms and Amulets*, 468.

28. Beck, "Goddesses in Celtic Religion—Cult and Mythology: A Comparative Study of Ancient Ireland, Britain, and Gaul," 442–448.

carved to represent heads, busts, and human bodies, some showing Celtic features such as torcs and the *bardocucullus*, a cowl-like garment. These represented the evidence of devotions dating from between the first century BCE to the fourth century CE, and seem to be focused on healing.

The pairing of Brixta with Luxovius may be an example of a Gallic pattern pairing water goddesses with gods of healing at sites like this. However, Luxovius may have been more than a god of healing; he may have been a tutelary deity as the community of Luxovium took its name from him and is the origin of the modern city of Luxeuil-les-Bains.

Brixta herself appears to have a profound association with water, and some scholars suggest the River Breuchin, which waters the area, takes its name from hers. The meaning of her name, however, points to magic. Brixta (or Bricta, as her name is sometimes spelled) comes from the same root as the Gaulish *brictom*, meaning "magic, enchantment, or charm." It appears in phrases in Gaulish magical tablets, such as *andernados brictom*, "the magic of the underworld," or *bnanom brictom*, "the magic of women." Cognate terms appear across the Celtic languages, such as the Old Irish *bricht*, "bewitchment," *brichtu ban*, "magic of women," Middle Welsh *lled-frith*, "charm," and Old Breton *brith*, "magic."[29] The suffix *-ta* on her name indicates action, so her name means "she who performs magic," or simply "sorceress" or "witch." So, while she seems to have a strong association with water, her name is connected to a profound tradition of magic.

During a pilgrimage in France, I spent a little time at another healing spring, Chamalières, which has a similar long association with Gallic magic and held its own temple and baths. This was early in my relationship with Brixta, and I hoped in contemplating her presence there to connect and learn a little more about her. I wanted to understand why she, and spring sites like hers, seem connected to both water and light, healing, and cursing.

Sitting in the warm water, I entered a meditative space and asked her to arise and speak with me. I saw her as a presence of light or flame emerging in water. She conveyed to me that her primary nature is as her name indicates,

---

29. Delamarre, *Dictionnaire de La Langue Gauloise*, 47, 90.

a goddess of magic. This magic moves in the waters that flow from the Otherworld especially at springs like this, and it is the presence of this magic and the connection to the Otherworld that make these sites places to access healing within the waters. At the same time, this is also what makes them powerful places to deploy spells and curses. "The magic is in the water," she said, "and it can both curse and cure."

Brixta blesses the waters for purification and healing. More than this, she is also a patroness of magic and the liminal spaces through which the powers of the Otherworld bubble up from the watery below into our world. Call upon her for water magic, sorcery, and connecting to the Otherworld. Her sigil combines the Gaulish letter-signs Sonnos, Bitus, and Lugion, representing light and healing, life and magic, and watery places and binding magics, and the ogham letters Sáil and Lúis. It incorporates both the water and the flame within which she moves. In the artwork, she emerges veiled from the pool of a sanctuary spring, bearing flame in one hand and water in the other. Her sigil can be seen inscribed on the stones framing the edge of the pool, and the sigil is also seen behind her.

Sorcerer's Toolkit
blessing waters

To begin to build your blessing and cleansing toolkit, let's look at the elements that make up a water blessing practice.

Water: Since its core virtue is the power to cleanse and to nourish, you can use any clean water that you would use for washing yourself or for drinking, such as tap water. Water absorbs the qualities of what it touches. This is part of why it works so well as a spiritual cleansing agent. It's also why so many folk traditions focus on how the water is collected. The more you attend to gathering the water from a natural source, and to how it is handled, the more of that natural virtue may be preserved in the water. If you can,

Sigil Illustration for Brixta

consider gathering water from a natural source such as a stream, river, or spring; rainwater; or water that has been in moonlight or sunlight.

Prayer: The simple act of praying over water is sufficient to charge it with holy power for blessing. Prayer combines the life force inherent in your breath, with the power and presence of the divinities that the prayer is directed toward. Your prayer could be a beautiful rhyming poetic charm, or it can be just a few simple words. The water is a being, so your prayer can simply be to the water itself, asking it to provide its blessing power. You can also think about focusing prayers toward divinities you feel close to, whose holy power you trust, or who you know to be helpful in blessing and cleansing.

Holy objects: To the basic elements of water and prayer, you can add in holy objects that bring their own virtues to the blessed water. Traditionally, materials that appear incorruptible, such as gold or silver, can bring this power of purity to the blessed water. Alternately, objects with an Otherworldly connection, such as holed stones or crystals, can help charge the water with their power.

Preservers: Tradition also favors materials that are known to disinfect and preserve, as these are seen to have the power to cleanse and ward away illness and rot. This is why spirits such as whiskey or wine are used in blessing waters, since alcohol preserves and disinfects. Salt has a similar property of disinfection and stopping decay. Salt may be especially helpful in contexts where the presence of alcohol may be harmful or unwelcome, such as around people in recovery.

Plants: Aromatic herbs and plants can be added into the blessing water and bundled herbs may also be used as an aspergillum to sprinkle the blessed water around. Any plant whose scent brings a sense of freshness may be of use. Plants such as mugwort (*Artemisia vulgaris*), juniper (*Juniperus communis*), heather (*Calluna vulgaris*), rosemary (*Salvia rosmarinus*), or other species in the

Salvia family are good choices for this purpose (see more about these plants under the section on fire rites).

There are a nearly limitless variety of options within this practice, so if you are just starting, it can help to begin with a very simple approach. Here is a pathway you can take to begin developing your practice:

Begin with just prayer and water. Take a bowl of clean water and hold it up so your breath reaches it as you pray: "May this water be blessed and bring blessing to all it touches." Breathe this prayer over the water and observe how the water looks and feels and how it changes as it absorbs the prayer. Do you sense power in it? Does it capture light differently? Sprinkle it over yourself and your space for a blessing. How does it feel?

Now, try adding other elements into your practice with blessing waters. Changing one thing at a time can help you to discern how each element adds to the practice.

Try adding physical elements. Put a piece of gold or silver in the water, then perform the same prayer. Bless yourself and notice how you feel.

Try adding a preserver. Pour a splash of whiskey into the water, then pray over it. Try stirring a pinch of salt into the water, then praying over it and performing the blessing. Do these feel different to you?

Try using an aspergillum. Find a suitable aromatic plant such as rosemary or juniper. Take a handful of plant stems and wrap them tightly with a bit of twine, leaving the leafy ends free to move a bit. Tie the twine off. Prepare your blessing water by praying over it. Dip the leafy end of the bundle in the water and sprinkle it over yourself and your space. Notice how the movement of the leaves propels the blessed water around, and how the aromatic scent of the plant feels in the air.

When you feel comfortable using each of these elements, try combining them. Experiment. Try singing over your water instead of just whispering a blessing. Get some water from a holy well, or a place that's particularly sacred to you. Make a big, lush blessing bowl with multiple elements together. Instead of just sprinkling it over yourself, try pouring some in your bath. There's no limit and your creativity is your guide.

Story
A water rite

It's Imbolc, a traditional time for purification, and I'm preparing a consecrated fluid for making blessing water I can use in my everyday cleansing rites throughout the year.[30] I've gathered all my things together: butter, mead and whiskey for the gods and spirits, herbs and plants for the mixture, a little silver pendant, a container of water from a holy well.

I begin by making a place for the divinities who will help me consecrate this: a little statue of Brigid with a candle inside it, and a piece of inscribed lead that represents Brixta, goddess of sorcery and healing. I pour mead and whiskey for them in little cups and lay a pat of butter on a little dish, asking them and my other spirit allies to bless the space I'm working in, bless all the materials, and bless the work I will do here.

First to go into the bowl are the plants and herbs. As I take up a small handful of each plant material, I whisper my request to its spirit to bring blessing into what I'm creating, then I pass it three times over the flame of the candle. Mugwort gathered from the plant I nurture in the yard; berries and crumbling needles of juniper; the last twigs and dried berries from a stash of rowan I'd collected on a trip to where it grows. Each is blessed and then goes into the bowl. Now I sprinkle in a few precious drops of holy water from Brigid's well and from a well

---

30. Adapted from Ronan, "Daily Purification."

in France where I'd connected with Brixta. A few drops from the offering cups, and then enough whiskey from the bottle to cover the herbs. Last, I take the silver pendant and whisper another prayer over it, pass it three times over the flame of the candle, and drop it into the bowl where it will give its power of purification to this mixture.

Now with everything in the bowl, I pass my hands over it, calling once more on the spirits for blessing. Gathering all the spiritual power I can into my breath, I whisper an incantation of peace and blessing over the intoxicating herb-scented bowl:

> *Síth co nem*
> *Nem co doman*
> *Doman fo nim*
> *Nert hi cách.*[31]
>
> *Translation:*
> *Peace up to heaven,*
> *heaven to earth,*
> *earth under heaven,*
> *strength in everyone.*[32]

With the final charge placed in the fluid, I carefully pour it into a jar, close up the jar, and tie a protective rowan cross on it with red ribbon. Then I place the jar with its crystalline golden liquid and floating bits of herbs on the altar amongst the candles and offerings, to sit in the presence of the gods and spirits overnight on St. Brigid's eve.

In the morning, it's ready to use. Throughout the year whenever I need water for blessing, I can pour a few drops of this potent fluid into a bowl of water, whisper a quick prayer over it, and sprinkle it about myself or anywhere I want to purify the space. I'll put some

---

31. Gray, "Cath Maige Tuired: The Second Battle of Mag Tuired," 72.

32. Mees, *Celtic Curses*, loc. 5234–5237.

into a spray bottle too, for a ready blessing I can carry in my ritual kit anywhere I go.

Fire Rites

Fire as a sacralizing element is attested from the earliest sources to contemporary folk practice. This aligns with practices found in animist and polytheist cultures worldwide, of course. Fire rites build upon the understanding that the fire itself is a living force. Fire operates on several levels, both physically and spiritually. First, it brings light and warmth, clearing shadows and darkness. This effect may matter less to moderns accustomed to artificial light at the click of a switch, but to the ancestors it meant safety. Fire can frighten away or hold at bay predators and other marauders that exploit darkness, and its power to exorcise and banish unwanted spirits follows as a matter of natural logic from this effect. Fire as a process also transforms as it consumes; its transformative and destructive power readily translates to use in a spiritual context to cleanse, consume, and transform the forces present in a space. Smoke, especially the smoke of aromatic plants or woods, is both purifying and preservative, clearing the air of insects, providing antimicrobial benefits, and helping to preserve food from decay. Similarly, aromatic smoke acts spiritually to clear spaces of unwanted presences or influences and prevent them creeping in.

The use of aromatic plant smoke for cleansing brings up issues of cultural safety and respect. When considering cleansing, many contemporary spiritual practitioners think first of the burning of sage for this purpose, often called smudging. This custom has been widely appropriated by white people and decontextualized from its origins in Native American religious cultures. The popularity of this decontextualized smudging practice among pagan and new age spiritual movements has led to the commodification and severe overharvesting of the white sage plant in many areas. This theft and commodification of a sacred practice by people who are not part of the cultures and communities it comes from is a clear example of harmful cultural appropriation. We can and should do better. And there is no need for Celtic polytheists and magical practitioners to appropriate ritual customs in this way. The Celtic cultures that form the foundations of our practice provide plenty of suitable and, in fact, quite similar traditions using fire and sacred plants for cleansing and blessing.

sacred fire and the seasons

The use of sacred fire is often tied to seasonal customs. Early literature highlights the making of sacred fires at seasonal points and folk custom continues this practice. For example, fires at Samhain (traditionally November 1) are mentioned in texts such as *The Destruction of Dá Derga's Hostel* as a practice that memorializes mythic history while providing a sense of protection: "It was on the eve of Samain (All Saints' Day) the destruction of the Hostel was wrought, and that from yonder beacon [fire] the beacon of Samain is followed from that to this, and stones (are placed) in the Samain-fire."[33] The Samhain fire mentioned in this story is called the "Boar of the Wood," and it is described as being a mighty, blazing fire built with logs to have seven sides letting the flames out. An early medieval poem describing the ritual customs appropriate to the major Celtic seasonal festivals mentions offerings being given to sacred fires at Bealtaine (traditionally May 1): "I tell to you, a special festival, the glorious dues of Mayday: ale, worts, sweet whey, and fresh curds to the fire." In the same poem, the Samhain fire is also mentioned: "Meat, ale, nut-mast, tripe, these are the dues of summer's end [Samhain]; a bonfire on a hill pleasantly, buttermilk, a roll of fresh butter."[34]

These seasonal fires were felt to have purifying and protective powers, a tradition that continues into more recent folkloric customs. The practice of leading the cattle between two fires is mentioned in the same early text about the seasonal festivals: "For the druids used to make two fires with great incantations, and to drive the cattle between them against the plagues, every year."[35] This detail is borne out by archaeological evidence at some sites.[36] Later folk practices have also included walking the cattle over straw or branches lit in

---

33. Stokes, "The Destruction of Da Derga's Hostel."

34. Meyer, *Hibernica Minora*, 49.

35. Meyer, "The Wooing of Emer," 232.

36. Sherwood, "An Bó Bheannaithe: Cattle Symbolism in Traditional Irish Folklore, Myth, and Archaeology," 189–225, 191.

these seasonal fires. Fire can also be carried around a space to cleanse and protect. Irish and Scots customs also include the carrying of lit branches from such sacred fires around farms and buildings to spread the blessing and protection of the fire.[37]

Sacred fires are often made with woods and plants chosen for their specific spiritual or magical qualities. Many sacred fire customs make use of rowan (*Sorbus aucuparia*, also called mountain ash)—a profoundly magical plant used extensively in protection and healing as well as cursing and other magical operations. Its red berries mark it as an Otherworldly plant, as red color is often portrayed as a marker of Otherworld presences in myth and folklore. In addition to being burned in sacred fires, twigs or staves are often woven into other magical items for protection or to increase their power.[38] Oak (*Quercus* spp.) would also be a popular wood for sacred fires; in addition to its religious association with druidic knowledge and holy power, it is long-burning and provides the best of clean heat.

Herbs and branches of smaller plants would also be added into sacred fires or carried as burning branches for blessing. In Ireland and Scotland, plants often preferred for this are juniper (*Juniperus communis*), mugwort (*Artemisia vulgaris*), and heather (*Calluna vulgaris*)—all aromatics that give sweet or musky herbal smoke that serves to freshen and bless the atmosphere. Mugwort is called *Mongach meisce* in Irish and associated especially with a protective power against witchcraft and harmful or unwanted spirits.[39] Fresh bundles would be hung about homes and farms, and the burning branches would be carried through to allow the aromatic smoke to clear the air and protect the place.

Many traditions also attach to the method of collection of these sacred plants. For example, in Ireland it has been customary to gather them especially on St. John's Eve (June 23, near Midsummer), or in some districts at Beal-

---

37. Campbell, *Witchcraft & Second Sight*, 241–242.

38. Carmichael, *Carmina Gadelica*, Vol. II, 241.

39. Mac Coitir, *Ireland's Wild Plants*, 114–116.

taine.[40] This Scottish custom for collecting juniper provides a spoken charm and ritual actions to be performed as it is gathered: "It must be pulled by the roots, with its branches made into four bundles, and taken between the five fingers, saying: 'I will pull the bounteous yew, through the five bent ribs of Christ, in the name of the Father, the Son and Holy Ghost, against drowning, danger, and confusion.'" [41] Here the spoken charm mentions yew, because juniper was also known as "mountain yew."

Sorcerer's Toolkit
Fire and Smoke Blessing

The practice of blessing with sacred fire is incredibly adaptable. It can be as simple as a candle or stick of incense, or it can be a great seasonal bonfire steeped in ritual. Here are some considerations toward building a sacred fire blessing practice.

Consecrated fire: What distinguishes a sacred fire from an ordinary one is the sacralizing act of blessing the fire. This is true whether the fire is a small candle or a huge communal bonfire. Even without prayer, fire has transformative and cleansing power, but consecration ensures that its action is aligned with our needs. Fire is itself a living thing, so consecration of fire is firstly about petitioning the fire and coming into relationship with it. You can also consecrate the fire with prayer to divinities you are close to, whose powers you trust, or whose spheres of influence relate to fire, cleansing or protection.

Materials: As discussed earlier, traditional materials for cleansing and protection by fire are often aromatic plants, or wood from trees that have special power. As a guide to choosing plants, consider

---

40. Mac Coitir, *Ireland's Wild Plants*, 116.

41. Campbell, *Witchcraft & Second Sight*, 105.

that while each plant has its own particular traditional virtues, such as the magical potency of rowan, or the protective power of juniper, a great deal of the vibrancy of this practice will come by way of relationship, because again we are dealing with living beings. You will get the greatest benefit from a plant you have been in relationship with, whether that is by growing it in a pot or garden, tending to the places it grows wild, or even working with it in a medicinal context. Attending to this relationship in the way the plant is gathered will help bring greater sacredness and virtue to the blessing practice. Branches, leaves, or material directly from the plant will have more virtue than packaged incense, if they are accessible to you. For interior spaces where it's not feasible to have smoke, you can still employ the sacralizing power of fire by using a candle. After all, a candle is just a flame fed by wax instead of wood. Just as with plants, attending to the source of the materials helps bring us into a more effective relationship with the fire—perhaps seek out local beekeepers, for example.

Beginning with the core elements, here is a pathway toward building a practice with fire and smoke blessing.

Start with a simple flame blessing rite with a candle. Place your hands over the candle and pray, perhaps starting with a simple prayer such as, "May this holy fire bless and protect all its light touches." Light the candle and take a moment to receive its light and heat. Take the candle, and with a measured pace, carry it around your space in a sunwise (clockwise) direction, attending to how its light touches everything. After completing a circuit, set it in the center of the floor and let it burn to the end (or as long as you can before needing to extinguish it for safety). How does the space feel after this blessing?

Try a blessing with sacred smoke. To begin, choose one plant to burn so you can attend to its particular qualities. Consider starting with juniper, as one of the traditional plants for this purpose. Take some charcoal and pray over it for the blessing of fire, then light it and place it in a censer. Give the charcoal a moment to fully light. You can also blow on it to help it along, while also giving it the gift of your breath. Taking up the leaves, offer a prayer to the plant spirit, asking it for its blessing, and drop a small pile onto the glowing charcoal. As the smoke begins to rise, take a moment to draw in the blessing of the heat and smoke. Pick up the censer, and with a measured pace, carry it around your space in a sunwise direction. You can waft the smoke with your hand or by using a tool such as a fan or feather bundle. When the space is fully resonant with the blessing of the smoke, let it burn out naturally. How does this feel compared to blessing with the candle flame?

Try the same smoke blessing with different plant sources. How do they feel differently and how do the scents shift the way the space feels after each blessing? Try fresh versus dried leaves, or try a packaged incense and compare its effects. When you have a sense for how different plant smokes work, try combining them. Try the traditional practice of lighting whole branches of a sacred plant and carrying the burning branch around the outside of your house. (But be mindful of fire danger—don't do this in dry regions unless there is plenty of moisture in the environment.)

Make a seasonal sacred bonfire and use it to perform blessings for Bealtaine or Samhain or another holy day. Gather seasoned firewood, sprigs or branches of sacred plants, a fire source, and offerings to feed the fire, such as alcoholic spirits, butter, flowers, or the like. Lay a structured base of wood and kindling with space for air flow. Pray to the spirit of the fire and to any other gods or spirits you wish to petition for help sanctifying the fire, then light the dry material and kindling. You can help it along with the gift of your breath or feed it air with a hand fan; having a few friends along to keep the prayers and songs going as you do this can help. As the fire strengthens, start adding sprigs of sacred plants, with prayers to each plant spirit as it goes in. Once the fire is well established and has a base of good red coals, so you don't risk smothering it, you can add any other offerings to feed the fire spirit. Blessings can begin once the fire is strong and fed with offerings. You can bless tools by wafting them through its smoke; traditionally, one would drive livestock near to let them receive the smoke blessing too. You can also take branches of wood and light one end in the fire, to carry its smoke around buildings (again, being mindful of fire safety as you do this).

Story

A smoke cleansing Rite

It's time for a good seasonal cleansing of the house. For ordinary, weekly cleansing I've been just sprinkling a little blessing water into the mop bucket, but it's been a busy summer and it feels time for a more thorough cleanse for the change of season.

I start with gathering the aromatic plants I'll use. Pouring a little milk into a cup, I take that with a sharp herb-cutting knife and go out to the yard. I say hello to the juniper tree that arches over the front steps and pour a little milk beside her roots. Grasping a low-hanging spray, I whisper, "May I take this branch for the blessing of my home and may there be peace between us." Then I give thanks and cut the twig. Round to the back yard where I greet the haunted mugwort plant that lives in the herb patch, again I pour a little milk, whisper my prayer, and cut a handful of the stalks with their fuzzy, gray-green leaves.

Inside I've also gathered the heads of roses that had been offered to the spirits and then let to dry. I begin crumbling the dried rose petals into a bowl. Then the juniper, its segmented needles breaking apart easily and its berries dropping into the bowl too. The fresh mugwort I have to tear, and its fuzzy leaves create a sticky, heady-smelling residue on my fingers. The floral scent of the roses, the piney, fresh juniper, and the herbaceous mineral tang of the mugwort begin to blend into a potent scent that sets my head spinning a little.

Once the plants are prepared, I take a little circle of charcoal and light it in the bottom of a hand-sized incense cauldron. While it sparks and begins to glow, I address the spirits in the house. "All you here with me, let this house be cleansed. If you are here in peace, please receive this smoke and aid me in cleansing this space. May all that brings harm or illness be burned away and made clean by the powers of holy plant and bright fire."

Rich aromatic smoke begins to waft up from the little cauldron as I lay a generous pinch of the plant mix on the red-hot charcoal. Carrying the cauldron by its little handle I begin sweeping it round the room, wafting the smoke into every corner while continuing to whisper to the spirits. Each room of the house will be cleansed this way with a fresh pinch of plant smoke and sparkling fire till the whole house is scented of incense and the air feels bright and strong. Then I'll thank all the spirits and the plants who helped me and let the last of the charcoal and herbs burn themselves out.

THE NOURISHMENT OF MILK

Milk and the products of milk as agents of healing and purification are a pervasive theme in the Irish literature and Celtic traditions in general. In part, this appears to stem from the fundamental connection in Irish tradition between nourishment and healing. This larger theme is emphasized by, for example, the names of the family of healing deities Dían Cécht, Airmid, and Míach, each of which has a meaning related to agriculture and food.[42] The insight seems to be that what nourishes the body heals the body. Additionally, milk, and its products, is associated with the ability to soothe, to neutralize poison or contagion, and to make whole and purify. Milk appears in many places in Celtic traditions as a condensed representation of the fertility of the

---

42. For a discussion on the meanings of these names, see Carmody and Thompson, "The Story of Airmed from Cath Maige Tuired."

land—nourishing, edible, gentle enough to soothe, rich with life from the land. Where the fertility of the land occurs as a plot point in myth, it is often represented by the phrase, "grain and milk," or "corn, milk, and fruit."[43] Similarly, the phrase "cows without milk," appearing in the prophecy of the Morrígan, is symbolic of total loss of fertility from the land.[44]

The symbolism and spiritual qualities of milk connect them with similar beliefs about water, particularly flowing sacred waters, such as springs and rivers. This is in part reflected in the associations that tie both milk and flowing water to the beneficent powers of life and renewal, and also in the deities that share associations with both. For example, the Gallic goddess Damona, whose name means "Divine Cow," and who was worshiped at a healing spring.[45] Similarly, the river goddess Bóann, namesake of the Boyne River, is also associated with a holy well and its inspiration, as well as with cattle and the milk of cows, and their associated fertility. The earliest reference to the Boyne River gives the name as Buvinda, from archaic Irish *bó*, cow + *vinda*, a term that can mean white, bright, or having wisdom (and sharing its root with that of the poet-warrior Fionn).[46] Her name and symbolism parallel several Continental and British goddesses associated with cattle and healing wells. In the myths and symbolism that attach to Bóann and similar goddesses, there are wells of knowledge whose waters pour forth with wisdom, nourishment, and healing, like streams of milk pouring from the body of a cow, and that become the river that carries her name.

Similarly, Brigid, a goddess deeply associated with waters and springs, healing and purification, combines many of these same symbols and modes of action. She is also a poet and the streams of water arising from the holy wells associated with her are imbued with inspiration, as well as healing, purifying, and renewing powers. At the same time, she is profoundly connected to cat-

---

43. Borsje, "Supernatural Threats to Kings: Exploration of a Motif in the Ulster Cycle and in Other Medieval Irish Tales," 173–94, 186.
44. Gray, "Cath Maige Tuired," 73.
45. Beck, "Goddesses in Celtic Religion," 352.
46. Beck, "Goddesses in Celtic Religion," 352.

tle, held as their protector, invoked in dairy rituals, and attached to blessings and nourishment provided by milk and dairy products.

Myths and folktales instantiate this belief in the healing and purifying powers of milk to counteract contagion or harm. The *Lebor Gabála Érenn* recounts an episode revealing this belief in the Battle of Ard Lemnachta. In this battle, a people called the Tuath Fidga are said to be in the habit of poisoning their weapons, so the Laigin and their allies make trenches in the battlefield and fill them with milk. This ensured that when warriors fell after being struck by poisoned weapons, they would fall into the milk and be healed: "Doomed was everyone on whom they should inflict a wound, and they would not take to themselves any but poisoned weapons. All those who were wounded with their javelins in the battle had nothing to do but lie in the milk, and the venom would do them no hurt."[47] This tale also provides a suggestion that the milk was not just any, but specifically from sacred cattle: the milk of white hornless cows is selected for this purpose.

There is also an episode in the *Táin Bó Cúailnge* in which a wounded Cú Chulainn is healed of his wounds by being given milk to drink at the hand of the Morrígan. Receiving the milk, he recites what sounds like a blessing: "May this be swiftly wholeness for me."[48] In another version, the blessing references poison directly: "May this be safe to me from poison!"[49] Here, again, the milk is special in that it comes from a cow with three teats. This detail is preserved across different variants of the story.

I've mentioned already the purification practice associated with Imbolc: "Washing of hand and foot and head."[50] The connections between purification and the milk associations of Imbolc are not not coincidental but are intertwined in relationship with the mythology of Brigid. As St. Brigit, she is profoundly associated with milk, beginning with her birth tale and a baptism in milk. She also has a role in cleansing warriors of a kind of mark, referred to

---

47. Macalister, *Lebor Gabála Érenn: The Book of the Taking of Ireland*, Part V, 175–177.

48. O'Rahilly, "Táin Bó Cúalnge from the Book of Leinster."

49. Stokes, "Cóir Anmann (Fitness of Names)," in *Irische Text Mit Wörterbuch*, 355.

50. Meyer, *Hibernica Minora*, 48–49.

in the hagiographies as a *signa diabolica*, and that can be understood as a warrior's mark.[51] As washing in milk is part of St. Brigit's own story, it is known throughout the tradition to have the power to purify. Irish literature scholar Phillip Bernhardt-House suggests this might be based on a ritual of cleansing that would make use of milk. This would parallel the Lupercalia, a Roman tradition associated with a similar time of year in which a blood mark made on the foreheads of young men is washed away with milk.[52]

Given that such practices pertaining to warrior bands, seasonal rituals, and the power of milk to purify are also attested in Irish tradition, it is not unreasonable to look at this as a reflection of an ancient strain of Indo-European ritual culture in which milk is used to wash away the spiritual contagion associated with violence and to renew the person bathed by it. It is easy to reimagine a rite in which the milk is used to wash or anoint the head, hands, and feet as in the Imbolc poem.

Story
blessed butter

It's February, and Brigid's time, and I've been inspired to make charmed butter. My ritual group and I will be hosting a temple space at a big pagan conference later that month. Since this conference takes place during the winter and involves many hundreds of people sharing air in a hotel, it's notorious for spreading "con crud," that is to say, nasty cold viruses that no one wants to come home with. I've had a nudge about making this blessed butter and offering it to temple visitors as a bit of hospitality, which can also bring the protective blessings sacred to milk, and hopefully help to ward off the crud.

I gather things for the butter-making. A sprig of rosemary for protection and flavor, gathered from the garden with a small prayer and

51. Macquarrie, "Insular Celtic Tattooing: History, Myth and Metaphor," 159.

52. Bernhardt-House, "Imbolc: A New Interpretation," 64–65.

a gift of cream to the plant before taking it. Salt that's been stored in the Dagda's shrine since being blessed for a feast. A silver ring I often use to bless water. Heavy cream and a large canning jar. And of course, blessing water.

First, I cleanse myself and all my gathered things, so that everything I do can proceed from a clean condition. At the shrine space Brigid shares with the Dagda in my house, I light the candles and begin by offering them both some of the cream. I offer a blessing: "Holy Brigid who blesses the herds, great Dagda who offers protection to the people, be with me now: receive these offerings and please pour your holy blessings into this cream, these herbs, this butter, and onto all who will receive it. Keep us from illness and from harm, may all who receive this blessing be whole and well in body and in spirit."

As I begin the process of making, I pass each thing I use over the flames of their candles for the gods' blessing. First the jar, then the cream is blessed and poured in to about halfway full, leaving plenty of room for the cream to expand. Then the sprig of rosemary and silver ring are blessed and dropped in, and finally I close the jar tightly.

Now I'll have about half an hour or so of shaking the jar. To make it easier, I'll sing a little spell-song: *Ith, blicht, síth, sáma sona* ("corn, milk, peace, prosperous wellness."). But you can be sure by the end my arms are feeling it and I'm remembering times when this was made easier by doing it as a group ritual and passing the jar from hand to hand. I shake and sing to the clicking and clacking of the silver ring that I've added as an agitator to churn the milk faster. In a few minutes, the clicking becomes muffled as the jar has filled with whipped cream. I shake and sing and shake and sing and after what feels like a long time, things begin to shift and the whipped cream fluff breaks into clumps of thick butter and a wash of watery whey. One more push of shaking the jar with tiring arms till the clumps gather themselves into one lump. It's butter!

I tip it out into a big bowl and with clean hands and the coldest water my faucet will produce, I wash the butter, massaging the soft mass with my hands under running water to wash away the whey, until the water begins to run out of it clear instead of milky. (Washing out the whey improves taste and helps the butter keep longer.) While I'm washing it, I'm also pulling out larger twigs and bits of the rosemary sprig that are too big to be pleasant in a bite. Once it is clean, I add the salt, mixing it into the still-soft butter with a spoon until the taste is just right: fresh, creamy, with a lovely herbal savor. Then I store it cold until it's time to use.

At the conference, every guest who came into our space was offered a taste of this butter on a bit of bread or cracker as a hospitality blessing. I'm sure there was still con crud at the event that year, but at least nobody from our suite came down with it.

CHAPTER 2

Apotropaic Charms and Protection Magics

Protection magic is the domain focused on shielding from or turning away harmful influences. It is a huge domain of folk magic, as throughout history people have relied on magic to protect them from forces both seen and unseen. This chapter will not attempt to cover all aspects of protection magic, but simply focus on a few core practices that I have found particularly useful.

The term "apotropaic magic" comes from Greek *apotropaios*, "to turn away." This term is often used by scholars of folk magic. It alludes to the worldview prevalent in animist magical cultures in which the world is understood to be inhabited by forces, powers, and beings besides us. It is not necessary to see any of these beings or powers as inherently or morally evil in order to recognize that there is potential for them to do us harm. The animist worldview is an ecological one, and it recognizes that like any ecology, some of the beings and powers around us may be potential allies, but many may be dangerous to us. Spirits may be predatory or destructive or simply hungry; forces and energies may be unleashed by other people around us even without intention, and yet can still cause harm. And of course, we may experience physical risk in our daily lives from ordinary mischance, dangerous occupations, predatory or pathogenic beings in nature, and casual or structural violence from our fellow humans.

All these dimensions of risk can be aided with protection magics. For experienced practitioners, the use of protection magics becomes a matter of everyday practice, like locking the door of your house.

Loricas and Shielding prayers

It is not surprising to find verbal protection charms occupying a prominent place in Celtic magics, given the importance of poetry across all aspects of these traditions. In this section, we'll look at lorica prayers and other forms of poetic spiritual armors.

Loricae are part of a class of protection prayers that invoke armor to shield the person; the word *lorica* is from Latin, often translated as "breastplate," and more generally referring to armors of various kinds worn by Roman soldiers.[53] Lorica prayers, and similar poetic armors, typically use verbal incantation to invoke divine protection, drawing these protections specifically to each of the parts of the body to build spiritual armor of protection over the person.

A typical example might read like this:

> *May the blessing of God be on my shoulders,*
> *May the blessing of Mary be on my head,*
> *May the blessing of Christ be on my forehead,*
> *May the hearing of the Holy Ghost be in my ears,*
> *May the vision of the celestial hosts be in my eyes,*
> *And the language of God in my mouth.*

---

53. Tuomi, "Parchment, Praxis and Performance of Charms in Early Medieval Ireland," 69.

As these examples show, most extant lorica prayers are generally Christian in framing and in the type of divine protection being invoked. It is not known if lorica prayers of this sort were used in pre-Christian contexts. Some scholars, such as medieval magic specialist Jacqueline Borsje, posit lorica prayers as a hybridization of Celtic pre-Christian and Christian cultural elements, and that their use originated in Roman Britain, possibly as protection against pagan sorceries.[54] It has been observed that the overall structure of lorica prayers follows a similar pattern to that of the typical Celtic and Mediterranean curse tablet texts: invocation of divine aid, followed by the detailing of the body parts to be affected, and ending with a closure that may take the form of a pact with the divine entity invoked for aid. In view of these patterns, scholars have suggested that the lorica prayer developed as a Christianized protection magic, following a familiar and culturally ingrained magical formula while weaving in the religious iconography of the new faith.[55] Linguist and Celtic scholar Pierre-Yves Lambert comments: "It is as much the sheer use of repetition and the formal stylization as the holy names invoked that generate the protective power of these texts. This feature of the loricae may derive from an ultimate origin in pagan defensive magical practice."[56]

Another way in which lorica prayers appear to inherit aspects of pre-Christian cosmologies lies in the iteration of the parts of the body. Many Celtic cosmological myths, as part of their inheritance in the Indo-European culture family, contain similar litanies of body parts in the context of the creation of the physical world from the body of a primordial sacrificed being. These litanies convey a cosmological construct in which the world itself is life created from life, matter from matter, following the sacrifice of a first divine being. They often follow a pattern of sympathetic linking of similar things: earth made from the being's flesh, mountains from its bones, plants from its hair, and the like.[57] In a similar vein, lorica prayers often sympathetically link divine qualities to the parts of the body

---

54. Borsje, "Celtic Spells and Counterspells," 19–20.

55. Mees, *Celtic Curses*, ch. 7.

56. Lambert, "Celtic Loricae and Ancient Magical Charms," 646.

57. Lincoln, "The Druids and Human Sacrifice," 388–389.

being protected. In a sense, this type of prayer invokes a microcosmic mirroring of the divine act of cosmological creation into the building of spiritual armor.

Other types of poetic shields exist that invoke more general spiritual shielding and protection, rather than focusing on building armor to a litany of specific body parts. A famous example of this type of protection prayer is the Spell of Long Life. This excerpt illustrates its poetic recitation of luck and protection:

> *I invoke the seven daughters of the Sea*
> *who fashion the threads of the sons of long life:*
> *May three deaths be taken from me!*
> *May three periods of age be granted to me!*
> *May seven waves of good fortune be dealt to me!*
> *Phantoms shall not harm me on my journey in flashing corslet*
> *   without hindrance!*
> *My fame shall not perish!*
> *Let old age come to me! death shall not come to me till I am old!*
> *I am an indestructible stronghold,*
> *I am an unshaken rock,*
> *I am a precious stone,*
> *I am the luck of the week.*
> *May I live a hundred times a hundred years, each hundred of*
> *   them apart!*[58]

Here this prayer shifts the formula to include an invocation of divine protection, and an enumeration of the types of protection being called for, including a lorica (here translated "corslet") of protection, but without the typical litany of body parts seen in most lorica prayers. It closes with a recitation of faith and invocation of divine blessing.

Another form of shield prayer is the *caim*, known primarily from the Scottish Gaelic tradition. It is also called a "circle prayer," as it invokes a spiritual shield encircling the body. *Caim* can mean a "loop or circle," and is also

---

58. Meyer, "An Old Irish Prayer for Long Life," 231.

sometimes translated "sanctuary" or "encompassing" (in the sense of encircle-ment).[59] Caim prayers invoke a ring of protection that centers on the body and moves with the person as they go about. Folkloric collections such as the *Carmina Gadelica* indicate that the incantation was performed along with a physical ritual. The verbal incantation invokes holy powers to enchant an encircling shield of divine protection, while the invoker "stretches out the right hand with the forefinger extended, and turns round sunwise as if on a pivot, describing a circle with the tip of the forefinger while invoking the desired protection."[60] This ritual of encirclement certainly suggests a pre-Christian ori-gin to the practice—the turning in a sunwise direction to invoke blessing is a practice found across many Celtic cultural sources, including the earliest Irish mythological texts.

Several examples of the incantation are preserved, including this one from the *Carmina Gadelica*:

> *The compassing of God and His right hand*
> *Be upon my form and upon my frame;*
> *The compassing of the High King and the grace of the Trinity*
> *Be upon me abiding ever eternally,*
> *Be upon me abiding ever eternally.*
> *May the compassing of the Three shield me in my means,*
> *The compassing of the Three shield me this day,*
> *The compassing of the Three shield me this night*
> *From hate, from harm, from act, from ill.*
> *From hate, from harm, from act, from ill.*[61]

Again, these incantations as found exist in a highly Christianized form. Given how much pre-Christian cosmology is contained in many of these prayers, it is blessedly easy to reengineer them for use in a pagan context. This can be as simple as replacing the names of Christian powers with other deities

---

59. Carmichael, *Carmina Gadelica*, Vol. II, 236.

60. Carmichael, *Carmina Gadelica*, Vol. III, 102.

61. Carmichael, *Carmina Gadelica*, Vol. III, 103.

and adjusting a few images, or simply writing new ones on a similar structural formula.

Sorcerer's Toolkit
spiritual Armor

Here is a simple approach you can use to develop a practice for spiritual armoring.

To start, create a lorica prayer for yourself. It should open with an invocation of the holy powers you are petitioning for protection and proceed with applying that protection throughout the parts of the body, finishing with an invocation of being wholly encircled by protection. If you need somewhere to begin, try this template, feeling free to alter it and make it your own:

> *Holy gods be with me today*
> *Guardian spirits be with me today*
> *Be my shield and my armor against all harm*
> *May your holy power be over each part of me*
> *Over my head and spirit*
> *Over my eyes and ears and each of my senses*
> *Over my mouth and throat and in my voice*
> *Over my shoulders and arms and in my hands*
> *Over my heart and encircling my body*
> *Over my limbs and in my feet*
> *May each part of me be encircled by your protection*
> *From rising to the end of day and in my sleep.*

You can add in the names of any gods and spirits you feel close with and trust to aid you in protection. If you're feeling inspired, get creative with the poetry and make it your own. Alternately, you can find a traditional lorica prayer and use that, swapping out any of the Christian imagery and names to suit the divinities you trust. Post your lorica prayer somewhere you will see it, like over an altar or beside your mirror. Say it aloud each day to get accustomed to the rhythm and pattern. In this way, when you need to invoke protection, the words will come easily instead of drawing a blank.

Try adding visualization of spiritual armor when you perform your lorica prayer. During the invoking lines at the beginning, visualize your gods and spirits appearing around you, their numinous power gathering to create the spiritual armor. As you name each part of you, visualize shining pieces of armor coalescing out of this divine power and wrapping themselves around you. Take your time and try to feel this in your body; the strength and sense of protection that flows into you from wearing this armor. It may help to touch the parts of your body as you invoke the spiritual armor onto them.

Try adding a caim shield. In the prayer template, focus on the line near the end that reads, "May each part of me be encircled by your protection." Ritualize this as an invocation of the encircling shield. As you say this line of the prayer, stretch your dominant hand out and turn in a steady circle sunwise (clockwise) so that your hand describes a complete circle around your center point. Visualize the same divine power that formed your armor flowing through this arm and forming a shining protective shield that arcs above and below as you turn, forming a bright, spherical shield.

Release your spiritual armor. It's wise to be able to disarm when you don't need to be carrying spiritual armor—when you're in your safe place, or when you want to be more open, vulnerable, or intimate. To release the caim, simply extend your hand and turn widdershins (anti-clockwise), visualizing the shining shield dissipating as you go and flowing back to the gods whose power it came from. To release the armor, go backwards and visualize each piece releasing and lifting away, the shining power that formed them dissolving and flowing back to the gods. Finish by giving thanks for their protection.

Practice is helpful! You can practice the caim part separately from the rest of the lorica, too. How do they feel differently from each other? What do they offer you separately and together? Keep practicing your lorica and caim invocations until they flow easily and the visualizations come readily. It can help to do this in the morning, or before you leave the safety of home. The ideal is to be able to instantaneously reinforce your spiritual armor the moment you need it.

Story
poetic Armor Rite

I'm in San Francisco on a chilly November day, marching in a large protest against the Dakota Access Pipeline, which oil companies are attempting to force through Native American lands. Everyone is talking about the efforts at Standing Rock Reservation to resist the pipeline. Out here in California, I'm joining local efforts to support the water protectors of Standing Rock to stop the pipeline being built. There are thousands in the streets today, and I'm marching with a small cohort of clergy folks from local churches, synagogues, and temples, as well as pagan and polytheist groups.

There's been a call from the organizers for volunteers willing to risk arrest shutting down the offices of the Army Corps of Engineers, the agency that permits the project. Today I feel able to take this risk so I've stepped forward to volunteer. We've arranged ourselves in ranks in front of all the entrances of the building and sat ourselves down blocking the doors. Sitting beside me in protest solidarity are a mix of other folks: a young minister of some stripe with his black shirt and white clerical collar, a gray-haired woman whose background I don't know, a dark-haired woman whose woven shawl suggests perhaps Jewish clergy, students with backpacks and scarves, folks of all kinds. We sit for a long while, passing the time between chatter and friendly silence.

Then word comes through the crowd that a police unit is incoming. That choice to risk arrest looms a little closer and we all get a little quieter. Arms are locked to make us that little bit harder to move. Some of the clergy folks around me are going into prayer. I begin arming myself spiritually in case police violence comes. I realize that I've never taken the time to memorize a traditional lorica prayer, so I just start making one up. Of course, I don't remember it, but it went something like this:

> *Mighty Morrígan, bringer of victory, be with me*
> *Macha, protector of sovereignty, be with me*
> *Badb of the battlefield, be with me*
> *Guardian spirits, wolf pack, be with me*
> *Spirits of the land I sit for protection of, be with me*
> *Courage of the Great Queen be in my heart*
> *Your Hero's Light be on my head*
> *Your spear be the strength in my spine*
> *The iron of Ernmas be my armor*
> *Protecting me from harm.*

I keep praying like that, holding the images in my mind as I invoke divine blessings onto each part of myself, till I feel covered in a shining armor of protection. Then I sit in meditation waiting for what might happen next. I'm not keen to get arrested but in the moment, I feel held by the gods and spirits and the solidarity of everyone around me and I'm at peace with what might happen. Eventually though, we get word that something's changed: a decision's been made that arrests won't be happening for the sitting clergy. I whisper another prayer of thanks. The feeling of walking with a shining armor of spirit presence wrapped around me will stay with me all day.

THE EVIL EYE

The link between the spiritual and emotional aspects of malevolence is evident in the folklore of the evil eye. Folk traditions in many cultures worldwide recognize and ward against this form of spiritual harm that comes from being overlooked, that is, being the subject of a malevolent glance. The ability of someone's glance to cause harm when it falls on a person hearkens to that animist worldview, which recognizes that we become connected to things we experience. Many evil eye beliefs center on the concept of spiritual or physical harm that arises from the emotion of an envious glance. To be looked on by someone feeling envy, suspicion, or hostility transmits a spiritual force arising from those emotions at the target of the gaze. Such a harmful glance can even be cast inadvertently by someone looking with too strong an appreciation, as this can verge close to envy, with the malevolence that rides along with it. In many Celtic sources, evil eye is also attributed to glances from Otherworldly, one-eyed, or monstrous beings; any kind of being whose glance might be thought to have power outside the norm. The young and new, or any being seen as particularly full of life, are thought to be especially vulnerable, such as babies and the young of livestock.[62]

Evil eye protections in folk practice are often focused on counteracting the danger of this kind of malevolent envy. Even a compliment might be counteracted with a subtle charm or apotropaic gesture, as a compliment can provide the focus for envy. In Gaelic folk traditions, this is often warded against by saying a blessing whenever a compliment is given to the practitioner or one in their care. These blessings often invoke the name of a protective spirit, saint, or deity. Sometimes they contain phrases meant to turn aside the power of the envy, like this one from a Scottish Gaelic charm: "Against small eye, against large eye, against the eye of swift voracious women ..."[63]

If someone is thought to have been overlooked, or even as a preventive, water rites are often turned to for relief and protection. There might be a blessing with consecrated waters, such as church-blessed holy water, or water from holy wells, collected in a sacral manner (as discussed in chapter 1). Incantations against evil eye often call upon a higher power felt to be able to interrupt its effect. There is also a custom of spitting to avert harm when

---

62. Borsje, "The Evil Eye," 3.

63. Black, "A Scottish Gaelic Charm in the North Carolina State Archives," 53.

there is thought to be a risk of evil eye.[64] A great many physical charms and talismans for protection in the tradition are also understood to protect against evil eye, in addition to other kinds of harm and trouble. These can include carrying a sprig of a sacred plant, or any number of the talismans discussed in the next section.

Apotropaic Charms and Talismans

The body of material relating to protective charms in the various Celtic cultures is far too massive to attempt to cover exhaustively here. Instead, I focus on a few themes that are prevalent in many of these traditions, and the types of charms and talismans I have found most helpful from this body of material.

Bright metals are often used in such protective charms. Silver objects are perhaps the most prevalent of this type. Silver has been perceived to be, in a sense, incorruptible because it does not rust. Its capacity to tarnish without corroding has sometimes been seen as reflective of the metal absorbing harmful spiritual forces directed at the wearer; then instead of being harmed, the black tarnish can simply be polished away to renew its protective function. Traditionally, medallions, pendants, or simply silver coins would be used as protective talismans; carried in the pocket, sewn into a corner of clothing, placed in the bottom of the shoe, or even buried with the dead to protect them.[65] Copper has sometimes also stood in for this function, especially in the form of copper pennies.[66]

Pendant talismans hung on a light chain, cord, or thread have the additional function whereby the chain can break if a spiritual attack or blow comes against the wearer, as a sign that the talisman has absorbed the blow. Talismans like this are functioning as a sort of magical analogue to an electrical fuse: an intentionally weak link designed to break when absorbing force, and so provide a signal of attack while also diverting the harm.

---

64. Borsje, "The Evil Eye," 32–33.

65. Black, *Scottish Charms and Amulets*, 518; Gilchrist, "Magic for the Dead? The Archaeology of Magic in Later Medieval Burials," 141.

66. Campbell, *Witchcraft & Second Sight*, 102.

Red color appears very frequently in protective charms in Gaelic folk culture; perhaps for its connection to Otherworldly forces, and for its association with life and blood.[67] Typically, red thread or cloth might be used in charms: a bit of red yarn tied round an animal's tail or a child's wrist; red thread wound around rowan crosses or woven into corn dollies or *brídeogs*.[68] Trees and plants naturally bearing red berries, especially rowan and to a lesser extent holly, find their way into protective charms, and this is likely due in part to the magical power seen to be inherent to these plants.

iron in protective magic

Articles made of iron or steel have long been felt to hold protective power, especially against Otherworldly or chthonic forces. There is a constellation of reasons why this is so: Iron's natural red color that emerges with rust aligns it with the broad folk pattern of using red items in protective charms. That red color associates it with blood—even in times before there was medical knowledge of the connection between iron and hemoglobin, anyone who has left water in a cast iron pot will have seen how iron appears to turn water to blood. Iron seems always to hold a special connection with humanity; worked iron is the product of human craft in the hands of the blacksmith, always a figure of magic and sorcery as well as metalworking skill, especially in Celtic cultures.

For all these reasons, iron objects of any kind are traditionally felt to be protective. This is especially true of iron worked by a blacksmith, such as nails, knives, tools, horseshoes, and the like. Folk practice seems to especially favor iron blades.[69] Beliefs and customs surrounding the protective powers of iron objects, especially sharp ones, date as far back as Pliny the Elder, a Roman author of the first century CE.[70] These customs are continued through Irish, Scottish, and British folk custom into modern times and reflected in contemporary folklore records.

---

67. McNeill, *Silver Bough* Volume 1, 96.

68. Black, *Scottish Charms and Amulets*, 477–478.

69. Campbell, *Witchcraft & Second Sight*, 185; Hoggard, *Magical House Protection: The Archaeology of Counter-Witchcraft*, 106–108.

70. Pliny the Elder, "Book XXXIV: The Natural History of Metals," 44.

For example, there is a pervasive practice of nailing horseshoes above doors for protection and luck—found in Irish and Scottish folk practice and continuing in contemporary farms and households even in the New World.[71] Iron objects such as pins or brooches might be sewn into clothing, stuck in caps, or otherwise carried on the body for protection; parents would leave a pin or a sewing needle pushed into the fabric of a child's clothes for protection. Orkney folklore details the practice of using an iron blade to guard the birthing bed during childbirth.[72] Other traditions include using iron nails embedded round the frame of a child's bed, or a reaping hook or iron knife secreted beneath the bed. Pins, nails, and all manner of other sharp metal objects are commonly used inside witch bottles, a type of protection spell made inside a bottle or jar (for more on this, see the section on spirit traps).

Iron and steel blades are particularly excellent as apotropaic charms in that they offer both passive and aggressive protection. A blade can be hung over doors or windows or secreted somewhere as a passive apotropaic charm to keep harmful spiritual influences at bay. In a moment of need, however, the same tool can be taken up and used aggressively—either physically or ritually, as the need dictates. Blades can be used to cut magical bindings and break curses. Iron's natural affinity for fire means that a blade can be heated in flame to consecrate and charge it with the power of the fire, enhancing its warding properties and imbuing it with the fire's spirit. An account from Scotland details a procedure for waking up a blade: "Certain magic words were muttered to the blade of a knife or axe (the more steel the better), which was held for the purpose close to the mouth, and then, the blade being applied to the sore place …"[73] In this instance, it is for use in healing, but the principle here is animism—awakening and instructing the spirit in the blade to aid in the magic. The same process can be applied to preparing a blade for protective magic, as demonstrated in the next section.

---

71. Campbell, *Witchcraft & Second Sight*, 12–13.

72. Towrie, "Orcadian Childbirth Traditions."

73. Campbell, *Witchcraft & Second Sight*, 99.

Sorcerer's Toolkit
ιroη protectioη cHarms

As shown in the preceding discussion, there are an endless variety of forms that protection charms can take. In this section, I'll offer a simple ritual template you can use to create an iron protection charm.

For this ritual, you'll need:

- Something made of iron or steel that has a blade or point, such as an iron nail, railroad spike, knife, arrowhead, or tool bit.
- Blessing water (see chapter 1 for instructions on preparing this).
- A candle.
- An offering, such as spirits, milk, or butter.

First, make sure to cleanse yourself and your tools by sprinkling with the blessing water.

Then, you'll waken the blade. To do this, hold the iron so its point touches the flame of a candle. You can wrap the end in a bit of leather to buffer your fingers from the heat. Keep it there just long enough to warm the metal a little; no need to get it red hot or risk burning yourself. When the metal is warm, pull the blade from the flame and bring it close enough for your breath to flow over it. Speak to the spirit in the iron so that your breath enters the metal while it is still warm, as you instruct it to protect you. You can instruct it however you choose; for example: "Awake, blade, waken and hear me. I ask you to guard me. Turn your point against all who would harm me and mine. Be you fierce and sharp to guard us."

The next step is to feed the spirit with an offering. You can put a few drops of something nourishing or enlivening on the metal. Whiskey or other spirits or wine are suitable offerings. Alternately, a few drops of milk or a little butter rubbed on the metal are nourishing. Metal objects also appreciate oiling with a blade oil as this literally feeds and protects the metal.

Finally, set the charm where it will protect you. There are many options for where to set the charm for greatest effect. You could hang it over a door, window, or other entry point. To guard you during sleep, attach it on or place beneath the bed. If you've used a nail, it can be hammered into any spot where you want to create protection. A small item can be hung on a cord to wear or slipped into clothing. You may wish to periodically retrieve it and repeat this ritual of wakening, instructing, and feeding the blade, so its protective power stays vibrant and attentive.

I encourage you to feel free to elaborate on this practice and to let your creativity and your spirits guide you. In the next section I share an account of a ritual to create iron protection charms with a few more magical components and layers added in.

Story
An Iron Charm Rite

We're gathered in a workshop room to practice making iron blade charms. We've chosen our materials: a handmade iron arrowhead or a favorite little steel blade; lengths of yarn and fabric in bright apotropaic reds; a bit of something to gather in our guardian spirits, a claw or tooth, feather, bone, or bit of plant. We've lit the candles and made offerings to our spirit allies. Now we begin the rite, lifting the bowl to sprinkle blessing water over all our tools and materials as they sit laid out before us.

I've chosen a little antique iron knife someone gave me as a gift. Breathing a whispered invocation to my spirit allies, I pick up a canine tooth and red thread and begin winding and knotting to bind them together. I wind round the roots and points of the tooth, and round the tang of the knife, make a knot, wind round again, making a webbing that will hold them fast together. I gather in a little crow feather, wind the thread tight round its shaft, and laying it along the blade of the knife continue winding and knotting them together. Each knot I make, I breathe power into with a little wordless prayer for protection.

Near me, someone's chosen an iron arrowhead; they've gathered a bird's claw and a bit of mugwort and secreted them inside the hollow socket with a whispered prayer. A little piece of red silk wraps neatly over the socket, and then they've begun to wind and knot, round and round with red thread to bind it all together. The space is full of whispered prayers and the winding and binding of knots as each completes the making of the charm.

When we've each finished and sit holding a completed blade charm, we ready to consecrate them. One by one, we bring the blade to the candle, carefully holding by its tang or shaft while we warm the point and blade in the candle's flame. Not too much to burn ourselves or to ruin the temper of the metal, just enough to warm and enliven the blade so that when we speak our instructions into the blade, our breath and life force are absorbed into the metal and our instructions are coded into it as it cools again. Finally, just while it is still warm but cool enough to touch, we feed the spirit in the blade with a few drops of whiskey.

The blades fairly vibrate now with life, and one thinks of the stories of weapons that were alive and jumped about ready for battle. After we close our space with the usual offerings of thanks and final cleansing, this lively little knife charm I've made will go and live above a door or window to guard my home. If I need to, I can also pick it up and carry it with me as a spirit weapon, warming the blade in my fingers or at a candle to waken it up. It will be a friend to me for a long time to come.

meeting Tlachtga

Tlachtga is an Irish goddess whose stories link her to druidic magics, fire imagery, and the sacred site of Tlachtga, now known as the Hill of Ward, in Ireland. I connect with Tlachtga for guidance in learning and practicing magical techniques especially when my practice brings me to experimenting with new innovations. Her story deals with themes of undertaking risk and facing magical danger, and so I also associate her with protective magics.

She is one of several goddesses whose names are attached to sacred assembly sites of early Ireland by way of myths that tell of their deaths, a characteristic she shares with Tea, the namesake of Tara, Macha of Emain Macha, and Tailtiu, among others. Each of these sites were traditional places of ancient assembly where great ceremonial bonfires were lit. Tlachtga is distinctive in her association with druidic magic, however. Her story contains parallels to an Irish mytheme in which a goddess undertakes risk in the pursuit of magical knowledge, succeeds in unleashing this magical knowledge, and dies as a result of this effort, becoming identified with a landscape feature in this process. In this respect her story is similar to the river goddesses Bóann and Sinann.[74]

In *Dindshenchas* tales that describe her, Tlachtga is said to be the daughter of the legendary druid Mug Roith, accompanying him on a journey to the East to learn all the world's magic. On this journey they involve themselves with Simon Magus, a magician character imported into Irish mythology from early biblical traditions.[75] From this journey and magical learning, Tlachtga is said to have created the Roth Ramach, "rowing wheel," a mysterious druidic artifact that is sometimes framed as a type of vehicle, and at other times a magical weapon. This wheel could be deadly to those who came near it: "Blind is each that once sees it, deaf is each that hears it: dead is he that aught touches of the rough-jagged dreadful Wheel."[76] Some interpret this as a reference to the thunder wheel, like those wielded by certain Continental Celtic thunder gods. Others have proposed that the wheel might refer to the *clairín*

---

74. Chadbourne, "Giant Women and Flying Machines," 107.

75. Stokes, "The Prose Tales in the Rennes Dindshenchas," 61.

76. Gwynn, "The Metrical Dindshenchas Volume 4," 189.

búirthe or bullroarer, an instrument that mimics the sound of thunder, and is known to have been in use in early Ireland.[77] Tlachtga is also associated with other druidic artifacts, such as a pillar-stone called Cnámchoill that is connected to the wheel.[78]

The end of Tlachtga's story attaches her to the Hill of Ward, an ancient site featuring a wheel-like multivallate rath system. The story tells that she was impregnated by the three sons of Simon Magus (by rape, in some versions), and after returning to Ireland, she died giving birth to her three sons at the Hill of Ward, which then takes her name.[79]

Tlachtga's name and lineage link her to celestial powers, which suggests another interpretation of the wheel. She is the daughter of Mug Roith, whose name means "servant of the wheel."[80] Some Irish texts have interpreted the wheel in his name to mean the "wheel of the heavens" as a reference to celestial powers or astronomical knowledge: "Because it was by 'wheel incantation' that he used to make his observations."[81] The name element *mug*, "servant," could suggest the title of a priest or votary of a sky god—something that may be reinforced by Mug Roith's frequent employment of weather magic in other tales. Tlachtga's name comes from *tlacht*, "surface, covering, protection, ornament" and *ga*, "spear"; contextually the first element is usually interpreted to refer to the surface of the earth and so her name is typically read as meaning "Earth Spear," which may be a reference to lightning (though an argument could be made for "protecting spear" or "ornamented spear").[82]

There are many more layers of complexity to the stories of these figures as represented in medieval Irish literature, but what strikes me and has driven my relationship with Tlachtga as a divine being is the through-line of magical innovation and celestial fire. Their lineage includes the Servant of the Wheel

---

77. Macalister, "Temair Breg: A Study of the Remains and Traditions of Tara," 345.

78. Gwynn, "Metrical Dindshenchas Vol. 4," 189.

79. Stokes, "The Edinburgh Dinnshenchas," 491.

80. Macalister, "Temair Breg," 345.

81. O'Grady, *Silva Gadelica (I–XXXI): A Collection of Tales in Irish, Vol. 2: Translation and Notes*, 511.

82. Royal Irish Academy, "EDIL 2019: An Electronic Dictionary of the Irish Language, Based on the Contibutions to a Dictionary of the Irish Language, s.v. *tlacht*."

and his daughter Lightning, who are originators of druidic magical technologies associated with fiery celestial phenomena such as lightning, storm, thunder, or meteor strike.

She is a magical innovator. Her connections with magical weaponry and protective ritual boundaries make her a powerful ally in both warding and aggressive magics. Her sigil features a wheel shape, for her fiery wheel and the multivallate rath at her sacred site, and a spear shape that references her name. It incorporates the Celtic letter-signs Orbion (the wheel, tradition, legacy); Dubnos (druidic magic, powers that can both heal and harm); and Ratis (the rath, hidden knowledge, Otherworld powers). It also includes the ogham letter-signs Tinne (metal, craftsmanship, weapon); Straif (occult power, transformation); and Onn (wheel, movement). She is illustrated as the stormy wheel of the heavens and the fire of the sun, and that fire striking the earth as lightning to connect with the sacred fire within the rings of the protective rath.

spirit traps

Spirit traps comprise a wide genre of protective magics and come in many forms. The basic principle is to draw an unwanted spirit or presence in through attractive or mesmerizing elements, and then to bind, entrap, or destroy it. This can be accomplished through a variety of different approaches and folk magical traditions have devised a profusion of creative methods.

In the folk traditions, spirit traps are often found in the form of complicated, tangled, woven, or mazelike structures. Spirits can be attracted to complex designs, drawn in and mesmerized by their patterns just as people may be when viewing something intricate. The understanding is that spirits will be compelled to try to trace the complex patterns or tangled lines, and in so doing they enter the spirit trap and become lost in its complexity and trapped like an animal in a maze. Some types of spirit traps found in folk magic operate on the related principle that a mass of small individual items, like seeds or beads, will cause spirits to be compelled to try to count the uncountable profusion of things, and will get stuck endlessly counting and never reaching the end of the tally. Both are examples of the use of complexity in a spirit trap.

Sigil Illustration for Tlachtga

Protective woven charms found throughout folk traditions exemplify the complex spirit trap. For example, in a pervasive custom found across Britain, Ireland, Scotland, and even imported to the New World, twigs (typically of rowan wood) placed in the form of a cross and bound round and round with red yarn would avert the evil eye and protect against harmful spirits.[83] This charm employs multiple forms of protection: the cross shape, the sacred wood, the red color all contribute to its protective power, while the winding round and round of the yarn (itself composed of myriad fine fibers) forms a trap for spirits. Similarly, the custom of making *brídeogs*, crosses, corn dollies, and similar protective charms from grain stalks or reeds creates several layers of protection.[84] These charms employ the complexity of the woven stalks to create a spirit trap, while their form and consecration—often named for and consecrated to Brigid, the Cailleach, or another deity—augment their protective power.

Ornamental interlace patterns and knotwork found on early architecture, monumental stones, as well as medieval books and reliquaries can function as an apotropaic device. Yes, that Celtic knotwork that is so beloved may often have been intended as a magical device. Medievalist Diego González Hernández has noted that the placement of interlace patterns and knotwork panels is often not random; instead, they are found more frequently at boundaries and other liminal points. For example, medieval doorways and other entrance points carry a higher occurrence of such art relative to other parts of buildings, as do boundary markers and even the exterior plates and transitional pages of medieval books.[85] The intricate, interwoven patterns of the knotwork form natural spirit traps to draw in and entangle harmful spirits. Often, this art includes animals and other beast guardians within its structures, who may be there in part to devour and destroy trapped spirits.

---

83. Black, "A Scottish Gaelic Charm in the North Carolina State Archives," 45; Black, *Scottish Charms and Amulets*, 477–478.

84. Black, *The Gaelic Otherworld*, 11; National Folklore Collection UCD, "The Schools' Collection," 211.

85. Hernández, "The Apotropaic Function of Celtic Knotwork in the Book of Kells," 40.

Witch-marks can often be found scratched, carved, or burned on the doorways, walls, or other surfaces in old buildings such as homes and churches—or even in caves. While some witch-marks appear to be used more as sigils or protective symbols, some of the more complex ones can also serve as spirit traps. These sometimes take the form of boxes, mazes, complexes of overlapping diagonal lines, daisy wheels, or circles.[86]

Starting in the late medieval period, witch bottles become a popular form of spirit trap, and though they postdate the Celtic period, they are exemplars of similar principles.[87] In the case of witch bottles, instead of using hypnotic complexity to draw the unwanted spirits in, the trap is baited with the bodily residues of the person being protected. Hair, fingernail clippings, and urine are often put into the bottle, so that a spirit seeking to harm a person will follow their scent into the trap. Of course, hair can also serve that entangling function at the same time, and sometimes knots of tangled thread are found in witch bottles as well. The bottles are also filled with sharp or jagged objects: pins, needles, nails, broken glass or ceramics, thorns—objects to wound and kill the harmful spirits once trapped there.

Like a physical trap, spirit traps may need maintaining. What happens next after a spirit is entrapped? In a spirit trap without a destructive mechanism, the forces trapped in it will simply stay there, but as they are living entities this isn't necessarily a stable situation on its own. Over time, spirits trapped (especially when multiples are present) can bond together, complexify, feed on one another, or organize to form something more dangerous. Even solitary spirits may become more dangerous over time through containment. With time the boundaries of the spirit trap may weaken, or the spirits left in it can overwhelm it. Even if spirits are eaten or destroyed, as in weaponized traps or those with guardians installed within, there still may be spiritual residues that over time can cause harm to the trap or weaken its ability to function.

It is, therefore, a good idea for spirit traps to be periodically emptied, cleansed, and their powers refreshed. Some folk traditions accomplish this by

---

86. Hoggard, *Magical House Protection*, 76–102.

87. Hoggard, *Magical House Protection*, 18–23.

tying the use of spirit traps to seasonal customs, where old apotropaic charms are burned or in some other way destroyed on a recurring holy day, thereby also destroying the spirits and forces contained in them, and fresh charms are made and blessed. The *brídeog*, corn dolly, or woven cross style of spirit traps lend themselves well to this approach. More permanent types of spirit trap, such as the kind inscribed or carved into structures, can't be destroyed, but can be cleansed and renewed. Here, the spirits held within it are forcibly banished, often by the use of spiritual cleansing methods like water blessing and sacred smoke. Often this would be combined with petitioning the blessing of divine powers understood to be stronger than the unwanted spirits, to make sure that anything released from the spirit trap isn't free to return to causing harm. The renewal of protections may be part of the reason why, where witch-marks are found, there are often many overlapping iterations of them inscribed in the same spot. Most of these apotropaic charms, perhaps with the exception of witch bottles buried or walled up inside houses, are not one-and-done methods, but instead are part of an iterative and cyclical practice.

Sorcerer's Toolkit
spirit Traps

Of course, as you've just seen, there are many, many forms spirit trap charms can take, from woven charms to seed jars to witch bottles. To get started with this practice, I'll offer a simple method here for creating a woven cross type of spirit trap protection charm.

For this ritual, you'll need:

- A few twigs of a sacred wood.
- Red yarn, twine, or heavy thread.
- Blessing water.
- An offering, such as spirits, milk, or butter.

In sourcing the twigs, a very traditional wood to use for protection is rowan (*Sorbus aucuparia,* also known in some places as mountain ash). For a spirit trap with some aggressive qualities, you could use twigs from a thorny plant such as hawthorn (*Crataegus* spp.) or rose (*Rosa* spp.), for their associations with Otherworld powers, or blackthorn (*Prunus spinosa*), which is associated with cursing. Alternately, you can choose twigs of a plant you have a strong spiritual affinity with and feel you can count on the plant spirit to help you. I have even made protection charms with dried stems of mugwort!

To begin, cleanse yourself and your materials by sprinkling the blessing water over everything.

Then, weave the charm. Take two twigs and hold them firmly in a crossed position between thumb and fingers. Pick up the end of the yarn and lay it against the crossed twigs, leaving a tail of a couple inches long that you can use later to tie it off. Adjust fingers, so that you can hold the yarn in place with the twigs. With your other hand, pick up the yarn and begin winding around the join where the twigs cross. Wrap the yarn around all directions of the crossing so that the twigs begin to be held in place. It's okay to let your pattern be somewhat random. Remember, the idea is for this weaving to confuse and entangle the spirits! A little chaos is just fine. When the join is held firmly with enough wrappings of the yarn, you can also expand down the length of the twigs, wrapping around them and crossing the space between them. While you are doing this weaving, speak to the spirit in the plant, asking it for its help to create a powerful spirit trap that will help keep you safe. Finish off by tying the end together with the tail you left at the start.

Awaken the charm. When you finish weaving, breathe over the charm to give it life, and communicate your instructions for its work. You can use words of your own, or start from this template: "Be a trap to mesmerize, to entangle, to gather, and to bind, may all spirits and powers who would bring harm be drawn in and trapped, and with your holy power held and bound without escape so that none can do us harm."

Feed the charm. A few drops of spirits, wine, milk, or a bit of butter rubbed on the twigs will do, as an offering to the spirit of the charm.

Set out to protect your home by hanging the charm over a door or window, bed frame, or any place you want extra protection.

You can build layers onto this practice in a variety of ways. Try adding a third twig so you create a triangular structure you can fill with a webbing of yarn. Or try adding other magical components that will diversify or enhance the powers that make up the trap. A tooth or claw from a predatory animal to help devour spirits that enter the trap, like the beasts inside apotropaic knotwork art. Or a bit of something silver or iron for general protection, or sharp items like pins, needles, or nails. You could even weave in some of your own hair as an attractant to draw in spirits that might otherwise be after you, similar to the way that witch bottles would be filled with hair and nails of the person they are meant to protect.

A trap of this kind is usually good for at least a year. If it becomes clotted with dust, falls down or breaks, or just begins to feel spiritually dead or inert, burn it and replace with a fresh charm.

Story
A spirit Trap Rite

We have inherited a hefty little bundle of blackthorn twigs that had been pruned from a tree grown by a friend. A perfect resource for making a spirit trap. Plus, Samhain is just around the corner and it's a good time for reinforcing the house protections.

First, as always, we start with cleansing: ourselves, the blackthorn, and the red yarn, nails, and other bits we've gathered. I've also brought a bit of whiskey and we feed our spirit allies and ask them for their help. I then take a little butter and (carefully!) rub it into the stems of blackthorn while giving thanks:

Blackthorn friend, thank you for this gift of your branches.
In thanks, please receive this offering of nourishment.
I ask you to join me in protecting this house;
bring to bear your winding withes to snare and bind,
your thorns to trap and pierce, your spirit to enchant
so that no hostile being may enter this place.

We begin winding the blackthorn stems together, thankful that they're still green and flexible, but needing to be very mindful of the thorns. At first, it's an awkward and flimsy circlet, but with each stem woven in, under and over, it grows sturdier. With its structure set, we can attend to placing the remaining twigs into a spiraling pattern with their thorns stabbing inward. When it is done, it has the shape of a small, compact wreath that spirals inward, drawing spirits into its thorny center.

Now I take the red yarn and tie its end round one side, then weave it across the center of the wreath. As it crosses the center, I knot it round an iron nail, breathing a breath into the knot. Then I pass the yarn through and round the other side and repeat the process, forming a loose web of red crossing the center of the wreath that suspends three iron nails in its weave. As I complete the weave and tie off the red yarn onto the blackthorn structure, I hang a little charm decorated with an eye, asking: "Keep watch always on this house."

It now feels like a living, breathing creature. A mouth with many thorny and iron teeth waiting to swallow and entrap, and a watchful eye that gazes out. We give it a sprinkle of whiskey as another offering to feed its spirit, then hang it over the front door. It fits right in with the Halloween decorations that adorn the porch: skeletons, bundles of bones, corn dollies, Blair-Witch style twig dolls, chalked sigils, spiderwebs and creepy lights. Only a trained eye would pick this one out as magically active among the others.

A few times a year we'll take it down and sprinkle it with blessing water to cleanse away residues from anything it's caught, and give it a fresh offering of whiskey, milk, or butter. It will stand and protect our house for years to come.

protective and Apotropaic spirits

Here I will cover the employment of apotropaic and protective spirits—that is, spirit allies who are recruited specifically to serve a protective function or to turn away unwanted forces. In such an animist and polytheist cultural framework, there are an enormous variety of forms these relationships can take and the types of magics they can support. I'll just look at some examples and ask what they can teach us about how spirit work can enhance and support protective magics.

Protective spirit allies in early Celtic cultures seem often to be recruited through sacrificial killing. This is not surprising, given the pervasiveness of sacrifice as a mode of ritual and devotion in the ancient world. It's wise to be cautious about interpretation of this pattern, however. The evidence for historical spirit practices is limited to that which tends to survive physically, such as bone and metal; or is documented by observers in some way. Many of the examples of apotropaic spirit work in Celtic cultures come from funerary contexts with artifacts, bone deposits, or from surviving bog burials. Many of these examples preserve evidence of sacrifice, such as cut marks. This apparent prevalence of sacrifice as a mode of recruitment for spirit allies may belie many other methods that are not as well documented, however. A folk tradition involving nonmaterial practices, or offerings that degrade and leave no trace, may easily escape ever being documented. Similarly, artifacts in a variety of contexts may have served a function related to apotropaic spirits, but without preserving evidence that allows them to be interpreted in the right way.

Many students of Celtic cultures will already be familiar with the traditions of sacral kingship and king sacrifice. Evidence from some preserved bog bodies from Ireland and Britain has been read as substantiating the mythic and literary portrait of kingly sacrifice—as highlighted by the famous exhibit of Irish bog bodies in the National Museum of Ireland, for example.[88] Specifics about the way these bodies and other objects are deployed also points to a protective function that they were intended to fulfill after death. A meaningful proportion of sacrificial bog body deposits are found along territorial borders between kingdoms, and some scholars interpret this to indicate that after death, the body of a sacral individual would be placed along the boundaries in order to recruit their spirit as a territorial spirit guardian.[89] There is also evidence to suggest that these sacral bodies would sometimes be dismembered so that parts of that individual could be placed in guardianship in multiple locations.

This type of sacrificial spirit guardian practice is not limited to the sacred kingship model, however. Remains of animals and sometimes human beings have been found in a huge number of contexts suggesting spirit guardianship. Bones from sacrificed animals were placed into intentional arrangements in rath ditches defining sacred enclosures, to act as guardian spirits for the sanctuaries. This practice is seen across a broad range of Celtic sites. Archaeologist Jean-Louis Brunaux, writing of this as seen in Gallic sanctuaries, calls this deployment of animal remains in the boundary ditches the "apotropaic cordon," a continuous boundary formed by the skulls and bones of sacrificed animals, including cattle, horses, and others, whose spirits served an apotropaic role following sacrifice.[90] In Ireland, a similar practice is in evidence at sites such as Temair, Emain Macha, Crúachan and the like: bones of animals including cattle, sheep, pigs, horses, and dogs, along with human bone, and in one case even an infant, were placed into boundary ditches at consecrated sites.[91] In Britain, there are also a number of hill-fort sites featuring an association of corvid and dog remains placed in ritual pits in intentional configurations, which may have in part served an apotropaic function.[92]

88. National Museum of Ireland, "A New Theory of Sacrifice."

89. Kelly, "An Archaeological Interpretation of Irish Iron Age Bog Bodies," 237–238.

90. Brunaux, *The Celtic Gauls: Gods, Rites and Sanctuaries*, 25–33.

91. Waddell, *Archaeology and Celtic Myth*, 72–73.

92. Serjeantson, "Ravens and Crows in Iron Age and Roman Britain," 94–96.

Perhaps the most spectacular example of apotropaic spirit guardians is the famous "Ghost Cavalry" at the Gallic oppidum of Gondole (in the Auvergne region of France). Here a large pit was found just outside the walls of the hill-fort with the carefully placed and aligned bodies of eight men and eight horses, lacking any grave goods and bearing no signs of violence.[93] The burial took place at about the time of Caesar's conquest of Gaul, and archaeologists have theorized that this apparently willing mass death and burial may have been undertaken in order to install a spirit army outside the gates to guard the hill-fort.

Not all apotropaic spirit practices are so grand and impressive. Domestic spaces have also traditionally received spirit guardians. Many houses from the medieval to early modern period in Ireland and Britain have been found to have horse heads buried beneath the floors.[94] There are multiple possibilities as to why this practice was prevalent, but archaeologists see protection as a likely one. It is also not uncommon in medieval houses to find animal remains entombed into the walls or beneath thresholds—often smaller domestic animals such as cats or dogs. It's theorized that these domestic helper animals who guarded the home in life from intruders, vermin, and other harms, were simply being recruited to continue protecting the household in death.[95] Many of these domestic animal guardians may not have been sacrificed—they may have been recruited to spirit guardianship following a natural death at the end of an ordinary domestic relationship. This is indicated, for example, by some of the horse remains mentioned previously, which showed advanced age, evidence of the wear of labor on the bones, and a lack of evidence of violence.

The principle at work in all of these examples is the understanding that the spirits attached to the bones of these beings would remain and could be recruited to protect the place where the bones are kept. Most instances of this practice in the archaeological record lack evidence as to how the ritual aspect of this was conducted. Reciprocity is key in all spirit relationships, and so part

---

93. Aldhouse-Green, *Caesar's Druids: Story of an Ancient Priesthood*, 63–64.

94. Hoggard, *Magical House Protection*, 60–66; O'Sullivan, "Magic in Early Medieval Ireland," 110.

95. Hoggard, *Magical House Protection*, 51–53.

of the ritual would likely have involved giving something to the spirit being recruited as guardian, in payment or tribute. In the case of domestic animals, this is merely the continuation of the reciprocity that has existed in life where domestic or farm service was exchanged for food and shelter.

Outside of the use of living animals, spirit guardians can also be established through the placement of artifacts. It may be that some of the votive artifacts found deposited in lakes, bogs, rivers, and other such subterranean or watery sites may have had such a function. It has been widely noticed that in many instances of Celtic votive deposition, the object is intentionally broken; this is understood as a means of sending it to the Otherworld for the use of the spirits or deities by destroying its use in the world of the living.[96] There may be another layer of meaning here: in an animistic culture, objects, particularly consecrated ones, are understood to contain a spirit. Early Irish literature documents, fairly thoroughly, a belief that weapons, armor, and other objects could be inspirited and that people were in relationship with these spirits (a topic I will take up in more depth in the next chapter). This being so, the physical destruction of the object would be a form of object sacrifice, where it is being ritually killed in order to send its spirit to the Otherworld where it can be of service. This provides a helpful model for working with spirit guardians for contemporary practitioners who may prefer not to deal with animal sacrifice.

---

96. Beck, "Goddesses in Celtic Religion," 335–336.

CHAPTER 3

spirit work and spirit alliances

Relationships with spirits undergird nearly all aspects of Celtic magic. In the last chapter, I shared some examples of how spirit relationships can enhance and integrate with protection magics. In this chapter, I will focus on spirits and spirit alliances. When looking at frameworks that Celtic traditions offer for relating to spirits, several themes emerge.

Animism and Reciprocity

Spirit practices in the Celtic traditions arise out of an animistic worldview within which spirits are understood and recognized as living, sovereign beings. The model of spirit work here is distinct from the approach of conjuration, commanding, and binding spirits to do the magician's bidding as found in some expressions of the Western ceremonial tradition. Rather than dominating spirits, most examples of working with spirits found in the Celtic cultures and literatures are built upon entering into reciprocal relationships. These relationships proceed from a relatively equal footing, and often arise out of long-term bonds between practitioners and spirits. Offerings and sacrifices are a recurring theme whereby reciprocity is enacted, sometimes framed as payment or tribute that is owed to spirits. In other instances, dedicated service has been given to spirits, their associated deities, or the places they call home, providing the basis for relationship and the ability to call on those spirits. Relationships with spirits are not only reciprocal, but in many cases are contractual in nature, and these contracts with Otherworld powers form the backbone of many myths, folktales, and folk practices.

Families and Retinues of Spirits

Spirits are often aligned into groups or families, and these collective relationships help direct how we work with these spirits. Some groupings of spirits are rooted in ordinary human relationships, such as the ancestors of a family line, clan, or tribe. Others may form around relationship to landscape and environment, such as groups of spirits relating to waters and rivers; sky and weather spirits; spirits in plants, stones, and other natural land features; and spirits of place. These traditions also strongly feature collectives of Otherworldly spirits, such as fairies, sprites, Otherworldly beasts, and the terrors or battle spirits. Relationships with animal spirits are also prominent in the tradition and may be personal, familial, tribal, or shaped by a person's role.

Within the realm of spirits, the gods are also an organizing force. As with many polytheistic and animistic traditions, deities tend to be associated with groups of spirits who in some way share aspects of that deity's nature and powers, or who may represent a minor aspect of their presence or identity. There is indication that the human dead, in some circumstances, may go with a deity in the afterlife and become part of their spirit cohort. In contemporary polytheist communities, these collectives of spirits are often referred to as the "retinue" or "court" of a deity—those spirits who are connected or aligned with that deity may appear alongside them, and may carry messages from or help accomplish the work of that deity. When we enter into relationship with gods, these retinues of spirits often present themselves as well.

There are several fascinating and well-described examples of deities with retinues that can be studied for knowledge of working with spirit collectives. A highly visible example are the battle spirits associated with weapons, war gear, and the battlefield, which the tradition positions in relationship with Badb as a goddess of battle; she is found among them in lists of spirits of the battlefield, and the descriptions portray a similarity in nature, appearance, and function between goddess and spirits.[97] Similarly, the various spirits associated with the Morrígan partake of her nature and appear similarly: eel spirits associated with sorcery and who echo her taking eel form; wolves who are associated with the cave where she makes her home, and who echo her taking wolf form, etc.[98] Spirits of air and wind are conjured by Mug Roith, whose name connects him to a storm or sky god.[99] Horses are associated in ritual with sovereignty, and horse spirits are found among the retinues of sovereignty deities such as Macha, as evidenced by the discovery of horse bones in the boundary ditches of royal sites.[100]

Celtic sorcery is a magic of spirits, a polytheist magic proceeding from spirit relationships that are themselves held and overseen by the greater powers of the gods. In a sense, gods can be understood as simply big spirits—spirits marked by a greater sphere of influence and more potent powers than those of common spirits. In consequence of their greater degree of power and influence within the spiritual realms, deities can be called on to help us establish alliances with spirits within their retinues. They can also come to our aid if we get out of our depth or need backup. When we understand what family or group a spirit belongs to, we can call in the cavalry, so to speak: invoke the aid of a greater divinity who can help us into the right relationship with the spirits, negotiate with them, or protect us from their influence.

---

97. Borsje, "Omens, Ordeals and Oracles: On Demons and Weapons in Early Irish Texts," 239–241.

98. Mees, *Celtic Curses*, 3930; Stokes, *Acallamh Na Senórach*, 264.

99. O'Grady, *Silva Gadelica* Vol. 2, 511.

100. Waddell, *Archaeology and Celtic Myth*, 144–145.

environmental sorcery

A recurring theme in myth and folklore concerns sorcery performed through calling on spirits in the land, waters, or sky. I think of this as environmental sorcery. Several stories in the Irish and Welsh corpus describe the rituals associated with this type of sorcery.

In the *Táin Bó Cúailnge*, there is an episode of environmental sorcery performed by Cú Chulainn. He is embattled and facing too many enemies to hold off on his own, so he performs an invocation for aid, calling on heaven, the earth, and the river. His petition focuses especially on the river, asking that the waters rise and create a barrier to his enemies: "'I beseech the rivers to come to my help. I call upon heaven and earth and especially the river Cronn to aid me.' Thereupon the river rose in flood as high as the tree-tops."[101] This story doesn't provide much ritual detail, but there are some things to be learned from it. One is that Cú Chulainn, while not often thought of as someone specializing in magic, has the ability to call upon spirits of the land, sky, and waters and that they will answer him at need. This leads me to wonder what reciprocity may already exist in his relationship with these powers that provides a reason for the river to respond. His contribution here may be his defense of the province of Ulster, placing himself in harm's way as a warrior to protect the province, which creates a debt of reciprocity with the spirits of the landscape he can call upon at need.

Another, rather spectacular type of environmental sorcery is described in the Irish sagas where characters acting in the role of druids conjure supernatural atmospheric phenomena such as thick clouds of mist, bloody rain, and showers of fire. This type of atmospheric sorcery is attributed to the Morrígan and her sisters in *The First Battle of Mag Tuired*, and also to the druids in *The Siege of Knocklong*.[102] The stories are mythological in nature, but the recurrence of this motif and the specific, granular detail by which the ritual technique is described suggests that it could contain elements of folk memory. Authors writing about druids in the ancient world recorded that they were

---

101. O'Rahilly, "Táin Bó Cúalnge Recension 1," 157.

102. Fraser, "The First Battle of Moytura," 27; Ó Duinn, "The Siege of Knocklong," 37.

believed to be able to control the heavens, and certainly, the Knocklong story provides a fully realized example of what a weather conjuration ritual might look like.

First, to prepare a magical fire, rowan wood is ritually gathered from special places in the landscape and is arranged into a burn structure. Shavings are taken from the wood of spear handles and this material is rolled with butter into a combustible ball. Mug Roith then begins to chant poetic incantations over the ball, which is then lit afire and hurled into the rowan wood burn structure to cause it to explode it into flames.[103] The smoke of this fire is then used to conjure atmospheric spirits and create the supernatural weather effects to be sent against enemies of the king that Mug Roith serves. In his incantation over the fire, Mug Roith blows his druidic breath over it, while petitioning the wind spirits and a god to aid his attack: "God of druids, my god above every god, he is god of the ancient druids. The wind will blow, may it blow a low flame to burn the young vegetation, a high flame for the old vegetation, a quick burning of the old, a quick burning of the new …"[104]

Here is a druid engaging an atmospheric power as a spirit ally alongside a deity. Not only is this an example of atmospheric sorcery through natural spirits, it also illuminates the relationship between deities and the spirits in their retinues. The god invoked by Mug Roith is not directly named, but there are some clues. His own name, Mug Roith, means "servant of the wheel." The first part, *mug*, means "servant, slave, or bondman," and also appears in early Irish names indicating a monk or someone who is sworn in service to a deity.[105] The second part of the name, *roth*, means "wheel" and appears to reference a sky god of some kind. Wheels are persistent imagery attributed to celestial deities across Celtic cultures; such as the thunder wheel of the Gallic Taranis, or the Welsh Arhianrhod whose name references the wheel of the heavens. Mug Roith's service to the "wheel" has been read by some scholars as indicating service to an

103. Ó Duinn, "The Siege of Knocklong," 97–99.

104. Ó Duinn, "The Siege of Knocklong," 99.

105. Royal Irish Academy, "EDIL 2019: An Electronic Dictionary of the Irish Langauge, Based on the Contributions to a Dictionary of the Irish Language, s.v. *mug, mog*."

Irish storm deity similar to Taranis, or even as a reference to a solar wheel and solar god.[106] Whoever this deity is, the story presents a druid who is in a lifelong relationship of service to a celestial god, calling on that relationship to petition his god to engage the wind spirits of his retinue, to aid in the conjuration of supernatural storm phenomena.

There is also a recurring motif of spirit armies conjured from the land. I think of this as a kind of environmental sorcery as these phantoms often arise or are conjured out of elements in the natural environment. Several examples of this phenomenon appear in the mythological literature: in the death-tale of Cú Chulainn, a phantom army is conjured from "leaves and stones and ferns" by the daughters of Calatín.[107] In the tale of *Cath Finntraga*, a similar host of spirits is conjured from stalks of grass and tops of watercress.[108] I will return to this motif in the last chapter of the book, on war magic.

stone veneration

Stones frequently function as loci of spirit alliances in both literature and folk tradition, and in the lore of stone reverence is a rich vein of material about the practices used in these spirit relationships. The veneration of stones appears to be a very ancient tradition reflecting the animistic roots of Celtic cultures, and given the background of preexisting megalithic cultures across the region, may well be inherited from pre-Celtic societies. There are many examples of this stone veneration in both mythological literature and continuing to recent folk practice; it seems to represent one of the continuous through-lines in Celtic tradition.

Stone worship is described in the *Dindshenchas* as part of ancient and medieval practice. For example, this description from the *Dindshenchas* of Druim Tairleime:

> There was a talking stone there, since the time of the Tuatha De Danann, and a demon used to give answers from it. He

---

106. Macalister, "Temair Breg: A Study of the Remains and Traditions of Tara," 345.

107. Mullally, "The Phantom Army of 1169: An Anglo-Norman View," 93.

108. Meyer, *Cath Finntraga*, 7.

used to tell everyone to halt at it, to worship him. So that everyone who passed by dismounted at it, and they used to worship him. Hence grew up the custom that none from that time onward approaches the hill without dismounting, as if they were under a ban not to pass by without stopping there.[109]

Here, several aspects of practice are being described. The stone is understood to contain a spirit that is capable of communicating with worshipers and it's implied that it provides oracular answers to questions. In reciprocity, it is offered worship, and there seems to be a cultural prohibition on passing by a standing stone understood to be alive in this way without stopping to honor it. There is a clear through-line from this early medieval description to a late eighteenth-century custom recorded on the isle of Inisglora, where the forms of worship of sacred stones are described in more detail: such living stones were washed regularly on certain days of the week or season, fed with butter or ale, and clothed as a sign of honor.[110]

It is interesting to consider the association of druidic magic with pillar stones in light of this information about animistic stone veneration. Early Irish literature makes an association where druids practicing magic are positioned on or near standing stones. From *The First Battle of Moytura*: "Their seers and wise men stationed themselves on pillars and points of vantage, plying their sorcery, while the poets took count of the feats and wrote down tales of them."[111] Pillar stones are also associated in the same text with what appears to be binding magic: "They [the Túatha Dé Danann] fixed their pillars in the ground to prevent any one fleeing till the stones should flee."[112] The Morrígan also lights on a pillar stone on more than one occasion when speaking prophecy.[113] These actions can seem obscure, but in light of the ani-

---

109. Gwynn, "The Metrical Dindshenchas Vol. 4," 297.

110. Wood-Martin, *Traces of the Elder Faiths*, Vol. II, 67.

111. Fraser, "The First Battle of Moytura," 43.

112. Fraser, "The First Battle of Moytura," 45.

113. O'Rahilly, "Táin Bó Cúalnge Recension 1," 152; Meyer, *Fianaigecht*, 16.

mistic tradition of reverence for spirits inhabiting stones, perhaps this use of stones is intended to align with and draw upon the power of the spirits in the stones.

Smaller and more portable stones also appear in magical practices, similarly framed as loci or instruments for contacting spirits. A vividly described example concerns the handstone of Mug Roith, my favorite druid sorcerer. He keeps a special stone in his possession, apparently of a size that could be carried in the hand. The medieval tale *The Siege of Knocklong* shows him using it as a kind of portal to activate a spirit alliance and summon the spirit. Revealing again the animism that underlies these practices, Mug Roith speaks about his stone as a person and addresses it directly in an incantation:

> *Bring me my poison-stone, my hand-stone, my hundred-fighter,*
> *my destruction of my enemies.' This was brought to him and he*
> *began to praise it, and he proceeded to put a venomous spell on*
> *it, and he recited the following rhetoric:*
> *I beseech my Hand-Stone –*
> *That it be not a flying shadow;*
> *Be it a brand to rout the foes*
> *In brave battle.*
> *My fiery hard stone –*
> *Be it a red water-snake…*[114]

I will return to this incantation later as it concerns that "red water-snake" he mentions. What I want to point out here is that the handstone is clearly being addressed as the vessel of a spirit being. Mug Roith offers this spirit praise and veneration and by means of an incantation, is able to rouse the spirit within the handstone and call upon its aid. I think of this in light of those pillar-stone veneration practices—the regular honoring, feeding, and anointing of the stones. I imagine that Mug Roith's conjuration of the spirit probably arises from an ongoing practice of this kind that has established the spirit alliance he is now calling into action.

---

114. Ó Duinn, "The Siege of Knocklong," 77.

Contemporary Irish and Scottish folk magic (and that of other European cultures) also preserve practices around the use of bullaun stones. These are sacred stones kept in holy places, often alongside saint cults such as at holy wells. The bullaun stones are typically about hand sized and often sit in hollows atop a larger stone, hollows that have been formed over centuries by the repeated turning of the bullaun stones under many hands.[115] Folk visit the stones and turn them in their hollows by means of traditional patterns for magical aid, sometimes along with a prayer or imprecation, for cursing or for healing.[116] There is an association between these bullaun stones and monastic or ecclesiastical sites where they are often found, but in practice their folkloric use reaches beyond Christian practice and takes in elements not condoned by the church, such as cursing. It seems to me that this engagement with stones may arise from the same animistic recognition of spirits within stones that underpins the ancient examples of stone veneration as well.

Animal Spirits

A great deal could be written about relationships with animal spirits in Celtic traditions as a whole, and this would be beyond the scope of this book. Here I want to focus on spirit work in these traditions as it relates to the practice of sorcery specifically, as well as some observations about models of relationship for working with these spirits.

It is important first to make a distinction between working with animal spirits in Celtic sorcery, and the idea of totemism or totem animals. The term "totem" has been appropriated and anglicized from Anishinaabe Native American peoples.[117] As part of this misappropriation, a variety of meanings have been projected onto it, most of which are not authentic to its meaning and function in Anishinaabe cultures—nor would it be ethical for a non-Native practitioner of Celtic sorcery to be adopting a Native practice without a strong grounding and relationship within the community and culture it originates

115. Dolan, "Mysterious Waifs of Time: Some Thoughts on the Functions of Irish Bullaun Stones," 42.

116. Wood-Martin, *Traces of the Elder Faiths*, Vol. II, 59.

117. Livesay, "The Ojibwe People's Dictionary."

with. Similarly, I will not be using the term "spirit animal" in the context of Celtic sorcery, as this is also lifted and misappropriated from Native American traditions.[118]

As popularly misappropriated in much of contemporary paganism, totems or spirit animals are often treated as a sort of personal symbol representing the individual personality type, or personal spiritual imprint of the individual practitioner—something like an astrological personality profile. This isn't accurate to how the original concepts function in Native cultures. It is also not accurate to Celtic paradigms about animal spirits. Much of the evidence about working with animal spirits in Celtic traditions points toward the tutelary model, which is focused more on kinship and functional relationships and is typically collective rather than individual. A tutelary spirit is a patron or guardian linked to place, kinship, function, or occupation. That is to say, in this cultural framework one comes into relationship with animal spirits by way of family lineage, by way of vocation or specialization, or by way of relationship to place—all of which are collective forms of relationship and not personality-driven.

The famous example from Irish literature that is often held up as an example of totemism is of course Cú Chulainn, the legendary hero who has a prohibition against eating dogmeat, because the dog is his name-animal. This prohibition arises from his being identified as a hound, and is reflected in his name—*cú* meaning dog, hound, or sometimes wolf. A deeper grounding in the Irish tradition reveals that this is in fact not a personal identity but a vocational one. Many warriors in Irish literature have names that reference hounds or wolves, such as Cú Chulainn's greatest rival, Cú Roí.[119] The tale of how Cú Chulainn gets his name appears to be a warrior initiation during which he kills a guard dog, takes on its role of guardianship of the settlement, and subsequently is granted the title Cú by a druid, along with the prohibition against ever eating dogmeat.[120] This is just one example of a vast pat-

---

118. Smithsonian Institution, "Native American Relationships to Animals: Not Your 'Spirit Animal.'"

119. Hickey, *Wolves in Ireland: A Natural and Cultural History*, 35.

120. O'Rahilly, "Táin Bó Cúalnge Recension 1," 141–142.

tern expressed throughout the whole Indo-European culture family where the canine tutelary spirits are attached to the vocation of warriorship.[121]

The example of the canine tutelary spirits as articulated in Irish tradition is helpful to look at, as it is detailed enough to illuminate a model for developing relationship with such tutelary animal spirits tied to a vocation. There is a practice or training period where the ways of that vocation and its spirits are learned, and an initiatory process in which the person must confront or engage with the being itself, ritually internalizing some aspect of its nature while formally stepping into the vocational role. With this a name might be ritually conferred, along with a lasting obligation to the animal, which can include behavioral prohibitions intended to preserve the sanctity of the relationship (such as that against eating the animal—although this could look different for different animal spirit relationships).

Another model for animal spirit relationships is based on kinship. Here the bonds of relationship with a given collective of spirits may be inherited through family lines or other forms of lineage. The stories present a cautionary picture of what may happen if these bonds are ignored or disrespected. An example of this is illustrated in the story of Conaire Mór, in *The Destruction of Dá Derga's Hostel*. Conaire is the child of a human woman and an Otherworldly man who has a bird skin that enables him to take the form of a bird. This bird-man is part of a tribe of bird-folk of the *síd* whose kinship Conaire inherits. He is given by them a blessing and prophecy for kingship, and also prohibitions, including that he may not kill birds.[122] When he violates this prohibition, he loses all the other blessings of his kinship with the bird-folk. The value of this story is its lesson about maintaining the bonds and blessings of spirit relationships through respect and honoring of our obligations to them.

More directly relevant to the practice of sorcery is the alliance of Mug Roith and the she-eel. In this story mentioned previously, the druid Mug

---

121. Powell, "Wolf Rites of Winter."

122. Stokes, "Da Derga's Hostel," 20; O'Connor, *The Destruction of Da Derga's Hostel: Kingship and Narrative Artistry in a Mediaeval Irish Saga*, 87.

Roith works with a giant she-eel spirit who can be conjured to help in fighting his enemies, using incantations and his druidic handstone. To conjure her, a spell is chanted over the handstone that functions as her talisman here:

> *I beseech my Hand-Stone . . .*
> *Woe to him around whom it coils,*
> *Betwixt the swelling waves.*
> *Be it a sea eel —*
> *Be it a vulture among vultures,*
> *Which shall separate body from soul.*
> *Be it an adder of nine coils . . .* [123]

This activated stone is then put in the hand of Mug Roith's student Ceann Mór, who deploys the conjuration by throwing the stone in a river ford. When she arrives, the conjured spirit is described as a giant female sea eel, large enough at least to coil nine times around the body of a man, strong enough to fling a man's body violently with a blow of her tail, and delivering poison with the bite of her teeth. She is addressed as a person with a name and an identity: her name is Mongach Maoth Ramhar (meaning "long-maned, wet, sleek"). This mighty she-eel spirit fights on behalf of the forces Mug Roith has allied himself with, and it is clear in the narrative that she has agency. After helping the druids succeed in the initial fights she was conjured to aid in, Mongach takes off after the rest of the army, and she has to be called off from attacking more than intended. Ceann Mór talks her down, "explaining the position to her, and saying: 'Easy, easy, O long-necked Maoth Ramhar . . . lie down now in the gentle hand of great Mogh Roith, calmly and quietly.'" [124]

This episode reveals a number of valuable lessons for working with such an animal spirit in sorcery. First, this story strongly emphasizes the point mentioned previously that spirit-work here is conceived as an alliance of peers, and not an instance of binding command as is often found in the Western ceremonial approach to spirits. Mongach, while she responds to the conjuration

---

123. Ó Duinn, "The Siege of Knocklong," 77.

124. Ó Duinn, "The Siege of Knocklong," 87.

and fights the enemies of the druid who called her, has her free will and it is through negotiation and communication that she agrees to stop attacking. It is also clear that the primary relationship or contract is between Mongach and Mug Roith. Even though his initial invocation of her is sufficient to allow his student to send her against their targets, when she must be called off, Ceann Mór the student has to invoke Mug Roith's name to succeed in calming her. This suggests that she recognizes the hierarchy of druid and student and that her actions are arising from an agreement or contract with Mug Roith himself. Again this story demonstrates that conjurations like this are underpinned by preexisting ongoing relationships, rather than a model where spirits are instrumentalized only in the moment when they are needed.

With animal spirits, it is possible to engage with their living counterparts and there is some precedent for that within the Celtic source cultures. Ravens and crows provide an interesting example that is relevant to the practice of sorcery. Perceived across Celtic cultures as connected with death and the Otherworld, communication with spirits, and therefore the power of prophecy, there is evidence that practices around these beliefs may have sometimes included living animals as well as their spiritual counterparts. Ritual deposits at a number of Iron Age sites in southern Britain included corvid remains, some of them in a condition that suggested the birds may have been domesticated companion animals. Some of these sites are associated with funerary excarnation, so one of the theories proposed by researchers has been that these crows and ravens were companion animals to the priests overseeing these funerary rites, and whose remains were ritually deposited after death as part of that ongoing relationship.[125] Possibly related, the Irish practice of raven-lore, or divination by observation of raven behavior, may have been practiced with domesticated ravens. The primary text describing this raven-lore includes descriptions of behavior that are clearly taking place inside houses, suggesting that diviners may have kept companion ravens for this purpose.[126] There is a continuity between these practices involving living ravens and those placed as ritual deposits. As animals

---

125. Serjeantson and Morris, "Ravens and Crows, in Iron Age and Roman Britain," 100.

126. Best, "Prognostications from the Raven and the Wren," 120.

associated with a spiritual power of communication with the Otherworld and its spirits, in life they could act as divining assistants, assist in carrying the dead to the spirit world through excarnation, and live as companion animals alongside ritualists; while in death these same animals might be deployed as allies in the spirit realm through ritual deposition.

meeting the she-wolves

Wolves figure very strongly in Irish spiritual traditions, although sadly the wolf has been extinct in Ireland since the mid- to late eighteenth century. The mythology and folklore of wolves remains strong, tying them to liminality and warriorship and the power of the land.

As I touched on in the previous section, many of the Irish wolf myths are centered around the identity of warriors with wolves, and canines in general, as part of the culture of the Fianna, or wandering warrior bands. Warrior bands were spoken of as wolves, and their hunting and raiding activities called "wolfing."[127] They haunted caves, like Kesh Corran where the mythic King Cormac mac Airt was said to be raised by wolves, a mark of kinship with the Otherworld and with the land.[128] In Irish one of the names they are known by is *mac tír*, "son of the land."[129] Much of this material is gendered, as the warrior role and participation in war-bands was historically a predominantly (though not exclusively) male activity. However, there are also female wolf myths: the Morrígan takes wolf shape, and there is a myth that tells of three she-wolves who lived in the Cave of Crúachan, the home of the Morrígan; these Otherworldly women came out of the cave in the shape of wolves to hunt and kill livestock around the area.[130] Traditions also exist that speak of wolf-identities that attached to whole families, such as the wolf people of Ossory, who are said to have the ability to leave their bodies in a kind of

---

127. O'Connor, *Da Derga's Hostel*, 82–83.

128. O'Grady, *Silva Gadelica* Vol. 2, 287.

129. Hickey, *Wolves in Ireland*, 29.

130. Stokes, *Acallamh Na Senórach*, 264.

trance or sleep while traversing the land in wolf shape, a condition that is described as in their nature "from ancestry and birth."[131]

The Irish wolf-people stories align with a huge body of European folklore of the werewolf, much of it centering on the idea that people may voluntarily change their shape into the wolf, or may put on a wolfskin. What I find most compelling in these stories is the specificity with which they describe the experience of out-of-body spirit travel in animal shape. At the same time, they paint a vivid portrait of spirits who are at once wild and untamed, and also can be protective and loyal guardians. In my practice, wolf spirits have come to be treasured companions who have taught me a great deal about the practice of spirit travel, while also walking with me as beloved protecting spirits.

The wolf spirits are loyal allies, guardians, and guides through the sometimes treacherous spirit worlds. They can help us to find our way safely through the Otherworld, and teach us to unlock latent powers and instincts. Their sigil is shaped after the image of snapping wolf jaws. It also incorporates the ogham letter-signs hÚath, which is for hawthorn with kennings that speak about wolves and liminality, and the Gaulish letter-sign Corios, which refers to wolves and warrior imagery. While the sigil is for wolf spirits in general, the illustration highlights the she-wolves of Rathcroghan in particular. It shows a pair of she-wolves before the stone marking the entrance of the Cave of Crúachan, with the hawthorn tree growing over the cave threshold.

Sorcerer's Toolkit
spirit Alliances

Spirit alliances are foundational to building a strong magical practice. Your spirit allies can watch your back and help protect you, allowing you to take on more consequential and risky efforts; they also can help expand your reach and sphere of influence; and they can help you see what's coming.

131. Boyle, "On the Wonders of Ireland: Translation and Adaptation," 248.

Sigil Illustration for the She-Wolves

Of course, spirit work carries its own risks. There are as many kinds of spirits as there are living creatures, and some are dangerous to us. How do you know which spirits you can trust to build friendships with? If you're new to working with spirits, I suggest an approach that builds from relationships of trust that you already have, such as trusted ancestors or gods. Think about any gods you may be in relationship with, and consider asking the one you trust most or feel closest to to introduce you to a spirit you can build alliance with. If you don't have any gods you feel close enough to to ask this, consider your ancestors; they usually have our best interests at heart. If you have a good relationship with your ancestors, you can ask them to connect you to a spirit who can help you in your magical work.

Here is a pathway you can begin from, toward building a set of spirit alliances to support you in your magical work.

Seek Contact through Trusted Guides

Begin by making prayers to the god or ancestor you've chosen to ask. Make an offering and ask them to introduce you to a spirit who you can trust to build alliance with.

Spend some time in meditation listening for messages you may receive in answer to your query. If there's a spirit they can introduce you to, what should you know about them? How will you recognize them? Are there certain offerings they will prefer? You can use divination tools to help clarify information.

If the spirit itself shows up immediately during this ritual, you can proceed directly to the next step. If not, you can plan another ritual to contact the spirit.

Beginning a Spirit Alliance

Call to the new spirit by whatever identifying information has been given to you by your trusted guides. If you've been given a name to contact it by, use that. Introduce yourself. To help establish trust, mention who referred you, as well as any important spiritual connections or lineages that help the spirit understand who you are and what to expect from you.

Present offerings. If you're in doubt about what to give initially, perhaps start with a simple cup of water. Alternately, if this is a spirit from the court of a particular deity, try giving a similar offering to what you would give that deity.

Seek to build rapport. Talk to the spirit about yourself and what you hope to do together with them. Ask the spirit how they prefer to communicate, and what kind of relationship they may want to have with you. Ask what feeds them, what they like for offerings, and what reciprocity might look like for them. Remember also to talk with them about limitations and boundaries—yours and theirs. You can also use divination to help you clarify your communications with them.

Perhaps the most important piece of advice I can offer is to give it time. Spirit relationships build over time just like human ones. If answers to some of your questions aren't clear right away, try again another day. You can continue to build trust by showing up to the relationship over time, by giving gifts and offerings, and by undertaking shared activities or doing meaningful work in the spirit's name. Start small and build up to larger undertakings once you feel more confident about how to contact, communicate, and collaborate with the spirit.

Story
A Ritual for Spirit Alliance

I begin in the dim light of my shrine room, having refreshed its air and my own self with blessing water. I am here to seek contact and enter into relationship with Mongach, the eel spirit I have been reading about and feeling drawn to work with.

I pour an offering of whiskey to the Morrígan, my guiding goddess in whom I trust. I begin to call out to her and to pray.

Hail to you, mighty Great Queen, bringer of victory, sorceress,
     fearful goddess.
You who rise as the coiling eel, the shaggy wolf, the horned
     heifer.
I seek you in your form of the mighty she-eel, eel of many coils
     who binds and bites aggressors.

I pray till I can feel my whispered prayers filling the shadowy room, till I can feel the presence of Herself looming near and drinking in the prayers. I ask her to open the way for me to greet the eel spirit Mongach and to bless the friendship I hope to make with her. I speak the name: "Mongach Maoth Ramhar. Mongach, I invite you." Then I go quiet, slowing my breathing, entering into a meditative communion.

There are coils moving in the shadows around me. I am neither here in my shrine room nor elsewhere. The darkness is like water, and in the water there are great muscular coils. I cannot see her clearly; I could not tell you where she begins or where she ends; I have not seen her face. The shadows slip and bulge, fluid and heavy.

I breathe out slowly and I speak her name again. *Mongach.* I'm suddenly mildly afraid she'll just eat me, but I proceed. I pour water into a bowl and add the bit of fish I've brought as an offering. I whisper to her: "I come in friendship, I bring this offering. I am under the Morrígan's protection and I seek an alliance of friendship." I go on speaking to her quietly. I sense a face, eyes studying me, toothy jaws. I feel her assent and sense the offering is received.

I ask her to show me how I might connect with her and what she might want from me. There is a rush of imagery: I will go to the nearest riverbank; I will find a branch from the trees there with a sinuous, serpentine curve to it and consecrate it to her. I will carve her name along its length in ogham; I will anoint and feed her through this tool and when I need to reach her I will be able to use it to make contact. We go on speaking for some time as I learn from her what kinds of magics she is willing to aid me in, and what I will owe to her in reciprocity.

When it is done, I give my thanks and feel the sinuous motion of the watery darkness slip away to stillness. I thank the Morrígan too, and once again cleanse myself as I leave the consecrated space.

weapon sorcery and inspirited objects

It is not surprising to find within these animist cultures a strong interest in inspirited objects. The Irish literature has a great fondness in particular for warrior gear inspirited by spells or inhabited by demons. Even where weapons are not explicitly described as inspirited, they are often named, which is an indicator of being seen to contain a being with personhood. There is also some material evidence that aligns with the practices described in the literature.

Many passages in the literature describe spirits or demons residing in weapons and armor, such as this, from the *Táin Bó Cúailnge*: "Such was the closeness of their encounter that sprites and goblins and spirits of the glen and demons of the air screamed from the rims of their shields and from the hilts of their swords and from the butt-ends of their spears."[132] The beings seem to be not just present around the warriors in the story, but specifically inhabiting the weapons and armor. This reflects a belief that weapons, armor, and other gear could be inhabited by spirits and that those spirits involved themselves in the work of the weapon or the events taking place around those who carried them. In the example, the particular type of spirits that are inhabiting these arms are spirits of the battlefield, showing a functional relationship guiding the type or family of spirits understood to belong to such armaments, or chosen to inhabit them.

Artifacts from across the Celtic cultures, particularly the exquisite metalwork for which the Celtic peoples are so famous, show that it was common to adorn valuable items with figures. Pieces of armor from early Celtic cultures, such as helmets and shields, are often found with animal forms sculpted on them—ravens, eagles, boars, etc. The great carnyces (war horns) were often

---

132. O'Rahilly, "Táin Bó Cúalnge from the Book of Leinster," 228.

fashioned with the heads of boars, serpents, or wolves.[133] And of course, there are many examples of the anthropomorphic sword type from the Iron Age—swords whose hilts were sculpted to look like little persons, more or less stylized to show simple arms and legs and often also a face with human features.[134] Other valuable items not specifically related to violence were also adorned with animal or anthropomorphic features, such as faces on the handles and grips of cauldrons and drinking vessels. Many archaeologists have interpreted these to indicate such an animistic belief in spirits inhabiting objects.

The Irish literature makes it clear that this is not a fanciful interpretation on the part of modern archaeology, because the belief in spirits inhabiting objects is made explicit in the texts. It also makes clear that this is not simply the generalized animism of believing that everything is alive—there appear to be ritual practices by which objects were intentionally inspirited. Fragments of this ritual culture of object sorcery are preserved in various manuscripts and tales, and when they are pieced together, a fairly clear picture of a system of spirit work emerges.

A passage from *The Second Battle of Mag Tuired* presents the first major piece of the picture. After the battle is over, the Tuatha Dé Danann recover an inspirited sword and it offers a description of how such a relationship might work:

> Now in that battle Ogma the champion found Orna, the
> sword of Tethra, king of the Fomoire. Ogma unsheathed
> the sword and cleaned it. Then the sword told what had
> been done by it, because it was the habit of swords at that
> time to recount the deeds that had been done by them
> whenever they were unsheathed. And for that reason swords
> are entitled to the tribute of cleaning after they have been
> unsheathed. Moreover spells have been kept in swords from
> that time on. Now the reason why demons used to speak

---

133. Aldhouse-Green, *Caesar's Druids*, 62–63.

134. Ross, *Pagan Celtic Britain: Studies in Iconography and Tradition*, 101.

from weapons then is that weapons used to be worshipped
by men and were among the sureties of that time.[135]

There are several valuable bits of information presented here. First, the sword has a name and is presented as a person. This is the first clue that there is a spirit in the weapon. It also relates that "spells have been kept in swords" and that the reason why "demons used to speak" from them is because they were worshiped. This seems to indicate a ritual or spell whereby the weapon has been inspirited, and that it is from this point the spirit can communicate with its holder. This ritual seems to include worship of the spirit, and it seems likely that it included some kind of spell of speech or opening of the mouth, and that the weapon would also be given its name. This passage also indicates that the relationship between weapon spirit and holder was a contractual one, engendering a duty to offer it tribute by cleaning it whenever it is unsheathed. In other words, this is an ongoing and reciprocal agreement that is renewed by veneration and the tribute to which the sword is entitled. In exchange the sword's spirit offers oracular knowledge through its recitation of the deeds done by it in the battle.

Other passages of literature expand on this concept of tribute owed and offered to inspirited weapons. Offerings are referenced in some cases; several instances describe spears that will move of their own power and cut people if they have not given it offerings. The spear of Maelodrán mac Dimma Chróin is one such weapon: "Everyone who did not leave anything with it—it would leap among them and make a slaughter of them."[136] The implication is that a tribute of blood is required to be fed to the spear, and in the absence of this being given, it is taken. Elsewhere, in *The Destruction of Dá Derga's Hostel*, there is a reference to some type of poisonous fluid used with a spear called the Luin, either as a substitute offering for blood, or simply to quench it from catching fire: "A caldron full of poison is needed to quench it when a deed of

---

135. Gray, "Cath Maige Tuired," 69

136. Meyer, *Hibernica Minora*, 81.

manslaying is expected. Unless this come to the lance, it flames on its haft and will go through its bearer or the master of the palace wherein it is."[137]

The weapon spirit's ability of oracular speech is also highlighted in many of these passages. In some instances, part of the tribute owed to it is the holder's listening to a sword's recitation of deeds done with it.[138] In that first passage quoted, it was said that "the reason why demons used to speak from weapons then is that weapons used to be worshipped by men and were among the sureties of that time."[139] That is to say, an inspirited weapon could serve as a surety—a guarantee of truth. It was understood to be a keeper of truth by observing deeds and revealing them through its oracular speech. This served as a check on boasts made by warriors about their deeds.

In the tale of *The Wasting Sickness of Cú Chulainn*, a truth ritual is described as part of the annual Samhain feast: "They laid their swords over their thighs when they declared the strifes, and their own swords used to turn against them when the strife that they declared was false; nor was this to be wondered at, for at that time it was customary for demon beings to scream from the weapons of men, so that for this cause their weapons might be the more able to guard them."[140]

In other words, when someone had carried a sword in battle, that sword's indwelling spirit knew the truth of their deeds. When those deeds were declared for the community they served, that declaration was made with the sword unsheathed and listening. If the warrior misrepresented their actions, the weapon spirit would know and could speak out against them. This is the basis for the custom of swearing oaths on swords as well. The weapon spirit was understood to physically enforce truthfulness and fidelity to oaths, as well as speaking out about them. "Their own swords used to turn against them when the strife that they declared was false." The weapon served as guarantor of fidelity because its indwelling spirit knew what was said and done, and

137. Stokes, "Da Derga's Hostel," 301.

138. Borsje, "Omens, Ordeals and Oracles," 225.

139. Gray, "Cath Maige Tuired," 162.

140. Leahy, *Heroic Romances of Ireland*, Vol I, 57.

if the warrior had been false, the next time they carried that weapon into a battle it would turn against them. This could serve as a very serious check on behavior for warriors who relied on their gear to safeguard their survival in the field. All of this also serves to emphasize that the spirits were understood to have agency and a will of their own, and while they did serve the owner of the weapon, that service was contractual and earned through reciprocal obligations, not simply a matter of command.

These examples center on weapon sorcery and highlight the sorts of battle spirits that would be inspirited into weapons and war gear. However, their example can be extrapolated to see that other kinds of gear can enshrine any number of other types of spirits appropriate to their particular function. I have seen hospitality and hearth-keeping spirits enshrined into cauldrons and fire tools, spirits of poetry and inspiration and knowledge enshrined into musical instruments, and many more. In an animistic practice, all your beloved tools can be inspirited so that they become not just instruments, but gateways to expansive spirit alliances.

Sorcerer's Toolkit
ınspiriting objects

Here, I'd like to offer a ritual template for inspiriting objects. Since the sword is a highly traditional type, this example is written as for inspiriting a sword, but you can easily adapt this practice for many sorts of objects.

Before beginning a ritual to inspirit an object, it's important to lay the groundwork by building up a relationship with the spirit whom you hope to install into the weapon. If you're new to working with this particular spirit, consider spending some time with the toolkit for building spirit alliances, presented earlier in this chapter. As part of this relationship-building, you should spend time in communion with them and also employ divination to determine what the shape of your agreements may be and any tributes that may be needed as part of your alliance. Remember, tributes aren't necessarily always going to be a physical offering or libation; just as often, they might be actions that you commit to doing in how you use the inspirited object. These actions in tribute both honor the spirit, and help to sustain and enhance its presence in the object.

For this ritual, you'll need:

- Cleansing tools, such as blessing water or incense.
- A candle.
- The weapon to be inspirited.
- A means of inscribing the weapon, such as a paint pen or etching pen.
- Offerings that appeal to the spirit or have been requested, such as spirits or a blade oil.

Cleanse your tools, yourself, and the space you will be working in by sprinkling with blessing water or fumigating with sacred smoke.

Awaken the blade. You can refer back to the section on working with iron in protection magic for a refresher on how to awaken a blade. Warm your blade in the flame of your candle to waken it. If you're inspiriting an object that can't be put in fire, you can warm it by rubbing it with your own hands. When it's warm, bring the weapon close and speak so that your breath enters the fabric of the warm metal, as you speak to awaken it and instruct it to receive the spirit that you're enshrining in it. You can use your own words or follow this template: "Awake, blade, waken and hear me. You shall be a shrine for [your spirit's name] and receive their spirit. Your body shall be their body. Their tributes shall be received through you."

Inscribe and name the weapon. Take the pen tool and inscribe the spirit's name on the weapon, saying "I name you [your spirit's name]. You are the body of [your spirit's name]." If the spirit has a sigil, you can inscribe that also.

Lay the spell of speech. Say, "You are the voice of [your spirit's name]. For spirits may speak from weapons when weapons are worshiped by us. Speak, speak, speak: I lay the power of speech in this blade. May you speak truth and fulfill this bond."

Make the tributes and offerings. Speak any commitments you may be making in the bond you're making with the spirit—what tributes it may be entitled to, if any have been asked of you. Seal the bond with an offering and touch the offering to the blade. Even if your tribute to the spirit going forward will be nonphysical, it's helpful in this ritual to feed the blade directly. For a metal object such as a weapon, anointing with blade oil is a good offering, or you can anoint it with a few drops of a liquid offering.

Story

A Rite of weapon sorcery

The sword is passed down to me by a friend's widow who is sorting through his treasured things and bequeathing them to members of his community. "He wanted you to have this sword. He thought it should belong to a shield-maiden like you." It's a good sword, not the cheap lightweight kind—well-balanced, and has been kept lovingly sharpened. It's a Celtic model, with an abstract stylized version of the anthropomorphic hilt.

I bring it home into my shrine room, unsheathe it, and sit with it across my knees, listening to the sword. What tale does it tell? It has been in the house of a witch who appreciated it but always felt he was holding it for someone else, so it has been waiting. It wishes to be carried by a fighter. It likes the feel of my hand. I give it a cleanse with consecrated water and a bit of oil on the blade.

I set the sword beside my shrine where I honor the spirits of fighting women: Boudica, Scáthach, the legion of women spirits. It feels at home there, but I need to give it time before I'm sure how I want to work with the sword. I visit it from time to time, touching its hilt when I visit the shrine. Periodically, it reminds me that it's waiting to be wielded. It's waiting for battles to help me fight.

A time comes when I've entered an intensive ritual cycle with the warrior women spirits, and it has finally come time to consecrate the sword. I'm working hard on transforming my own trauma and the rage I carry as a result of my history as a survivor of domestic violence, seeking both to heal my own trauma and to reorient my relationship with my trauma so that I can be of help as a priest providing spiritual service to others like myself, without entangling my own emotions into the help I'm offering. I've asked these warrior women spirits to help me in this work: to help foster the courage and resilience I need; to guide me in bringing wise strategy to the work I do; and to help me hold healthy boundaries and accountability around the work. In prayer and communion with the spirits, an agreement emerges: I will offer tribute of service in the name of these spirits, and when I need release for my own trauma, I will bring it to them. They will receive and transmute and offer strength and guidance. They will walk with me and help me in my battles. The sword will hold this bond; when I have been in this struggle, helping a survivor get safe, performing a binding or a curse to stop an abuser, providing pastoral care to a survivor. Whenever I've been doing this work, afterward I will come back to the spirits, unsheathe the blade, offer them tribute, and recount my deeds. If I have transgressed a boundary or conducted myself poorly, they will hold me accountable, and I will know. The sword will be both my sorcerous weapon and the guarantor of my honesty and accountability to the spirits who help me.

When the agreement has come clear, I formalize it. I invoke the women warrior spirits with prayer, chanting, and offerings of meat and bloody red wine. I call them into the blade and charge it with force conjured from a deep well of injured rage and passion for justice, emerging from my body in roaring screams. When this has run its course, I sit for a while in communion with them and then I speak aloud the terms of the bond of agreement. I inscribe the name and sigil of this spirit collective in consecrated oil on the blade. In a hoarse whisper I name the sword and speak a spell of speech over the blade:

> *I name you _____, sword of the women warriors. For spirits may speak from weapons when weapons are worshiped by us. Speak, speak, speak: I lay the power of speech in this blade. May you speak truth and hold the guarantee of truth for the actions I do in service of this bond.*

As time goes on, I will return again and again to my communion with the spirits through the sword. I can't always carry it with me when I'm going "into battle" against abusers in my community, but it's a touchstone for me. When I can, I visit the shrine and connect before going into this work, and it helps me to feel the spirits standing by my side strengthening me to the fight. When I feel the stress or the trauma rising, I take it to the spirits and let it pour out of me, transforming into pure force invested into the blade, and then I hold it in my hand and feel the comfort of the blade's strength. When I'm unsure where I stand and need to reconnect with my ethical foundations, I return and tell my stories in the presence of the blade, and listen to the counsel and wisdom of the spirits.

CHAPTER 4

επchαπτπeπτ απδ τhe
poetics of sorcerp

Poetry and incantation are threaded through nearly all forms of Celtic magics. This centrality of poetry is not unique to magic; it is reflective of the fundamental importance of poetry in Celtic cultures generally. I have mentioned several examples of magical ritual that incorporate some component of poetic incantation. In this chapter, I will focus on the role of poetry, the patterns and structures that give it form, and its use in ritual as an aid to trance.

poetrp in celtic societies

Historically, poets occupied a very high social status in the societies from whom these traditions emerge. Early Ireland is the best documented of these societies, so I will be looking at the role of poets and poetry in the Irish context, with some visits to other Celtic cultures to broaden the view. In Ireland, the social systems within which these poetic traditions operated were undergoing significant transformation throughout the medieval period, from pagan to Christian and from an Iron Age tribal-kingship structure toward the medieval Gaelic kingdoms and then the Anglo-Norman state. Poets retained a very high status until late in the medieval period, although the particulars of their roles changed as these transformations took place.

Early Celtic societies were highly ranked. In Ireland, poets belonged to the *nemed*, or privileged class. The root of the word *nemed* is "sacred, holy" and it seems to have originated as a designation for rank based in religious functions as well as material class.[141] The same root appears in words for sacred places like *nemeton* (Gaulish) and *fidnemed* (Irish). Within the *nemed* class were kings and lords, as well as the *aes dána* or "people of art": poets, druids, seers, clerics, and judges. The roles of poets included composition and performance of praise poetry, satires, elegies, and other forms of socially impactful poetic performance. In some periods, poets were also involved in judicial functions, such as law-speaking, recording of precedents and conveying of judgments. They also kept and performed vast bodies of traditional lore, including histories, genealogies, sagas, and the lore of places.[142]

This importance of poets and poetry is rooted in the oral nature of prehistoric pagan Irish culture, the core values and patterns of which were inherited into the literate, Christian medieval period. In an oral culture, poetry and poetic skill are central to encoding, transmitting, and retaining knowledge. When the body of lore that represents the culture's values, beliefs, and records is unwritten, it can only survive through memorization and person-to-person transmission. Thus, early Irish society before the advent of literacy was an oral culture with a strong emphasis on memorized oral literature and poetic performance, and this habit continued into the historical period. Poets would memorize massive volumes of material for public and ceremonial performance; poetic meter facilitates memorization and accurate recitation. Also, in a society so centered on the spoken word, word and poetry were understood

141. Kelly, *A Guide to Early Irish Law*, 9.

142. Kelly, *A Guide to Early Irish Law*, 43–48.

as formative of reality, and poets were seen as mouthpieces of divine and Otherworldly powers.

Poetry is ubiquitous in the early Irish literature, as the tales and sagas likely originated in forms memorized for oral performance. In their extant forms, many Irish tales alternate between narrative prose text and verse, with the verse segments often framed as spoken by the mythic characters themselves. In many cases, the language of the poems is much older than the surrounding narrative text.[143] Poetry is conservative; metrical form acts as a mnemonic device, tending to facilitate the text being transmitted in whole rather than altered and embroidered, since changes can readily be seen to disrupt the poetic structure. Thus, the poems within a story can sometimes be examined as the backbone of the story, conveying its thematic core and earliest components, providing a partial lens into what the earliest, oral version of the literature might have sounded like.

Ritual Poetry

Many of the oldest poems in the Irish literature are composed in a form called *rosc*. The word *rosc* has several meanings in Old Irish: it can mean a poem, ode or chant, or a legal statement, all of which directly reference it as poetry. However, it has a further meaning as an archaic word for "eye," or for the faculty of vision.[144] This secondary meaning is intriguing in light of the ways in which *rosc* is used in the mythic literature.

Passages of *rosc* poetry in Irish sagas generally are understood to represent an older stratum of the material. Medieval literature scholar Ralph O'Connor describes it thus: "A traditional metrical form characteristically used for prophetic utterances and typified by a succession of vivid haiku-like images. *Rosc* does not offer detailed explication, but rather a calculated obscurity."[145] This obscure poetic style stumps many language scholars in attempts to translate the poems, to the point that in many text translations, the poems are simply

---

143. Corthals, "Early Irish Retoirics and Their Late Antique Background," 18.

144. Royal Irish Academy, "EDIL 2019: An Electronic Dictionary of the Irish Language, Based on the Contributions to a Dictionary of the Irish Language, s.v. 1 *rosc*."

145. O'Connor, *Da Derga's Hostel*, 140.

left untranslated. The pattern of *rosc* is characterized by brief, terse lines of a few words each, typically centering on kennings, allusions, and metaphor. Its lines often do not form complete sentences, but rather conjure a sequence of cryptic, dreamlike images, as in this passage from the Morrígan's prophecy in *The Second Battle of Mag Tuired*:

> *A cup overfull,*
> *full of honey,*
> *mead aplenty,*
> *summer in winter…*[146]

The structure of this poetry favors multiple meanings densely interwoven together. Its rhythm is counted not by the number of syllables but by the stresses in the words (thus often referred to as nonsyllabic poetry). The lines are typically linked to each other by means of alliteration (use of similar sounds) rather than end rhyme, and the patterns of alliteration can be quite complex. Often the final word of one line alliterates with the first of the next line; for example, from another poem in *The Second Battle of Mag Tuired*:

> *mna can* **feli**
> **fir** *gan* **gail**
> **gabala** *can* **righ**
> **rinna** *ulcha ilmoigi*[147]

This cyclical alliteration pattern creates a sense of fluidity to the poetry in spite of the terseness of the individual lines. Alliterative sound-patterning is also used intentionally to highlight multiple meanings—clever use of alliteration can evoke similar-sounding words with different meanings to a native speaker of the language, so that there is both a spoken and an unspoken layer to the poetry.

The nonsyllabic meter of this poetry tends toward a rhythm that seems to roll or sway, carried along by the fluidity of the unstressed syllables and

---

146. Mees, *Celtic Curses*, 5237.

147. Gray, "Cath Maige Tuired: The Second Battle of Mag Tuired," 72.

punctuated by the stressed ones. This rolling rhythm, along with the cyclical patterning that is often created by alliteration, tends to give the poetry a fluid, mantic quality. All these characteristics, along with the archaic language style, point to the origins of *rosc* as poetry created for an oral, ritual context. Its fluid, incantatory rhythm lends itself well to trance induction, and in fact many of the *rosc* poems found in early mythological texts are presented as prophetic utterances spoken under a state of inspiration. As historian Bernard Mees frames it: "Such prophecies [the prophecies of the Morrígan] have long been linked with imbas forosnai and other early Irish expressions which suggest that there was a longstanding connection between the filid and divination, the simple form of the rosc or retoiric they evidence putatively a sign that such expressions are based on dreamy mantic utterances."[148]

It is believed that *rosc* derives from a very ancient Celtic poetic tradition of incantatory visionary poetry whose signature metrical forms can be traced to ancient Indo-European ritual verse patterns. Medieval literature scholar Johan Corthals has observed that its format and structure are remarkably similar to the earliest Welsh poetry as well as some Gaulish magical texts and early strata of Icelandic and Roman poetry, indicating an origin in ancient proto-Indo-European traditions.[149] As oral cultures, poetic recitation and transmission in a ritualized context would have been central to each of these societies. Thus it is within this poetry that some of the earliest memories of Irish culture are preserved.

In the medieval literature, *rosc* also takes on an association as the language of spoken judgments and other speeches in a legal context. This use of *rosc* relates to the importance of verbal contestation in a legal system that evolved within the oral culture of pre-Christian Ireland. Its role in the performance of law is not separate from its associations with ritual, prophecy, and mantic trance. Rather, it is precisely because of these ancient associations that the ability to verbalize an appeal or a judgment in *rosc* held value in a legal context. The specialized and cryptic nature of *rosc* speech represented a kind of code

---

148. Mees, *Celtic Curses*, 5272.

149. Corthals, "Early Irish Retoirics and Their Late Antique Background," 28.

that would be at least partly opaque to less-studied listeners. At the same time, its association with ancient tradition wrapped the identity of the speaker in a mantle of mythic authority.[150]

THE poetics of sorcery

These poetics that are found throughout the medieval literature are equally central when it comes to magic and sorcery in the Celtic context. There is a profound relationship between this Irish mantic poetry and the Celtic curse texts of Gaul and Britain as expressions of a distinctly Celtic poetic magic.

Those curse texts of Gaul and Britain represent an interesting fusion of Celtic with Mediterranean practices. As a literate form of magic built upon inscribing magical formula on metal tablets, the magical technology was adopted into Celtic cultural practices through contact with Greek and Roman customs. However, in the language of the texts, an indigenous Celtic poetics emerges that is recognizable from the study of poetic forms. In the words of Bernard Mees: "The reason why the Celtic curses which are metrical seem more removed from the [classical Latin curse tradition] is because there was an indigenous Celtic tradition that curses, as spells, were things that were usually sung."[151]

This relationship between poetry and magic is also encapsulated in the term *bricht* and its cognates in different Celtic languages. In Irish, the word *bricht* means "charm, spell," but also refers to a specific type of poetic meter, or the poem or spoken charm itself. Bernard Mees sees in this double meaning "evidence for a key Celtic relationship between magic and metrical form."[152] The importance of this dual concept of poetry as spell is also represented in the phrase *brichtu ban*, "spells of women," preserved in multiple medieval Irish texts—most famously in the context of the protection charm called the Lorica of St. Patrick, invoking protection against "the spells of women and smiths and

---

150. Stacey, *Dark Speech: The Performance of Law in Early Ireland*, 98–101.

151. Mees, *Celtic Curses*, 2145.

152. Mees, *Celtic Curses*, 4760.

druids."[153] Its importance is also signaled by its preservation across time and distinct cultures, as a precisely cognate phrase *bnanom brictom* is invoked in a Gaulish magical tablet from the first century CE, deposited several hundred years earlier in a tomb in France.[154] This phrase seems to have persisted as a way to describe a class of poetic sorcery especially associated with women.

What might this poetic sorcery look like? For vivid descriptions of the enactment of poetic sorcery, the Irish literature cannot be beat. It presents richly described examples of chanted poetic magics.

The Morrígan, while best known as a war goddess, is also prominent as a poet and sorceress of the Túatha Dé Danann and is several times portrayed chanting magical poetry. In one story recounted in the *Metrical Dindshenchas*, she lays an enchantment of sleep over a woman named Odras, in this fashion: "The owner of kine chanted over her, with fierceness unabating, toward huge Sliab Bodbgna every spell of power: she was full of guile."[155] This short passage concentrates a fascinating amount of descriptive detail about the practice of poetic sorcery. Her action in chanting over the sleeping woman "with fierceness unabating" evokes a sense of passionate or frenzied recitation, vocal intensity, and perhaps body movements in the chanting. It also mentions that in doing so she orients herself toward Sliab Bodbgna, a mountain named for a related war goddess, Badb—and thus perhaps a place of power for her within the landscape.

Another aspect of the practice of poetic sorcery is reflected in several tales that mention the performance of poetry or spoken magic "in one breath." This theme is reflected in an incident in *The Wooing of Emer*, in which Cú Chulainn is able to bind Scáthach to fulfill three wishes by speaking all of them in a single breath.[156] In another very vivid example of this, the war goddess Badb employs weaponized poetry to curse a king who has violated his oaths of kingship, in *The Destruction of Dá Derga's Hostel*. She chants a poetic curse while leaning in the

---

153. Mees, *Celtic Curses*, 1560.

154. Delamarre, *Dictionnaire Gauloise*, 90.

155. Gwynn, "Metrical Dindshenchas Vol. 4," 201.

156. Meyer, "Wooing of Emer," 300.

doorway, "standing on one leg, and in one breath."[157] In addition to chanting the poem in a single breath, this passage references ritual posture used in conjunction with poetry, and it is one I examine in detail in chapter 8 on justice magic and cursing.

Examples of prophetic, protective, and weaponized poetry can be found throughout the literatures of Celtic cultures. Even in the nonliterary cultures such as Gaul, there is evidence that poetry was in use, as reflected in the metrical curse texts with their *rosc*-like structures, which scholars read as indicating that poetic incantation would have been part of the performance of the spell. The metrical tradition of rhythmic or sung charms continues to present day in folk tradition, as reflected in many early modern to modern collections of folk charms. The loricas and poetic armors described earlier in the chapter on apotropaic magic are also examples of this tradition.

The continuity of these poetic magics from ancient traditions to contemporary folk custom is remarkable. One example that demonstrates this continuity well is the "joint to joint, sinew to sinew" healing charm. It was documented in use for healing sprains in nineteenth-century Shetland in the following form:

> *The Lord rade, and the foal slade;*
> *He lighted, and he righted,*
> *Set joint to joint, bone to bone,*
> *And sinew to sinew, heal in the Holy Ghost's name.*[158]

Other forms of this same charm using this "joint to joint" formula have been found in ancient Indian Vedic sources, the medieval German Merseberg Charms, and in the early Irish mythological tale *The Second Battle of Mag Tuired*, where the medicinal deity Míach heals a severed hand by chanting "joint to joint of it, and sinew to sinew," over nine successive days and nights.[159]

---

157. O'Connor, *Da Derga's Hostel*, 137.

158. Black, *Scottish Charms and Amulets*, 434.

159. Carey, "Charms in Medieval Irish Tales: Tradition, Adaptation, Invention," 17; Gray, "Cath Maige Tuired: The Second Battle of Mag Tuired," 33.

This ancient charm, which is thought to have originated within very ancient Proto-Indo-European societies, has continued to be used in folk custom into very recent times.

Sorcerer's Toolkit
poetic charms

This chapter has touched on a rich and very detailed historical tradition of metrical poetry. As a set of professional skills that took years of a person's life to master, it can be challenging to imagine how to adopt poetic sorcery into our own practices. What if you aren't a highly trained professional poet?

The good news is that you don't have to be able to achieve *imbas forosnai*, where perfectly formed metrical poetry flows from your tongue. Nor do you need to construct meticulously arranged *rosc* poetry in order to bring some of the power of poetry into your magical practice. Think of some of the folk charms found in the magical traditions of the common people. While they are often simpler in structure, these charms are powerfully effective as vehicles for entering a mantic state and encoding magical intention through breath and language. Using a little creativity, alliteration, and playfulness with language you can create simple charms for your own practice.

Here are a few steps to try your hand at working with poetic charms. We'll use some examples relating to healing as reference points for trying this out.

Try working from already-existing material. You can make use of phrases, charms, and poems that already exist in the literature. The "joint to joint, sinew to sinew" charm mentioned earlier is just one example of this great body of material. Consider any myths or stories that pertain to your magical work. Are there verses or even just phrases in these stories that you could adapt using repetition and variation? You may find usable bits of poetry in existing folk charm collections, such as the *Carmina Gadelica* and similar works. You can also try elaborating on what you find to make a longer charm: "joint to joint, sinew to sinew, skin to skin, blood to blood, breath to breath ..."

Try writing little rhymes for yourself. Remember, it's okay for them to sound simple or even childlike. Many traditional folk charms do. The point is to give you something to chant that can build rhythm into your ritual while encoding the spell in magical language. It doesn't need to sound sophisticated. Consider this simple rhyming charm for healing a burn, from Ireland:

> *There came three angels from the north*
> *One for fire and two for frost.*
> *Out, Fire! and in, Frost!*
> *In the name of the Father, Son, and Holy Ghost.*[160]

It consists of a simple rhythm with a bit of end rhyme, it invokes the chill of frost to replace burning, and it calls on the aid of divine powers. Can you create something simple like this?

Try experimenting with other poetic techniques. Here's an example that extends the "joint to joint, sinew to sinew" charm with added alliteration and repetition:

> *Health to heal, health to heal*
> *Bone to bone, well to feel*
> *Health to heal, health to heal*
> *Joint to joint, well to feel*
> *Health to heal, health to heal*
> *Sinew to sinew, well to feel.*

---

160. Hillers, "Towards a Typology of European Narrative Charms in Irish Oral Tradition," 88.

Feel for rhythm and where the emphasis naturally falls. You don't need to use formal metrical structures, but you do want it to flow so that it will roll off your tongue easily in ritual.

When you've created your charm, practice it. Recite the charm a few times till it flows easily, so that remembering it is not a distraction in ritual. Be emotive and fierce; let your body move with the incantation. This invites your whole being into the act of enchanting the charm, rather than just your voice.

A good verbal charm supports and enchants your ritual actions in sorcery. It is a vehicle for utilizing your breath and language to encode the intentions of the spell, while bringing your whole body into the act of magic, and inviting the attention and aid of spirit powers.

ттапсе ѕреесн

Several traditions reference a genre of oracular poetry emerging from a state of trance or sleep. This seems to be part of a continuum of spiritual techniques for obtaining prophecy through inspired speech; trance opens the practitioner to inspiration or possession by spiritual forces that speak truth through them.

In the Irish literature, one such form of trance-speech is called *búadris* and seems particularly associated with prophecy geared toward the outcome of conflicts. Examples of this type of prophecy are spoken by poets, kings, and warriors on the eve of battles: in the *Táin Bó Cúailnge*, trance-speeches by Dubthach, Láegaire, and Conchobor are described; similarly by Conaire in *The Destruction of Dá Derga's Hostel*.[161] In these stories, the seer speaks "in his trance" (*búadris*), or arises as from a deep sleep to chant a prophecy. A similar practice is described among the medieval Welsh where *awenyddion*, "inspired people," would give prophetic speeches, emerging from a state of deep trance.[162]

The word *búadris* has a meaning of frenzy, turbulence, or excitement, referring to the frenzied or agitated state of ecstatic trance; it can also be parsed as

---

161. O'Rahilly, Táin Recension 1, 219–220, 230; O'Connor, *Da Derga's Hostel*, 184.
162. Wright, *The Historical Works of Giraldus Cambrensis*. 501.

"victory-tale," emphasizing its connection with prophecy relating to the outcome of conflict.[163] In its history, *búadris* is also linked to intoxication, which could suggest the use of consciousness-altering agents as an aid to trance. The word is also used to connote the intoxication of the senses after drinking "streams of old mead." Such consciousness-altering practices may have included the use of herbal additives with psychoactive effects; for example, evidence of the use of henbane as an additive in mead and beer is broadly known throughout the period, including examples in Britain, Scotland, Greece, and Germany.[164]

This idea of ritual intoxication as a vehicle for prophecy brings to mind the attested Continental Celtic practice of armed councils before war with a ritual drinking component "aimed at making contact with the gods so as to be protected, helped and possessed by the supernatural forces."[165] *Búadris* seems to point to similar practices in Ireland—linking to a web of connections between warriors, female warrior-sovereignty figures such as Medb, mead, and prophecy. The trance-speeches in the camps suggest drinking sacred mead—perhaps also infused with herbs—to enter an inspired state in contact with spiritual forces, access prophetic knowledge expressed through oracular trance-speech, and to gain protection in battle.

A related trance ritual is the one called *imbas forosnai* ("knowledge that illuminates").[166] The phrase *imbas forosnai* is also used to reference a power or skill attributed to legendary poets; it is among the "three things required of a poet" in early Irish law texts, and is identified as the highest pinnacle of poetic art.[167] This skill must have been considered quite important, as it is mentioned in multiple sources; legendary seers including Fionn, Scáthach, and Fedelm, among others, are said to have possessed it. The literature on this is complicated and obscure but at its core, *imbas forosnai* appears to be a state

---

163. Royal Irish Academy, "eDIL 2019, s.v. *búadraise,* s.v. 1 *búaid,* and s.v. 1 *ris.*"

164. Nelson, *The Barbarian's Beverage: A History of Beer in Ancient Europe,* 12–13.

165. Beck, "Goddesses in Celtic Religion—Cult and Mythology: A Comparative Study of Ancient Ireland, Britain, and Gaul," 516.

166. Royal Irish Academy, "eDIL 2019,, s.v. 1 *imbas.*"

167. Carey, "The Three Things Required of a Poet," 41.

of inspiration that allows the practitioner to deliver prophecy through spontaneous and inspired poetic performance.

mantic trance incubation

Some sources describing the rites for cultivating *imbas* associate it with offerings to pagan deities and a kind of mantic sleep or meditation in darkness, which may correspond to the "sleep" from which trance-speech emerges.[168] In *Cormac's Glossary*, details of a ritual to engender this power of seership are described. The seer chews a piece of raw meat, and also offers some of the meat to the gods, "on a flagstone behind the door," with a series of sung incantations. The seer then goes to sleep, placing "his two palms on his two cheeks," and is watched over by others to ensure the visionary state is not disturbed until the prophecy comes.[169] This ritual might be conducted for as long as nine days, according to this glossary. As with the *búadris* rituals just described, the central feature here is a mantic trance, out of which the poet emerges with inspired poetry pouring from their lips.

This ritual seems to be part of a group of visionary incubation rituals that share some common features. The *tarb feis* (bull feast) ritual is another of these, described in at least two instances, in *The Destruction of Dá Derga's Hostel* and *The Wasting Sickness of Cú Chulainn*. *The Wasting Sickness* describes the ritual as follows:

> There was then prepared a bull-feast by them there, in order
> that they should discover out of it to whom they would give
> the sovereignty. Thus was that bull-feast prepared, namely: a
> white bull was killed, and one man eat enough of his flesh,
> and of his broth; and he slept under that meal; and a charm
> of truth was pronounced on him by four Druids; and he
> saw in a dream the shape of the man who should be made
> king there, and his form, and his description, and the sort of

---

168. Chadwick, "Imbas Forosnai," 97–135.

169. Stokes, *Three Irish Glossaries*, XXXVI.

work that he was engaged in. The man screamed out of his
sleep and described what he saw to the kings…[170]

The Destruction of Dá Derga's Hostel version repeats many of the same
details, adding that "the sleeper would perish if he uttered a falsehood."[171]

Some elements of ritual practice that appear in these narratives: The person undertaking the vision eats a full meal of meat, which would induce a heavy sleep and perhaps help to stimulate vivid dreams. The spell of truth that is chanted over the dreamer seems to be intended to evoke the power of prophecy, and perhaps also would include protections to ensure the visions are true ones. It is also likely by means of this spell that the dreamer is bound under curse to speak the truth about what is seen. As this was an act of public divination that would determine who was selected for kingship, clearly that element of truthfulness was important.

Another dream incubation ritual is described in *The Battle of Findchorad*. It is performed on behalf of Queen Medb of Connacht, and is structurally similar to the *tarb feis*, but the sacrifice is not a bull:

> They were telling their druids to find out for them what
> would be the consequences of the battle and which of them
> would be defeated … They offered sacrifices to Mars to
> Osiris, to Jove and to Apollo. These are the sacrifices they
> offered; the flesh of dogs, pigs and cats. Afterwards they
> went upon the hides of old hairless […] bulls and on hur-
> dles of the rowan tree, and their faces […] north towards
> Hell. The gods to whom they sacrificed told them to bring
> the Brown Bull of Cooley and the White-horned Bull and to
> start a fight.[172]

170. O'Curry, *On the Manners and Customs of the Ancient Irish*, Vol. II, 199.

171. Stokes, "The Destruction of Da Derga's Hostel," 22–23.

172. Dobbs, "The Battle of Findchorad." *Zeitschrift Für Celtische Philologie*, 399.

In this case, sacrifices of dogs, pigs, and cats are offered; it may be worth noting that all these are animals that are said to emerge from the Otherworld at Crúachan, the ritual center of Connacht.[173] The four classical gods named in the offerings may point to Irish gods reinterpreted through a classical lens here, as is often the case in the Irish saga literature. The detail in the preparation of the visionary bed is particularly interesting. It is woven out of rowan staves, and it must face north, "towards Hell." I think it likely that this references the Cave of Crúachan, Oweynagat, which has been called the "Irish entrance to Hell" since the medieval period.[174]

There is a core of consistent structures across these rituals for mantic incubation. There is an animal sacrifice and offering, the seer goes into seclusion in a specially prepared bed, and the seer receives visions from the gods. These rituals vary in the type of animal sacrifice involved and other particulars of the ritual, such as the orientation of the prepared bed and the use of poetic incantation to enchant the dreamer. These variations could indicate regional differences, or they may reflect the distinct functional uses of the ritual. Both bull-feast examples are divinations to determine kingship, and the bull may be symbolically related to that kingship. The ritual described in *Findchorad* and oriented so strongly toward the Otherworld is performed for the rulers of Connacht to divine outcome of a battle. These examples of mantic incubation ritual vary in their purposes, seemingly tied to specific occasions. Together, they illustrate how the particulars of this visionary ritual may be adjusted to context and need while supporting the core functions of the practice.

Some scholars regard these ritual details as little more than medieval retrospective fantasy about pre-Christian practices.[175] Other scholars note how many elements of this ritual are consistent across different accounts of trance practices and dream incubation and would see these tales as part of a common inheritance of Celtic ritual.[176] From a ritualist perspective, it is also a

---

173. Waddell, "Rathcroghan—A Royal Site in Connacht," 22.

174. Waddell, *Archaeology and Celtic Myth*, 58.

175. Carey, "Three Things Required of a Poet," 58.

176. Waddell, *Archaeology and Celtic Myth*, 137.

ritual structure that makes sense. It begins with offerings and sacrifices and an invocation to draw the holy powers close; consuming a part of the sacrifice in order to receive those powers within; then entering ritual darkness and seclusion in a prepared bed to seek an enchanted sleep and dream. This ritual may or may not be historical, but it's clearly potent.

Sorcerer's Toolkit
mantic trance

The mantic trance is something like a state of unordinary awareness or dissociation, which allows us to be more receptive to communication with spiritual powers. To access this state, we need to shift how we experience the relationship between mind, spirit, and body, entering into a state in which the incorporeal and numinous is sensed as immediately as the physical. There are many tools that can help us access this state, and societies round the world have developed thousands of culturally adaptive techniques for doing so. Trance practices merit a small library of their own, and a full exploration of this realm of practice is beyond the scope of this book. What I would like to offer here is just a ritual template that employs a few of my preferred tools for entering mantic trance, inspired in the traditions we've just been looking at.

Preparation

Offerings: Many of the examples from early literature describe animal sacrifices with offerings of meat from these animals. However, this doesn't mean your offerings have to look like that. If you, like many contemporary practitioners, are not able or choose not to participate in animal sacrifice, another food offering can be suitable. Try making an offering of ethically sourced meat, or another food offering you invested effort into preparing. Consider what offerings your gods in particular respond most to, or any agreements you have with them about offerings. You'll need to consume a little of the offering yourself, so make sure it is something safe for you as well as pleasing to the gods.

The spell of truth: In the literary examples, a "spell of truth" is chanted before entering into ritual seclusion. This provides an additional safeguard toward ensuring that visions coming through this ritual are truthful and directed by trusted spirit powers. The chanting of an incantation also helps you begin entering a trance state. The act of chanting and the effect of rhythm, gentle movement, and repeated words all act to help initiate the dissociation from ordinary consciousness and entry into the state of trance. As a starting point, you can use this chant, which uses phrases from Irish, or its English translation, or create one of your own:

rolá bricht, bricht suain
amru sceóil, scél becht
rolá bricht, bricht comga
amru sceóil, scél becht
rolá bricht, breth fíri
amru sceóil, scél becht

Translation: cast a spell, a spell of sleep
tale of wonder, tale of truth
cast a spell, a spell of warding
tale of wonder, tale of truth
cast a spell, a spell of truth
tale of wonder, tale of truth

The place of seclusion: The tradition speaks of a bed made of rowan staves, but this doesn't mean you must build a special bed just for this ritual. The point is to prepare a place to lie in vision where you will not be disturbed, and that has magical protection and connection to the Otherworld. Consider making some protective rowan charms such as outlined in chapter 2 and attaching them round the place you will lie in.

Mantic Trance Ritual

For this ritual, you will need:

- Cleansing tools, such as blessing water.
- Images of the gods and spirits you wish to seek visions from.
- Offerings.
- The prepared bed or place of seclusion.

Begin by cleansing yourself and the space where this rite is taking place.

Call on the gods and spirits you wish to seek visions from, and those you trust to safely guide you in the trance work. Ask them to help and guide you in reaching a visionary state. Ask them to protect you during trance so that your openness during trance is not exploited by any unwanted powers.

Lift the offerings you have prepared for the gods and consecrate them with praise. Place a portion of the offerings before their image, or by the door of your space. Eat a mouthful of the offerings while meditating on the presence of the gods. You are seeking to enter communion with them, to receive their presence within the body, and to prepare yourself for a state of trance incubation.

Chant the incantation to set the boundaries of the visionary state and begin entering into trance. Take time with the incantation, letting yourself sink into its rhythm, even move with it gently.

When you feel ready, darken the room and lie down in the prepared space. You can also cover your eyes with a veil or mask in lieu of blacking out lights. Let yourself drift in the trance state. You can continue the chant in a whisper to yourself, or silently, if it helps you to deepen into the trance state. Focus on the holy powers you called and from whom you are seeking a vision, but without tension. Just be with them, for as long as it takes, until messages or visions come.

You may find yourself called to journey with them in spirit. It's also okay if you drift into sleep, as the vision may come during a dream or a half-waking state.

When you emerge, it's helpful to move the body and eat a little something to help you ground back into ordinary waking consciousness.

Give thanks to all the divinities who guided and protected you during this trance journey.

Cleanse yourself again to ensure no unwanted spirit presences follow you out of the Otherworld.

Finally, I'd like to offer few more things to consider when undertaking this work. First, this kind of visionary seership really hinges on the ability to enter and sustain trance states. This is a learned skill that operates like psycho-spiritual musculature, and strengthens over time with practice. So, don't be discouraged if trance practice doesn't yield memorable results the first few times. It is an ability that needs to be cultivated over time.

Second, remember that in the literature describing these practices, the seer is accompanied by others who watch over them. Trance practices are always safer when we have support. Companions can help arrange things for the seer, so that you can focus on entering into trance. They can also help ensure you come back fully into your senses at the end of the session, and tend to your needs by making sure you have water, food, and anything else you might need to return fully to ordinary reality. They can also help with recording what was seen, at a time when you might not yet feel ready to start scribbling things down.

FEDELM AND THE CHARIOT

One of the characters who is said to have mastery of *imbas forosnai* poetry is the seer Fedelm. She is introduced in the *Táin Bó Cúailnge*; she identifies herself as *banfili*, "poetess," and appears in wealthy clothing, armed, and standing in a chariot from which position she chants poetry. The text clearly identifies her as a person with Otherworldly status or powers, having "three pupils in each of her eyes."[177] Her name traces from the proto-Celtic root *uid-* "to know," with a connotation of knowledge gained by visionary sight. Notably, her name is also cognate to the Gaulish Uidlua (or Vidlua), attested as a title for a female enchanter in a Gaulish curse-text.[178] Fedelm is also identified by Medb as a *banfáith*, the term for a female practitioner of the art of prophecy, and cognate to the Gaulish *vates*, diviners and sacrificers. Fedelm seems to represent an Irish reflex of a very ancient role or archetype, the high-status female seer and enchantress whose poetry reveals Otherworldly knowledge and power.

Fedelm's oracular poetic ability as described in the *Táin Bó Cúailnge* is worth looking at, as it offers a framework for constructing an oracular poetic ritual. In her scene in the *Táin*, which exists in two primary versions, she arrives dressed in resplendent garments befitting a poet of the *nemed* class, and she is standing in a chariot. Her power is signaled not only by her accoutrements, but also by her Otherworldly three-pupiled eyes. She also carries a weaver's beam, an artifact that is often associated with prophetesses in myth.[179] She is asked by Medb to give prophecy as to the prospects for her army in the coming war. The text suggests that before this, Fedelm has been practicing some form of trance incubation to access the power of *imbas forosnai*; she announces to Medb that she has this power and has come from Albion where she learned the art.[180]

A kind of rhythmic exchange occurs between Medb and the prophetess, which suggests ritual cues:

> *A Feidelm banfáid, cia facci ar slúag?*
> *Atchíu forderg forro, atchíu rúad.*

> *Translation: O Feidelm prophetess, how do you see our host?*

---

177. O'Rahilly, "Táin Bó Cúalnge Recension 1," 126.

178. Mees, *Celtic Curses*, 1582.

179. Enright, *Lady with a Mead Cup: Ritual, Prophecy and Lordship in the European Warband from La Tène to the Viking Age*, 187.

180. O'Rahilly, "Táin Bó Cúalnge Recension 1," 126.

I see it bloody, I see it red.[181]

This exchange continues with further questions from Medb, each time with the ritual cue: "But speak truth to us, Feidelm. O Feidelm Prophetess, how do you see our army?" After repeating this chilling phrase several times, "I see it blood-stained, I see it red," she continues with a longer poetic speech in which she gives a full prophecy of the fate of Medb's armies and the outcome of the *Táin*.[182]

The language of this exchange is interesting. Fedelm here makes use of the prophetic formula *atchíu*, "I see." This phrase also marks instances of prophecy by the Morrígan, also initiated by a question that seems to serve as a ritual cue: "Have you any story?"[183] The same phrase *atchíu* is also used by the seer Scáthach in her poetic prophecy.[184] It is a phrase that often appears in speeches of prophetic poetry. There is a way in which this scene strongly resembles another scene of poetic prophecy in which Cú Chulainn encounters the Morrígan on the road, where she is also dressed in fine clothing and in a chariot, identifies herself as a professional poet, and gives a poetic prophecy.

These seem to be cues that identify how such a visionary poet might be consulted to prompt a prophecy. The outlines of an oracular ritual are coming into view. The prophetess accesses the divine powers, possibly through trance or meditation. She is positioned in a chariot, a liminal vehicle, which could be seen as facilitating spiritual travel and Otherworld contact. Using ritualized cues, she is asked for prophecy and she answers in mantic verse.

meeting vidlua

Vidlua (or Uidlua) is a seer and a spirit of poetry, of enchantment through the spoken and written word, and of visionary seership and divination.

Her name is found on a couple of spell tablets from Iron Age Gaul. Where it's mentioned on the spell tablets it's not always clear if it's referring to a

---

181. O'Rahilly, "Táin Leinster," 143–144.

182. O'Rahilly, "Táin Leinster," 144–145.

183. Gray, "Cath Maige Tuired," 72.

184. Henry, "Verba Scathaige," 199.

person's name or a title—it is a word that means "seer." The name Vidlua is directly cognate to the Irish Fedelm, whom I introduced in the previous section; a seer and poetess with the power of *imbas forosnai*, who performs oracular prophecy for Medb in the *Táin Bó Cúailnge*.[185] So the name seems to refer to a role found in multiple Celtic cultural contexts in the historical record and mythological literature: a (usually female) seer who performs prophecy and is also connected with poetry and magic.

There are no recorded myths or stories for Vidlua; the closest we have are those brief descriptions of Fedelm in the Irish texts. Vidlua came to me when I began working on what became the Viduveletia Celtic letter-based divination system (presented in the next chapter). Her presence is characterized by a profound spiritual insight, giving impressions of brilliant, prismatic eyes with a penetrating gaze, reminiscent of the Irish description of Fedelm having eyes of many colors with three pupils to each eye.[186]

Vidlua is a spirit of visionary seership and trance, enchantment in poetry, and divination. She is a collective spirit who embodies and personifies the role of Vidlua, the seer, and she contains and accesses the collective knowledge of all the individuals who have served in that role in the past. Call on her to aid in poetic inspiration, divination, and visionary trance. Her sigil combines Celtic letters relating to her (Ratis and Vlatus) and the Ogham Coll, for wisdom. Its form is inspired by the story of Fedelm where she is described as having three pupils in each eye, as a way of conveying the visionary power of her sight. It is illustrated here in a scene illuminated by a full moon, evocative of her shining gaze, which is reflected in a bowl one might use for scrying, surrounded by the trees of a sacred grove.

---

185. Mees, *Celtic Curses*, 1575–1582.

186. O'Rahilly, "Táin Bó Cúalnge Recension 1," 126.

Sigil Illustration for Vidlua

Story
An oracular prophecy Rite

The candles are lit. The fresh scent still lingers in the air from the herbs we've used to sprinkle blessing water all around. The doors are closed. Prayers begin, calling on the protection and guidance of our spirit kindreds. We finish with invocations to the divinities who oversee prophecy for us in this rite: Vidlua, Scáthach, Manannán, and the Morrígan, pouring offerings to each.

> *Holy ones, guide us, bless this space and the work that we do here. May the ways to the Otherworld be opened so we may seek vision. May the ways to the Otherworld be guarded so we may be protected from harm and false vision. Bless our eyes for vision, our hands for prayer, our tongues for speech.*

In this room, some of us have chosen to seek vision and to become oracles. Others have chosen to serve as warders, watching over the rite and the safety of the oracles. As we ready to open the trance space, the warders take up seats around the sides and corners of the room, adopting a posture of meditative focus, alert for changes in the presences in the space. The oracles settle themselves in the inner ring, lifting veils and scarves to cover their heads—entering into a consecrated meditative darkness.

We begin the trance induction chant: *síd co nem, nem co doman, síd co nem, nem co doman.* Gently, beginning just above a whisper. Letting it gather a rhythm of its own, steady and swaying as our voices gradually strengthen. Harmonic layers arise in the singing and we begin to feel the shift as the ways to the Otherworld open: the dimensions of the room seem to expand, as if the floor and walls are dissolving away into a greater space.

Into the rhythm of the chant, I drop the first ritual cue: "Nach scél laut? Have you any story?"

It takes a little while longer as the oracles are still sinking into trance. In a little while, I ask again: "Nach scél laut? Have you any story"?

A voice responds from the circle of oracles, a little hoarse at first from chanting: "I have a story." She speaks in halting phrases, pausing to reach for words for the visions that are welling up through her. She tells us of what she sees in the Otherworld, things that may be real or may be yet to come. I hear the quick scratching sound of the pen from the participant who has volunteered to record the prophecies as they come.

The oracle who was speaking seems to have reached the end of her vision. I give some time for the chant rhythm to reassert itself before asking again: "Nach scél laut? Have you any story?" In this way, we will continue for some time, holding the trance space steadily while the oracles speak and then fall silent in turn.

When it seems the last vision has been spoken and no more are coming tonight, we will softly slow the chant and let it drop into silence. I will call the oracles back from the Otherworld paths, asking our guiding divinities and protective spirits to aid them in finding their way back to us. Our warders will check in with each of them, helping them with water, with salt, with food, with talismans to ensure they've safely recovered themselves. We'll carefully close the pathways to the Otherworld and give thanks to all our gods and spirits for their aid.

For these messages that have been given to us from the Otherworld, we'll each take time considering them. No prophecy is complete, final, or objective, so we'll check our understandings of them using divination and getting second opinions from those we trust.

CHAPTER 5

divination, sign, and sigil

Divination is a crucial skill set in sorcery as it allows us to consult the spirits for guidance and information in a more concrete format than intuition alone. In this chapter, I will look at methods and approaches to divination for sorcery practitioners, rooted in Celtic traditions, including augury, as well as lexical symbol sets. I will also explore the use of these symbol sets as magical seals and the art of sigil-making.

Divination can be found in an enormous number of spiritual traditions. In contemporary neo-pagan culture, it is ubiquitous, perhaps most commonly in the form of tarot and other divination card decks. As with many cultural practices, the belief system underlying its use is often unarticulated. Frameworks for understanding how divination works, why it is consulted, and where its insights come from vary. Some understand it as a method for consecrated communication with divinities of a particular tradition. Others describe it in terms of accessing the wisdom of "the universe/archetypes/collective mind." Still others simply see it as a tool for articulating what your own subconscious mind already knows.

For this practice, my intention is to develop an animist and spirit-based framework for a practice of divination. In Celtic cultural paradigms, the world is both alive and full of spirit beings. Divination exists to facilitate communication and communion with the holy powers of the gods, spirits, and living realms. In pre-Christian times, divinatory expertise was primarily the domain of the druids, who in early Celtic cultures seem to have been understood in part as natural philosophers, studying the nature and workings of the cosmos, the land, the heavens, the Otherworld, and all that moved within it.[187] Divination techniques rooted in these traditions are therefore outward-looking and animist in nature; they are methodologies for accessing knowledge and communication from gods and spirits understood to exist in both natural and Other worlds.

Augury and Omens

Augury, or the reading of omens through watching phenomena in the natural world, was a widely attested tradition in Celtic cultures, something they shared with many other ancient cultures. There seems to have been a particular focus on bird augury, at least in the records that remain.

Early Irish monastics condemned bird augury, particularly regarding the reading of omens in the voices of birds, suggesting pagan connotations. An early Irish lorica poem attributed to Columcille rejects the practice while associating it with divination: "I adore not the voices of birds, nor sneezing nor lots in this world nor a boy nor omens nor woman. My druid is Christ the Son of God."[188] Most of these items mentioned appear to be forms of divination that a proper Christian at the time would have abjured: the voices of birds, sneezing, drawing lots, the taking of omens, etc.

---

187. Koch and Carey, *The Celtic Heroic Age*, 18.

188. Best, "Prognostications from the Raven and the Wren," 120.

Ravens in particular seem to have been especially closely associated with divination: a branch of Irish augury was called *fiachairecht*, "raven-lore," and recorded in a medieval divination tract alongside another specifying augury through the behavior of wrens. The raven-lore text identifies auguries based on wild flight behaviors and calls:

> If it call from a stone, it is death-tidings of an *aitheci* [peasant]. If it call from a high tree, then it is death-tidings of a young lord. If from the top of the tree, death-tidings of a king or a youth of noble lineage. If it go with thee on a journey or in front of thee, and if it be joyful, thy journey will prosper and fresh meat will be given to thee. If thou come left-hand-wise and it calls before thee, he is a doomed man on whom it calls thus, or it is the wounding of some one of the company. If it be before thee when going to an assembly, there will be an up rising therein.[189]

Similarly, the text also specifies auguries on raven behavior within domestic spaces:

> If it call from above the goodman's bed, the place where his weapons will be, and he going on a journey, he will not come back safe; but if not, he will come back sound. If it is the woman who is about to die, it is from the pillow it calls. If it call from the foot of the man's bed, his son or his brother or his son-in-law will come to the house. If it call from the edge of the storehouse where the food is kept, there will be increase of food from the quarter it calls, that is, flesh-meat or first milking of kine.[190]

The assumption that ravens would be hopping about one's house commonly enough to develop a divination system on their behavior points to

---

189. Best, "Prognostications from the Raven and the Wren," 124.
190. Best, "Prognostications from the Raven and the Wren," 123–124.

domestication. It is thought that ravens may have been kept as partner animals for divination purposes. Archaeological evidence suggests a similar practice in Iron Age Britain; the remains of aged and apparently domesticated corvids have been found in burial pits in contexts that suggest intentional ritual deposition.[191]

Augury through the behavior of corvids may have been known among the Continental Celts as well. The historian Livy describes a duel between a Gallic warrior and a Roman tribune where the appearance of a crow that flew in and perched on the Roman's head during the fight was seen as an omen of victory.[192] It may be relevant to mention here that the foundation legend of the Gallo-Roman city of Lugdunum attributes its name to the appearance of a flock of corvids, interpreted as a message from Lugos, associated with ravens.[193]

Beyond bird augury, there are references to other animal omens in use in early Celtic cultures. Queen Boudica, in Celtic Britain, is said to have released a hare during her invocation before battle. The running of the hare across the battlefield was read as an omen for the coming fight; the army toward which it ran was thought to be the one favored for victory.[194] Sacred horses were kept in association with kingship rites in multiple ancient cultures and observed for omens. In the rites for the kingship of Tara, in Ireland, the behavior of the sacred horses was read for omens on the virtue of the king and the prospects for his reign. The Roman historian Tacitus's *Germania* describes the keeping of sacred white horses at sanctuary sites, which were held to have divinatory powers, and whose movements were read for omens.[195]

The operative principle here is that of animals who are particularly sacred to or felt to be in the retinue of the divinities from whom one is seeking signs. Their behavior, when contextualized correctly, can be understood as carrying messages from the realms they are in kinship with. Context is key in bringing

191. Serjeantson and Morris, "Ravens and Crows," 100.

192. Beck, Goddesses in Celtic Religion, 594–595.

193. Beck, Goddesses in Celtic Religion, 131.

194. Koch and Carey, *The Celtic Heroic Age*, 46–47.

195. Waddell, *Archaeology and Celtic Myth*, 108–109.

this into practice. The ordinary behavior of, for example, crows—who populate most cities—while going about their daily corvid business of living is not necessarily a message from the gods just for you. Augury works when we ritualize and contextualize our seeking for omens. This might mean opening the omen-taking with a prayer or other ritual framing action, and then the very next animal behavior seen might be read as an omen. In some instances, as noted, it might mean the ritualized containment or release of an animal, and its behavior observed in that context. Omens can come unasked, but usually not in the normal daily behavior of animals; your signal that animal behavior may represent a message is when it is unique and out of the ordinary for that species, or when it appears singularly focused on you.

casting in wood

Another recurring theme is the casting of wooden staves or lots for divination. Accounts of various kinds of divination using signs inscribed on wooden lots are found across Celtic regions from Ireland to the Continent.

Some early Irish texts mention divination using "keys of knowledge" made of wood. In *The Wooing of Étaíne*, the druid Dalan uses four yew wands inscribed with ogham signs to discover the whereabouts of Étaíne. "The druid took four wands of yew and upon them he wrote oghams, and by his keys of poetic wisdom and through his ogham he divined that Etain was in Bri Leith with Midir."[196] The term used for this practice is *crandchur*, literally "casting in wood," and is also a common term used to mean divination or lottery—its cognate in Modern Irish is the contemporary word for a lottery. Similarly, *The Second Vision of Adomnán* mentions *fidlanna*, "wood divination" as a practice of druids and pagans in early Ireland that is rejected by the Church.[197]

The references to ogham specifically are medieval, not pre-Christian, as the earliest documented use of ogham is about the fourth century CE. However, the cultural link between the use of wooden lots and divinatory knowledge is likely much older than ogham as a specific symbol set for the construction of

---

196. Leahy, *Heroic Romances*, Vol I, 21.

197. Volmering, "The Second Vision of Adomnán," 662–663.

these lots. Medieval Welsh sources also preserve this association of divination with wooden staves in the term *coelbren*, "omen stick."[198] Tacitus describes a rite among Continental tribes in the Iron Age: "They cut off the branch of a nut-bearing tree and slice it into strips; these they mark with different signs and throw them completely at random onto a white cloth. Then the priest … offers a prayer to the gods, and looking up at the sky picks up three strips, one at a time, and reads their meaning from the signs previously scored on them."[199] The preference here for a nut-bearing wood may parallel the traditional Irish belief in the hazel as a tree of knowledge.

Wood artifacts survive poorly in the soil, so the lack of any recognizable surviving wooden casting sets in the archaeological record is not terribly surprising. Still, the pervasiveness of this concept throughout Celtic as well as Germanic cultures seems to reflect a cultural association that is quite ancient.

viɒuveletia

The Viduveletia is a contemporary Celtic letter divination system that was created to fulfill the need for a letter-based symbolic divination tool similar to the Germanic runes, but suited to Celtic polytheist and magical practices and rooted in a broadly Celtic spiritual and mythic lexicon. It is a contemporary innovation, developed by me in collaboration with Viducus Brigantici Filius and Segomâros Widugeni, starting in 2015.

This system makes no pretense of being historical, but springs from a grounding in tradition. As noted in the preceding section, the idea of letter-symbol divination is ancient, apparently having been used in Gaul, Germania, and early Ireland. Divination using letters is also attested in ancient Greece. Details of the Gaulish system have been lost, however. To fill this gap, we have in a sense back engineered a system using an alphabet attested from the period, the Lepontic script.

This script, sometimes also called the Lugano alphabet (for the location in Switzerland where it was first identified), was used for writing Lepontic,

---

198. Mees, *Celtic Curses*, 4520.

199. Waddell, *Archaeology and Celtic Myth*, 27.

an early Celtic language spoken in the Alpine region in the last half millennium BCE, and eventually assimilated into Gaulish.[200] Lepontic was the first Celtic language to be written, and the letters of the script are thought to have developed based on the Etruscan alphabet. They share some letters and similar forms with runic scripts, as both are derivative from early Italic alphabets. Lepontic is extinct as a living language, but the Lepontic script has been revived by some modern Celtic polytheist practitioners (including myself) for use in writing, as magical signs, and in divination.

The Viduveletia is composed of eighteen letters called *prinni*. These are divided into groups based on alignment to the Three Worlds cosmology:

- The Lower World group, relating primarily to chthonic and ancestral powers.
- The Middle World group, relating primarily to human and social forces, and the beings that make up the living world.
- The Upper world group, relating primarily to celestial powers and deities.
- The Liminal group, representing forces that are liminal or mediate between the realms.

---

200. Stifter, "Ancient Celtic Epigraphy and Its Interface with Classical Epigraphy," 102–103.

The Lower World

Lower World Group of the Viduveletia			
Name	Symbol	Letter	General meanings
Dubnos	⋇	D/Z	Darkness, the deep, the realms below Druidic power arising from the Otherworld Chthonic powers and spirits
Corios	K	C/K	Army, band of warriors Battle, combat, conflict Courage, warrior valor Regalia of war Noise of battle Powers and divinities of battle
Lugion	L	L	Oath, obligation to the Otherworld Watery places of votive offering—lake, marsh, bog Lightning—light from the Otherworld Divinities of oath swearing
Orbion	O	O	Heritage, memory, transmission of tradition Ancestors and descendants Ancestral lineage or pathway Inspiration from Heroic Ancestors Divinities of eloquence, heroic inspiration
Iugon	I	I	Yoke, bondage, hard work Yoke of time—cycles of time Obligations passed down from old to young Hardness, binding, obstacles, stasis, fixed condition Divinities and powers of time, age

The Middle World

Middle World Group of the Viduveletia			
Name	Symbol	Letter	General meanings
Bitu	◇	B	Life—the living world Mother's milk, new life, nourishment, renewal Poetry—upwelling inspiration Springtime—rites of renewal Divinities of renewal, inspiration
Pritios	Γ	P	Creativity—shaping of new things Fire in the head, seat of creative inspiration Cauldron—place of creation and remaking Poet-hero divinities, divinities of cauldron and creation
Vlatos	F	W/V	The sovereign Feasting, generosity as an obligation of leadership Visionary seership that guides leaders Divinities of knowledge and prophecy Divinities of wealth and sovereignty
Gestlos	⇓	G/X	Guest/host obligations Reciprocity, contracts, exchange of pledges Hostage, pledge-bound guest Binding prayer, ritual obligation, prohibition Obligations and bonds transmitted through kinship
Touta	X	T	The tribe—bonds of community Skill, craftsmanship, technologies and arts that sustain the tribe Thunder—noise of hammers Divinities and powers of thunder and storm Smithing/craftsman divinities Tutelary divinities

The Upper World

Upper World Group of the Viduveletia			
Name	Symbol	Letter	General meanings
Albios	$\wedge$	A	Sky, heaven, celestial realm World tree that holds up the heavens Guardianship of people and resources Leadership; status earned through service Sacrifices by a leader in service of their people Divinities of leadership and sacrifice
Sonnos	ζ	S	The sun, solar power Solar cycles, seasonality, the year Summer—time of the sun Healing; purification, healing springs Divinities and powers of solar fire, heat, healing
Nemetos	$\wedge$	N	Sanctuary—sacred enclosure containing power Mystery, the unseen, night, darkness Initiatory mysteries, bindings and bonds Isolation, vulnerability, nakedness Stranger—one from outside the boundaries Divinities of sanctuary
Uros	$\vee$	U	Ancestors, elevated ones Ancestor veneration and honoring Primal bull—first being whose body forms the landscape of creation Strength arising from the land Ancestral divinities and powers Divinities of high places
Đira	$\bowtie$	Đ/TS	Star; river of stars Milky Way galaxy, "the Way of the White Cow" Serpents and regeneration Cow goddess/creatrix Divinities and powers of creation, regeneration

The Liminal

Liminal Group of the Viduveletia			
Name	Symbol	Letter	General meanings
Ratis	D	R	Rath, fortification, protection of the sacred That which is guarded, secret, hidden Law, right governance, sovereignty Chariot; liminal vehicle and symbol of power Divinities of sovereignty and Otherworld power Chariot divinities
Matir	M	M	Motherhood, maternal lineage Liminality, mediation between worlds, factions, powers "Lady with a mead cup" archetype The weaving of fate Mother and Matron divinities Mead, sovereignty, and fate-weaving divinities
Epos	E	E	Horse as symbol of power, wealth and fertility Horse as vehicle of warriorship, land and territorial protection Horse as psychopomp/spirit vehicle, spirit travel Horse divinities and powers of martiality and territorial protection

divination

Divination can be helpful to verify, correct, or deepen insights gained through any other form of spiritual practice. For the polytheist, divination is about relationship; it is a communication with a deity, spirit, or collective of spirits. It is helpful to bring this awareness of relationship to the practice of divination. Divination is then not simply a vague open-ended seeking, but a language for articulate conversation with the gods and spirits. Questions to ask to help develop the practice might include: Whom do you wish to consult? What is their domain of knowledge or influence? What is their native language or cultural context, and based on this, what tools may help translate their communication? How might you specifically invite conversation with this divinity rather than any others?

This polytheist approach can help in identifying tools and methods of divination that are suitable. Spirits and deities sometimes do find it helpful to have tools keyed to the language or cultural lexicon they are rooted in, allowing them a more finely tuned vocabulary to communicate with us. For example, Irish spirits may respond well to ogham, as a familiar symbolic lexicon. However, this doesn't mean we are limited to old or traditional methods. The ancients innovated and adopted new methods from other cultures they contacted, and we are free to do that too. The Viduveletia set described in the last section is an innovation of this kind. Almost anything can be effective as a divination tool, provided it is acceptable to the gods or spirits you wish to use it to communicate with. Divination systems are like modes of language, and their usefulness is proportional to the comfort level of the parties who are trying to communicate.

It is also helpful to think in terms of the different kinds of communication that divination methods offer. Message is always shaped by language—by the things that a given language has or lacks vocabulary to convey. I tend to classify divination systems based on the way that meanings are communicated, falling into three functional modes: *visionary*, *symbolic* or *verbal*, and *binary*.

Visionary divination modes rely on entering a receptive state and allowing impressions, images, or visions to surface. In this group, I place methods such as the traditional dream incubation and visionary divination rites mentioned earlier. Visual gazing methods such as scrying, and perhaps some forms of visual augury, would also fall within this grouping. The source from which meanings are drawn in this type of divination mode is the mind of the seer, and the powers they are in spiritual communion with. Visionary divination modes give the widest flexibility in what the spirits can show—being limited only by what the seer is capable of perceiving and articulating. However, with this flexibility comes risk, as these modes are especially vulnerable to projection and to being filtered through the seer's assumptions and cultural lenses. It is tantalizingly easy to see just the thing that one is looking for or already believes to be true. In part, this is why the ritualized trance state is important; it is what moves the seer into an unordinary state of consciousness in which, it is hoped, the contents of their seeing may be sourced not from within the personality itself but from the transpersonal Otherworld they have opened themselves to.

Symbolic or verbal divination modes rely on the use of a structured symbol set or lexicon from which messages are drawn, and that guides their interpretation. Traditional methods such as ogham or rune sortilege fall within this grouping, as would the unspecified "casting in wood" described in *The Wooing of Étaíne,* or the signs inscribed on nut-wood attributed to ancient druids and priests, and the modern Viduveletia. I would also include tarot and other oracle card decks in this grouping, as well as bibliomantic divination using texts or books. The functional core here is a predetermined and structured lexicon of meanings that are drawn from by means of some type of randomizing tool, such as tossed dice, stones, staves, or shells, or shuffled cards. The structured lexicon helps to organize communication, providing a ready, and often also culturally aligned, vocabulary of meanings and messages. Of course, this structure also delimits what can be conveyed with it.

Binary divination modes center on the use of items that provide two possible results and can thus produce a yes-no answer. This binary can also expand to represent a spectrum of answers, from strong-positive and strong-negative to weaker responses, as well as redirects such as "no answer" or "wrong question." Traditional binary practices often employ natural objects such as three to eight coins, shells, staves, or other two-sided objects where one side represents a positive and the other a negative. Alternately, binary mode found in both Irish and Scottish folk traditions involves the use of three stones of different colors instead of identical objects with two sides; here the three colors can stand for yes, no, and maybe (or the third may convey a lack of answer).[201] Binary modes like these can be very useful for clarity in answering direct questions, and they are also invaluable for testing and confirming knowledge gained from

---

201. Stokes, "The Irish Ordeals, Cormac's Adventure in the Land of Promise, and the Decision as to Cormac's Sword," 191; Richardson-Read, "Skyrie Stanes."

other sources. Being able to ask the spirits "Did I interpret this correctly?" is incredibly powerful as a tool against confirmation bias in all spirit practices.

Given that each kind of divination mode has is strengths and its limitations, a really robust divination practice ideally might include tools representing all three modes—visionary, symbolic, and binary divination. Of course, a polytheist approach will also take into account what divination methods are favored by the particular divinities you are consulting with.

This brings me back to that crucially important question of, "Whom are you consulting when you use divination?" As I've said, divination is a conversation with spirits. If you aren't specifying which spirits, the act of divination may not be much more than the spiritual equivalent of going into a crowded street and yelling your questions to anyone who might care to respond. You might get a useful answer, but it's not reliable. Some divination systems are a set of spirits in and of themselves, or may have a spirit or deity who oversees or rules them as a collective. For example, practitioners of the ogham recognize them as not just a set of symbols, but a family of spirits, traditionally created by and overseen by the god Ogma.[202] Similarly, the Celtic Viduveletia are spirits, named for and collectively overseen by Vidlua (who was introduced in chapter 4). In these cases, the spirits of the divination tool itself can be whom you are consulting for divination, or may act as helpful intermediaries with any other divinity you may be wishing to consult. The usefulness and precision of divination is proportional to how intelligently it's focused. So this question of whom you are consulting should be foremost both in preparing your divination tools, and each time you use them.

Sorcerer's Toolkit
divination Rites

Once you have your divination tool sourced, it needs spiritual preparation before you begin to use it. It is best to first cleanse the tool, to

---

202. Carey, "Ogmios and the Eternal Word," 3.

ensure that any unwanted spiritual residues from how it was made or from anyone's hands it may have passed through are neutralized. Then it should be consecrated, blessing it for divination with the divinities appropriate to it or whom you are in relationship with. This practice allows you to specify what entities can speak through it by placing the tool under the guardianship of gods or spirits you trust. It is the spiritual equivalent of installing a lock or password, preventing interference from random unwanted spirits when you sit down to divine with the tool. This protection can also be enhanced by inscribing the spirits' names, sigils, or other protective marks on the container.

Here is a template you can use for preparing a newly acquired or created divination tool:

Rite to Consecrate a Divination Tool

For this rite, you will need:

- Tools for cleansing, such as blessing water or incense.
- A candle.
- An offering suitable for the spirits whom you'll be consecrating this tool to.
- Your divination tool.
- A container to store the tool in.

Cleanse the tool, yourself, and the space you're working in by sprinkling the blessing water or wafting sacred smoke.

Invoke the divinities whom you're consecrating the tool to. Light the candle and speak a prayer to them. Ask them to come near, bless the tool, seat themselves in it, and take guardianship of it. If the tool is one that has its own set of spirits, include them in this invocation.

Make the offering, inviting the spirits you've called to receive it and be fed. Touch a bit of the offering to the tool as well, to consecrate it to them. You may wish to leave the tool sitting in the presence of the spirits for a period of time, to continue absorbing their presence and blessings.

When you're finished with the rite, put the divination tool into the container you've prepared for it, so that it is stored in a spiritually protected way between uses.

Similarly, whenever sitting down to perform divination, think about framing the practice in a polytheist mode of communication with the spirits. To ensure it's a conversation that can proceed clearly and articulately, prepare the communication space with spiritual practices just as you would if you were sitting down to prayer or meditative communion. Here is a simple template you can build on in your divination practice:

Simple Divination Rite

For this rite, you will need:

- A cleansing tool, such as blessing water.
- Your divination tool.
- A small offering for the spirits who oversee your tool.

Begin with purification of yourself and your tool by sprinkling the blessed water.

Offer a prayer to the spirits whom your divination tool is consecrated to. Ask them to speak through the tool, to help you receive the knowledge you need, and to prevent interference from hostile forces in the communication. Share a bit of offering to feed them.

You can now begin your divination. As you divine, think of it as a conversation with the spirits.

When you're finished, close your session with gratitude prayers to the spirits.

Cleanse your tools and yourself again before putting the tool away in its consecrated container.

This basic procedure for spirit-centered divination is highly adaptable and you can build on it based on what your spirits prefer, or what works best for you. It is worth noting that a ritualized approach like this doesn't have to mean that divination can't be performed quickly or on-the-fly when the situation demands it. I love being able to easily bring ritual with me, so I keep my most-used divination tools in a little kit, which also contains a small spray bottle with blessing water, and a little jar of herbs I can use for offerings. Then, wherever I happen to be, if I want to check something I can easily perform a quick purification with the blessed water, whisper a prayer and sprinkle a pinch of herbs, and I'm ready to toss my staves for a quick answer.

Going deeper with divination Tools

The animist worldview that underpins Celtic magic can inform how we adapt to working with divination tools. It invites us into ever deeper connection by taking divination as a mode of relationship. Think of how, in close friendships, people develop a sort of private memetic language over time, where condensed meanings can be conveyed with a single word or phrase that conjures a shared memory and everything that is attached to it. As we deepen into relationship with our spirits, divination can become this kind of intimate shared language that is particular to that relationship.

To deepen into this way of divination as relationship, consider ways of exploring beyond the standard uses and meanings of your divination tools. You can try interviewing your spirits using the tool. Ask questions that can reveal something about how they will communicate with you. For example, "Can you show me what sign you might use to signal X?" and then pull a card, stone, stave, etc. to see the preferred sign. In this way, you can begin to learn in more detail how your spirits use the language of divination to communicate. You can also accomplish this through performing divination in the usual way, and also employing a binary divination tool to confirm as you go: "I'm reading this sign I pulled to mean that you're saying X. Is that correct?" Over time, this habit will help you calibrate how you interpret messages through the medium of divination.

Another way of deepening into divination with symbolic systems in particular is to practice devotional meditation with them. It's often recommended when learning a new symbol lexicon (such as ogham, runes, tarot, or the like) to go through a study cycle and contemplate one symbol at a time each day or week. You can build on this learning technique as a mode of relational learning with the spirits. Taking one symbol of your divination lexicon at a time, open a devotional session with prayer and offerings to the spirits. In your prayer, ask them to reveal what this symbol means to them, and what they would like you to see in it when they use it to communicate. Spend some time in devotional meditation, and make notes of what you saw. Continue this through the whole lexicon of symbols in your divination system. This type of practice can add great depth and sensitivity to how you understand what the spirits are communicating in your divination practice.

Divination tools can also become a two-way conversation between you and your spirits. In a divination or prayer session, beyond receiving their messages through the symbols, you can reply back to them using the same language. Try selecting a symbol that conveys what you feel, focusing on it, and sending it outward like a prayer. When you feel it's been heard, sit and listen meditatively for the response; or you can do another divination pull to see the response.

Lastly, divination can be an incredibly powerful tool for guiding a ritual practice. A traditional way this has been implemented is the omen-taking associated with sacrifices, where the gods are asked how the offerings were received and whether they are satisfied. Beginning to employ this practice can help you learn a lot about what best pleases your spirits, and so deepen your bonds with them. You can also use divination to help articulate ritual practices with the guidance of your spirits. Consider asking things like, "For a ritual to accomplish such-and-such, what actions are indicated? What are my risk factors? What kind of protections or safeguards should I look at?" etc. For each question that you might mull over in the planning of a spell or ritual, your spirits may have helpful guidance for you. The meanings and images attached to the symbols that you draw for these questions won't necessarily spell everything out for you, but they can offer concrete ideas to build from in preparing your rites.

sigils: An Animist Framework

Since the symbol and letter sets used in divination are spirits, they are also magically active sigils in their own right. A sigil is a sign or symbol considered to have magical power. The name is from Latin *sigillum*, "seal," and comes into magical usage by way of Western ceremonialist occultism, rooted in medieval grimoire traditions that made heavy use of Latin texts and seals for conjuring spirits.[203] However, in the broader sense as signs used in magical or spiritual operations, sigils have appeared in many cultures and for thousands of years. In contemporary usage, when people speak of sigils they often mean compound symbols made by combining multiple letters or symbols, and they are often used in conjunction with ritual to invoke or evoke a spirit, power, or effect.

Many contemporary occultist approaches to the construction and use of sigils are heavily influenced by ceremonialist methods, reflecting the same medieval grimoire roots just mentioned. A method with wide currency in contemporary occultist and pagan circles is to write a name, phrase, or wish, reduce it by the elimination of duplicate letters and/or the use of numerology, and then combine the reduced group of letters into a sigil. In this way, the original phrase is "occulted," that is, hidden and no longer consciously readable. Many practitioners using this method might not know to credit Austin Osman Spare, the early twentieth-century British occultist, but this method of reducing a name or incantation by occultation was devised by him.[204] His theory and approach to the making of sigils is based in a very modernist understanding of magic as driven by will and intention; the occultation or disguising of the inscription is understood to shift awareness of the intention from the conscious mind to the subconscious, where it more directly and primally engages the magician's will.

---

203. Merriam-Webster.com Dictionary, "s.v. 'sigil'."

204. Grant, "Austin Osman Spare: An Introduction to His Psycho-Magical Philosophy."

I share this bit of history to provide some background and to contrast it with the approach I take to sigil work, which is a little different from this. Modern Western occultism works fine for those who choose it, but it is rooted in a worldview quite different from the cosmology we are operating within. Rather than focusing on the will and mind of the solitary magician, Celtic approaches to magic begin from an animist worldview and operate on a relational model. Every symbol we work with, including letters, is a being or at least a force we interact with. Instead of condensing and occulting the magician's will, the process of sigil creation is one of inviting spirits into relationship to form a shaped alliance that is visually encoded by the sigil. We are enabled to make contact and collaborate with those forces or spirits, to activate those relationships, through the use of the sigil. It is a magic of relationship and alliance.

symbol sources

Any lexicon of letters, numbers, or symbols can be worked into sigil creation. As a Celtic polytheist, I tend to work from alphabets and symbol sets that have some historical interface with one or more of the Celtic cultures. Some practitioners find it helpful to focus on those that have established spirits inhabiting them and traditions for working with them. However, there's also fun and fruitful work to be done in exploring with less established lexicons. In my own practice, I typically work with three primary scripts, adding other sources at times when I find it helpful.

The first is ogham, which you will also sometimes see in its older spelling of ogam. This is an Irish script dating from about the fifth century CE onward.[205] Ogham inscriptions have also been found in Scotland, Wales, and western Britain, as well as the outer isles between Britain and Scandinavia, including Shetland and even as far as Iceland.[206] Much of its early usage, at least that for which evidence survives, was in memorial inscriptions on stone markers, primarily in Primitive Irish. In the early medieval period, it came

---

205. The Discovery Programme—Centre for Archaeology and Innovation Ireland, "Ogham in 3D."
206. Institute of Archaeology—University College London, "Celtic Inscribed Stones Project."

into use also as a script for ciphers, messages, and records. Several systems of kennings, or individual letter meanings, were recorded in early Irish manuscript sources, along with extensive examples of how the script could be adapted to encode different types of information.

Second, I also employ the Iron Age Celtic Lepontic script, as seen in the Viduveletia divination system, presented earlier in this chapter.

Third, I also work with the runes, a Germanic alphabetic system historically used from the first century CE onward.[207] Originating in northwest Germany, it was likely based on Old Italic scripts brought into the region through contact with the Romans. The early Germanic runic alphabet developed into several variants, spreading into Scandinavia and in use with the Old Norse language, and continuing into the medieval period with Gothic and Anglo-Saxon forms. Early evidence indicates that the runes were used as magical signs as well as a script for writing; their historical use as divinatory signs prior to the modern period is a matter of scholarly debate.

There are of course many other sources for symbols that can be used in sigil-making for a Celtic magical practice. Greek letters were also used from an early period to write Celtic inscriptions, and the Greek alphabet has a rich history of its own as a lexicon for divination and magical writing. And we are not limited to alphabets—there are a wealth of other symbols that can provide material for sigil craft. The pictographic and abstract forms found in Celtic and pre-Celtic art can also inform the practice: spirals, wheels, key devices, cup and ring marks, and other patterns. Sigils can also weave in simple representational images, and many examples in history do so: eyes, suns or stars, serpents and other animals, and many more motifs.

It is worth dwelling for a moment on the combining of source motifs from different cultures. I've mentioned including signs from Irish, Gaulish, Germanic, Scandinavian, and Greek sources, and the interweaving doesn't have to stop there. This interweaving of cultures is not a modern phenomenon. Historically, many rich examples of sigil-making have occurred at the intersection of cultures. There seems to be a fertility that occurs when different

---

207. Museum of Cultural History—University of Oslo, "The Origin and Development of Runes."

cultural lexicons are brought together. In fact, when looking into the histories of these different scripts and symbol-sets, it's clear that they never did exist in isolation.

For example, there are fascinating examples of complex sigil creation at the intersection of Gaelic and Norse cultural influences. Historically, the intersection of these cultures is well attested, resulting from extensive contact between Scandinavia, Iceland, and the western islands including Ireland, Britain, and the Scottish isles. This intersection of cultures found its way into the patterns of use of written and magical scripts. Complex ogham appears in *The Book of Ballymote*, including versions that incorporate Norse runes, framed as a type of ogham cipher, *ogam lochlannach* or "ogham of the Norsemen."[208] There are combined ogham and runic stone inscriptions, such as the Killaloe stone in County Clare, Ireland.[209] Similarly, the Bressay Stone of Shetland features Pictish-style carvings with an ogham inscription recording a combination of early Gaelic and Old Norse language.[210] Paradise Cave, in Iceland, features inscriptions in both ogham and runes on its walls.[211] This cultural interweaving flowers vividly in the *galdrastafir* bind-runes found in medieval Icelandic grimoires—complex, beautiful magical sigils that appear to incorporate influences from both runic and ogham traditions.[212]

Some interesting compound symbols also appear in curse tablet inscriptions that are the product of cultural fusion. Called *defixiones* in Latin and *katadesmoi* in Greek, these inscribed magical petitions deposited in charged places originated as a magical practice in the Mediterranean cultures of Greece and Rome, but the practice was diffused out throughout the area of Roman expansion, including Egypt and the Near East, as well as Gaul and Britain. Along with the written curse texts, these inscribed objects often feature drawings, figures, and sigils, frequently with layered and interwoven symbolism

---

208. Royal Irish Academy, "The Book of Ballymote."

209. Moriarty, "An Unusual Ogham and Runic Inscription from Killaloe, Co. Clare."

210. Institute of Archaeology, "Celtic Inscribed Stones, BREAY/1."

211. Katla UNESCO Global Geopark, "Paradísarhellir."

212. Museum of Icelandic Sorcery and Witchcraft, "Magical Staves."

combining local deities, spirits, and iconography, with this Mediterranean style of magic.

I think what's most valuable to learn from this rich history of interwoven traditions is that magical practices are enlivened by these cross-fertilizations, and that we don't need to limit ourselves to a single lexicon for symbol-making out of a sense of cultural purity or to avoid crossing streams. Ancient practitioners seem to have felt free to weave together imagery and symbolism from the different cultural frameworks they were living in relationship to, and those fusions have offered up some of the most inspiring forms of sigils and magical signs.

sigils as magical engines

As an animist, I understand sigils not just as symbols, but as condensed magical engines animated with a spirit of their own. Like any organism, they are comprised of interconnected parts working as one whole being. Also like an organism, they live and act on different scales or levels, from their interwoven internal components to the whole.

There are three (or at least three!) levels of action in sigils, each of which may represent a distinct spirit or set of spirits. Here I describe them in sequence from the micro or component level to the macro or the level of the sigil as a whole.

First, at the root level, there are the powers of the individual component parts—the letters or signs we bring together to construct the sigil. It is not the habit of most westerners to see distinct powers within the individual letters of the Roman alphabet, for example. However, in a great many other cultural contexts, the individual letters or signs in the alphabet or lexicon often do represent distinct spirits or powers in their own right. This is certainly the case for the Germanic/Norse runes, for the Irish ogham, and many others. Whether or not they were seen to have these powers in their original historical context, they certainly do now after generations of modern practitioners working with them in a spiritual capacity. When you construct a sigil, you are weaving each of these component powers into the whole—like parts in an engine or organs in a body, their individual powers are focused into the working of the whole.

Second, a sigil may take its power from the word, name, or phrase it is built to convey. This may not be the case for all sigils, of course. Some may be built by selecting individual letters or runes and weaving them directly into a shape without consideration for what they spell together. The conventional Western occultist mode of sigil creation begins at this level with the written intention. For a devotional sigil, it might be the name of the being it is meant to invoke. For an operational magic sigil, it might be a word of power or a magical phrase or incantation.

At the third level is the shape given to the sigil as a whole—the pattern into which its component parts are bound together. In my approach to sigil creation, this level is crucial. It's here that the dynamics powering the sigil are generated, based on the shape and form it is given. That is to say, it's not just about sticking the component parts together any kind of way. To act as a symbol, it needs to have spiritual and emotional impact, both on the person using it and any others who see it, as well as the spirits. Its visible shape needs to conjure its intended meaning and impact. To act as a magical engine, it needs to have its parts bound together into a structure that allows it to move and shape spiritual forces in a given way. What do you want it to be able to do, and what structure will help it do that? The way in which it is built and the shape that it takes will determine how it in turn shapes and moves spiritual forces.

Sigil Functions

By way of example, here are some of the many different functions a sigil can be built for, and the kind of structures that help them function:

Shield sigils can create barriers to stop or disperse spiritual forces. They might visually imitate a physical shield, or they might employ a structure that gathers power and spreads it into a field or barrier.

Spirit trap sigils may use complexity to entrap, entangle, or bind. There might be a part of the structure that attracts, and another part that entraps. There might be barbs or weaponized parts of the sigil that employ directed force to harm or neutralize that which has been trapped.

Weapon sigils can be made to concentrate and compound force into a shape that can pierce, wound, or cut. They can be designed to direct and send forces toward a target, like a projectile.

Door and pathway sigils can be shaped to create openings or gateways, to lay out pathways for movement and return, or signposting and directionality.

Vessel, container, or well sigils may be geared to receive, gather, or hold power. Their shape might be designed for drawing forces inward, for containment, for intensification or magnification.

Sigils for vision and insight might follow the shape of an eye, pupil, or lens—opening, focusing, drawing in light. Similarly, sigils for fending off evil eye often take a form like this.

Sigils for growth and expansion might take their form from the sprouting and spreading of plants, from the rising of light, or a more abstract approach with a shape that broadens in space and pushes outward.

Devotional sigils might have the purpose of helping to seat a spirit or divinity in a place or within an object. Their design might focus on visual representations of symbols of that divinity, placed within a shape that is oriented toward structure and stasis.

These are just a few examples, not an exhaustive list. We are limited here only by our creativity and spiritual vision.

sigils are subjective

The structure and shaping of sigils for movement and shaping of forces is naturally subjective; that is to say, opinions vary on how any given shape affects energy. For example, in the school of *galdrastafir* Icelandic staves, there are conflicting views on how the structures within the staves shape magical dynamics. Does a crossbar at the end of a stave indicate a blocking of force or a redirection? If it has backward-pointing hash marks, does that indicate intensification of the energy or dispersal? Most historical sources of magical sigils do not explain how they were constructed, so we are left to hypothesize and different practitioners reconstruct these methods differently.

My approach is to accept this subjectivity as a given and work with it. From an animist spirit worker's perspective, this is about relationship, just as all animist magic is. When I create a sigil, I am conjuring a spirit entity into being, or weaving a spirit collective into operation from the spirits of the symbols being used. Or, in some cases I might be creating a form as an expression of a preexisting spirit or deity. Whatever the specifics, sigil work is rooted in communication with a spirit or group of spirits, and it's that communication that directs how the sigil should go together. This means that when it comes to questions about how a given shape affects or shapes magical forces, we are free to work from our own instincts and the directives of the powers we're working with.

Sigils may also encode ritual gestures in their shape. This can be an alternative method of design. It begins with a fixed visual framework within which the letters of the alphabet or lexicon are set out—this is often done by placing them around a ring or square, or multiple concentric shapes. The word or incantation is then spelled by moving from letter to letter around the framework, and the pathway taken to spell the word is recorded as a shape. This same pathway can be traced in the air as a ritual gesture using the hands or other body part, to invoke the spirit encoded in the sigil. Many of the Goetic sigils of grimoire traditions are created from the ritual gesture method. Some contemporary practitioners use Finn's Window, a medieval concentric-ring framework for the ogham letters found in *The Book of Ballymote*, to generate gestural ogham sigils.[213]

Whether or not a gestural method is used to construct the sigil, any sigil can be converted to ritual gesture for invoking and conjuring. The more com-

---

213. Royal Irish Academy, "Book of Ballymote, MS 23 P 12, f. 170r."

plex a sigil is, the more challenging it will be to translate it into a coherent ritual gesture. Hard-ended lines may need to be converted into more flowing, cursive forms that fit with the way a hand moves in space. From an animist perspective, it matters less whether the sigil gesture can be literally read as a precise imitation of the written one. What matters is that the spirit or spirits encoded in the sigil can recognize the gesture and will respond.

Sorcerer's Toolkit
sigil making

There are a thousand ways to work with sigils. Here, I'll just offer a pathway for making and charging a sigil, based in my practice and way of working. You can experiment and build on this in developing your own ways of working.

Creating a Sigil

Identify the components that will make up the sigil. Meditate on the purpose of the sigil, and consult with the deities or spirits you're working with. Questions to consider: Is there an alphabet or symbol source you wish to work from? Is there is a word, phrase, or name that is being encoded in the sigil? Are there letters or symbols appropriate for your sigil based on their individual meanings and powers?

Identify the shape the sigil should take. What visual impact do you want this sigil to have? Is there a being it should represent, and if so, what image will serve them? If the sigil is meant to deliver a magical effect, what shape will give it that impact? You can review the list of suggested shapes in the previous section for ideas.

Weaving the sigil. Begin with prayer or invocation to the divinities who oversee your work, so they are with you in creating the sigil. Start loosely sketching ways of combining the parts into a sigil, while listening for any guidance from the spirits. Try to keep in mind the overall shape you identified and aim toward that. If it doesn't come together immediately, just keep trying different configurations. At a certain point, the pieces will usually fall into place. You may feel a particular sketched configuration seems to stand out with a feeling of power or presence. If this doesn't happen, or you have multiple versions that you think might work, you can use divination to consult the spirits about which one is best.

Take a little extra time to refine the shape so that it is as graceful, beautiful, or striking as it can be. Play with proportions and line weight, or try decorative flourishes if they seem appropriate. Your sigil should not just efficiently combine its parts, but also feel artful and alive.

When the sigil is ready, it is time to put it into action by giving it life and consecrating it to its purpose. What this looks like will vary a lot depending on what you've made this sigil for. Here is a simple template for ritual you can build creatively on.

Rite to Charge a Sigil

For this rite, you will need:

- Tools for cleansing.
- A surface to inscribe your sigil on, such as paper, wood, soft metal, or another surface.
- Pen, paint, or a sharp tool for inscribing the sigil.
- An offering to feed the sigil, such as spirits, wine, milk, or oil.

Cleansing: As always, begin with purifications of yourself, your materials, and your space using blessing water or another method.

Call the spirits who are connected to your sigil or the work that it's for with an invocatory prayer. Ask them to be present and enter into the sigil that you've created for them.

Inscribe, carve, or paint the sigil on your chosen materials. While you do this, you can be speaking the sigil into life. If it encodes an incantation or a name, chant or recite that. If it encodes a magical function, you can speak instructions for that magical function.

Once inscribed, awaken the sigil and give it life. Breathe into it, tracing it with your fingers, as you say, "I give you life."

Feed the sigil with spirits or an offering that is suitable for its nature. You can sprinkle drops onto it, or dip your finger into the offering and use it to trace the sigil.

CHAPTER 6

ɳecroɱaɳcẏ aɳɗ Aɳcestor work

In this chapter, I will explore an area that is crucially important in many polytheistic traditions, and well represented in Celtic cultures: that of spirit work with the dead—the domains of ancestor veneration and necromancy.

Sorcery practitioners may want to include the dead in their spirit relationships for a variety of reasons. First, I think it's worth considering that the dead are all around us, whether we address them or not. This is the case not just at places considered to be haunted. We are surrounded by the spirits of the dead everywhere, as part of the general ecology of the spirit world, even if many people may only become aware of them when there is a spiritual disturbance. This becomes even more the case when we are engaged in an active magical practice, as these activities can stir up, agitate, or attract all kinds of spirits. It greatly benefits us to be conversant and on friendly terms with the spirits around us.

Ancestor work and communication with the dead can also be a rich source of mutual benefit to both the living and the dead. The dead are keepers of a vast well of knowledge—the collective lived experience and wisdom of hundreds of generations—and in general they *want* to share this wisdom with us. And having been alive, they often are closer to our experiences and may understand our needs better than gods or other nonhuman spirit beings might. Ancestors who are connected to you through family, lineage, common struggle, or other kinds of kinship tend to have a strong investment in your well-being and thus can be enormously helpful.

Finally, and perhaps most importantly, we are responsible for the dead, and especially our own ancestors whose heritage, burdens, and privileges we often carry. We may have ancestors who suffered harm and oppression and may have bequeathed generational traumas to us. In many instances, those ancestors may be as in need of healing as we are, and it is only the living who can help them access that healing. We are also responsible to our ancestors in terms of of what we do with privilege. For example, I am of mostly European ancestry, and folks like myself are inheritors of the privileges and generational benefits of whiteness, which in turn is the product of centuries of my ancestors' participation in oppressive systems. I have a responsibility to use that privilege toward dismantling those oppressions and, to the extent I can, making right the wrongs of my ancestors. This too can be part of an ancestor practice.

THE JOURNEY OF THE DEAD

Many of the stories relating to the dead center on rituals of sacralization or elevation. This is the means by which the spirits of the dead are aided to transition from the liminal and potentially dangerous status of newly dead, to the collective, stable, and sacred status of ancestors.

This domain of spirit work centers on the understanding that newly dead spirits are potentially in a vulnerable state, and that there are different pathways for the dead depending on how this period of transition is handled. Ideally, the dead should complete a transition to a stable, sacred, and empowered state as an ancestor; this transition may be framed as a journey to an ancestral realm, aided by psychopomp divinities, and/or a process of elevation into a sacred realm. Many contemporary folk traditions, especially where African Diaspora, Latin Catholic, or spiritualist influences are present, frame this process in terms of spirit elevation or ancestor elevation, in part reflecting the idea that the sacred ancestors would reside in a heavenly realm. Celtic cultures have tended to see the ancestors as residing in the Otherworld, which is often more likely to be situated within the land (as in the Irish Otherworld) or as an Underworld (as in the Gallic cosmology). Therefore in a Celtic context, these rites tend to focus more on heroization than on vertical elevation, though elements of elevation may also be present.

The vulnerability of the dead, especially those whose deaths are shaped by trauma or injustice, means that there is a risk of becoming lost, trapped, or unstable. Often the battlefield dead and those similarly associated with violence are framed within the tradition as ghosts or walking revenants. For example, *The Adventure of Nera* describes the talking corpse of a hanged criminal who entraps Nera into carrying it about on a lengthy and disastrous set of adventures.[214] Similarly, the Boyhood Deeds of Cú Chulainn (in the *Táin Bó Cúailnge*) describes a revenant with half his head missing, rising from the battlefield to attack the boy.[215] The hosts of specters and horrors that accompany war goddesses such as Badb may be understood as made up of such unquiet spirits who have become horrors.

In my view, part of the function of funerary traditions is to accomplish the proper transition of the dead so that they can reach the status of ancestors, and avoid becoming ghosts or horrors. This crucial transition depends in part on the living providing proper sacralization rites to assist them. We can identify several distinct elements in these rites, many of which are shared with other cultural approaches to ancestor elevation: separation or cleansing

---

214. Meyer, "The Adventures of Nera," 215–217.

215. O'Rahilly, "Táin Bó Cúalnge Recension 1," 138–139.

from the trauma of death, nourishment and healing, remembrance and praise rituals, and collectivization.

Separation

The first phase is separation from the trauma or confusion of the initial death state. This usually includes cleansing. Where this work is integrated into funerary treatment of the body, this can include physical washing of the body. In instances where this work is being done for the spirit at a later time, items belonging to the dead or otherwise representing them may be cleansed instead, or the process may focus on a place in the landscape where the dead are understood to be trapped or attached and needing release.

Separation may also involve grief rituals and lamentation. Rituals of grief and lamentation, such as the keening traditions of Ireland, serve not only as a catharsis for the living, but also to exorcise and transform the trauma of the dead. Thus, a dead person who has not been properly grieved may need to be keened or otherwise vocally grieved in order to be released from their liminal status and move forward in their journey.

This phase may also involve the aid of psychopomp divinities, to relocate the spirit to its safe and proper place in the ancestral realm. It is for this reason that imagery of birds and horses is often associated with places of ancestral veneration in Celtic contexts—these divinities were understood to literally carry the spirits of the dead to the ancestral realms.

Nourishment

The next phase of the sacralization process centers on providing nourishment and healing to the spirits. Here, offerings and sacrifices are typically included to feed the spirits of the dead and give strength, in the understanding that while the dead may not have living bodies, their spirits still need sustenance. The presence of food—often large joints of meat or whole slaughtered meat animals—in Celtic graves attests to the importance of feeding the dead. These offerings may both feed and heal. Irish tradition highlights the connection between healing and nourishment through food; many of its healing rites associated with death and rebirth involve food, such as the bath of beef and bacon in which Fraoch is immersed for healing.[216] Alongside these offerings of food and drink, fire is ever present, offering warmth and light to the space in which the dead walk, and also helping to light their way to the ancestral realm.

Remembrance

Remembrance and praise are also important in the rites of ancestral sacralization. The deeds of the dead or the stories of their lives may be told. Historically, for high status individuals, this was the role of poets who would compose praise poems telling the high deeds of the dead. For common folk, this might have taken the form of something more like the custom at a wake of telling tales about the dead. Keening customs also illustrate this, where some of the songs sung by keeners would include praise of the dead. These litanies of remembrance are not just about lifting up and praising the dead; they are also a crucial part of the process of transition. Telling the stories of the dead ensures that the deeds of their lives are not forgotten, which helps them to be fully released and therefore not remain as revenants. Further, these litanies are often composed so as to help to place the dead into the lineage of other ancestors who have gone before. The recitation of them therefore helps to weave the dead into relationship with the ancestors. Litanies for the dead can weave a kind of bridge of poetry or story through which the dead can find their way into collective remembrance as one of the ancestors.

Collectivization

These rites often include petitions and offerings to the ancestors, to ensure that they receive the dead into their realm and to help establish them within the body of the ancestors as a collective. In a sense they accomplish a shift or elevation of both identity and relationship to time, from newly departed dead person to revered and eternal ancestor. These rites also help to establish a stable spiritual framework for ongoing relationship between the living and the ancestors, and between the ancestors and other divinities in the spirit realm. This spiritual framework provides for reciprocity between the living and the

---

216. Waddell, *Archaeology and Celtic Myth*, 137.

dead: the ability for the ancestors to be heard and to share wisdom with the living through oracular rites, and to be able to offer aid and support to the living. This reciprocity is illustrated in the stories of the oracular head guiding communities through wisdom-speech, and of ancestral cult centers where the living gathered to celebrate with the dead.

Lamentation and the Spirit Journey

Ritual lamentation performances, also called keening, feature prominently in funeral traditions of the Celtic-speaking regions. This lamentation practice is a central through-line in the lore of funerary ritual from early texts right through into historic times. Early texts tend to describe vocal lamentation as the role of family members, with professional poets also composing elegiac poems to honor the dead. In historic times, the ritual lamentation was often performed by professional keening-women. It is notable that laments in the keening tradition employ a structured pattern, which often includes similar forms to *rosc* poetry—highlighting their antiquity and their role in ritual. Music researcher Narelle McCoy describes the structure of keening laments in this way:

> The use of recitative style with a falling inflection at the
> end of each line; the employment of *rosc* metre which had
> short lines of two or three stresses linked by end-rhyme
> and arranged in stanzas of uneven length which gave the
> *caoineadh* a raced and breathless style; and the three part
> structure of a keen which comprised of the salutation, the
> verse or dirge and finally the *gol* or cry which was taken up
> by the mourners.[217]

Lamentation opens up a dimension of funerary ritual that has both a social and a spiritual function. Its obvious social function is to channel and vocalize the grief of the community, and to open up a space of permission for expres-

---

217. McCoy, "Madwoman, Banshee, Shaman: Gender, Changing Performance Contexts and the Irish Wake Ritual," 211.

sive and embodied grief. It also has a spiritual way-opening function, being understood to help the spirit of the dead person to complete their transition. The keening is understood to open doorways, roads, or pathways through the spirit world and to aid in guiding the movement of the spirit. The *bean chaointe*, or keening woman, "inhabited a liminal state between the living and the world of the dead for the mourning period," allowing her to mediate between the worlds and help the dead to cross over.[218] Folk beliefs about the necessity of keening suggest that a person who has not been properly bewailed might be at risk of becoming a lost or disturbed spirit rather than transitioning as they should.

The spiritual function of keening is underlined by its association with spiritual beings in Irish tradition. Keening is described as having been established by Brigid when she began to mourn her son Ruadán; it is also performed by Badb and other spiritual beings who are said to keen and wail, especially in warning of a coming death.[219] Also, of course, there is the folklore of the famous banshee. The term is Anglicized from Old Irish *ban síd* or Modern Irish *beansidhe*, "fairy woman," a common epithet for Otherworldly women and goddesses in the Irish sagas. It appears that from this mythological tradition, through the late medieval and early modern period, folklore developed around this belief in Otherworldly female spirits who would appear keening and wailing to warn of an impending death. In the early modern and modern periods, these beings are tied to specific family lines. Sometimes also called *bodhbh*, "crow" or *bodhbh chaointe*, "keening crow," especially in the southeast of the country, these beings show a continuity of beliefs from ancient Irish goddesses to the contemporary notion of a being who performs a mourning role similar to that of a human keener.[220]

---

218. McCoy, "Madwoman, Banshee, Shaman: Gender, Changing Performance Contexts and the Irish Wake Ritual," 214.

219. Gray, "Cath Maige Tuired: The Second Battle of Mag Tuired," 57; Henry, "The Goblin Group," 408.

220. Lysaght, "Aspects of the Earth-Goddess in the Traditions of the Banshee in Ireland," 154–157.

Sorcerer's Toolkit
Ancestor Sacralization

There are many, many ways to approach rites of sacralization or elevation for the dead. Here, I'll present a simplified ritual cycle that you
can build upon in your practices. We'll construct a ritual for the dead
following the four steps identified in the previous section: separation,
nourishment, remembrance, and collectivization.

For this beginning ritual, let's imagine you wish to offer sacralization to a recently dead person. Perhaps this is a family member or
someone in your community, or simply someone whose spirit you
feel may need assistance. Perhaps the official funeral organized by the
surviving family is secular or of a different religious tradition from
the dead person, and so doesn't account for the needs of the spirit.
We will assume for this instance that you won't be handling the body
directly, since the considerations for that type of work are beyond the
scope of this book.

For this ritual, you will need:

- Cleansing tools, such as blessing water and incense.
- A consecrated space, such as an altar with images of the
  ancestors.
- Candles for light and warmth.
- Food and drink offerings.
- An image of the dead person, or an item belonging to them
  that can represent them.

Begin by cleansing yourself and your working space with the
blessing water.

Speak invocation prayers to the ancestors, as well as any divinities
whom you trust as psychopomps to aid and receive the spirit of the

dead person. Light candles for the ancestors and divinities, and place some of the offerings for them.

Separation and cleansing. Take up the object or image representing the dead person, and say their name. Speak to them directly so they know they are seen and honored, and so that you can communicate what you are doing for their spirit. Say, "I welcome [name], and I offer you the cleansing of holy water and sacred smoke, that your spirit be eased," or similar words. Wash or sprinkle water over their object, then pass it through the incense smoke.

You may wish to sing a lament or keen for them. This can begin with a song or chant that feels appropriate, or simply singing their name. As you sing, let yourself open to the emotion of grieving, not just your own but everything the world has lost in losing this person. Let your singing shift naturally toward wailing, let it be as formless and emotive as it wants to be. If you feel able, and with the aid of the divinities you've called on for help, reach with your heart across to the Otherworld and let your voice open a road that the spirit can cross. Keep wailing till you feel a shift and the spirit of the dead person feels more free, or until you sense that you have reached your own spiritual limits.

To fulfill nourishment, light a candle for the dead person, beside their image or object. Dedicate the offerings of food and drink and place before them. You can say words like, "[Name], I offer you food and drink, light and warmth. May this fire light your way to the realm of the ancestors, may you be nourished and fed, and may nourishment heal your spirit."

In this stage of ritual, remembrance, honor the dead by telling their story. You can speak aloud about beloved memories or anecdotes from their life; what they did that mattered, what they valued, and how those values will be carried forward by others. Remembrance is most effective when it is collective and lasting. If you are performing this ritual alone, consider writing a remembrance that can be published or posted later where others will see it. Commitments made in the name of the dead also serve as lasting memorials. What can you do to offer the dead assurance of lasting memory?

Collectivization. Now, gather the dead person into the arms of the ancestors. Address the ancestors in prayer and ask them to receive the newly dead. You can use this prayer as a template, or create your own:

> *Honored ancestors, I ask you to open your arms and receive*
> *[Name]. Take them into your halls and give them rest and*
> *renewal; let them be gathered into your glorious company and*
> *take their place as an honored ancestor. Help them to know*
> *wisdom and share wisdom with the living and those who will*
> *come after. May we always know the blessing of your guidance*
> *and kinship.*

Lift up the object representing the dead person and physically place it beside your ancestor images, visualizing the spirit finding its way to the ancestors and being received into their arms as you do. Place the dead person's candle beside them as well.

Give thanks to all the spirits and divinities who aided in this rite before closing your ritual.

Remember to cleanse yourself again after closing.

In some instances, particularly where there is trauma, harm, or deep-seated ancestral problems, ancestor sacralization can be a much more complex process that may not be accomplished in a single ritual. It may need to be performed over an extended period of time, and may require other offerings as well as spiritual and social work to address the particular needs of the spirits. Sometimes, the healing that the dead need is justice for wrongs done to them or done by them, and our offerings can include labor, donations, activism, making amends, or other acts of restitution and restoration. These more complex situations are beyond the scope of this chapter, but my hope is that this provides a template you can build on as you develop your skills in this work.

Story
A keening

I did not seek out the practice of keening; the spirits taught it to me. My keening practice began with a wound in the landscape.

I'm visiting at a spiritual gathering in Canada that is taking place beside a deep glacial lake. It's evening, after the scheduled rituals have concluded, and I'm sitting beside the communal fire. Around me festival folk are dancing, singing, drinking, enjoying the night. But I'm distracted—I can't seem to focus on what's happening around me. My gaze keeps drifting out beyond the firelight, out to the dark waters of the lake. Something is calling me out there.

I wander away from the fire to the shore of the water. The water is black and deep and shining like a mirror. A heavy, white moon pours down over the water's surface like a pillar of light. I hear whispering, whispering, and the whispering is pulling me into a deep trance. I follow it, stumbling along the shore path, seeking a quiet place further away from the fire and the noise of festivity.

Further out along the lakeshore the path takes me by a rock outcrop that juts into the lake. I clamber out and find a spot to perch myself among the rocks. The whispering is pulling my entranced spirit out of my body. I'm gliding far out into the black water, sinking deep. The mirror surface of the lake is still as glass and transparent so I can see into the spirit world through it. A thousand spirits teem in the deep, whispering, calling out to me. Something happened here. There are so many dead and suddenly I can hear them—they are telling me their stories, their deaths, their loss. I understand what they want from me now. They are asking me to keen for them. Whatever happened here trapped them and they need a keening to help them cross.

I don't know how to keen, but I just begin. A low humming lament that rises and gathers force as the weight of all their grief begins to

stream through me, first in rivulets, then a running stream, then a tor-
rent. My voice is rising in pitch, my mouth has opened, the humming
becomes a wordless song, and then a rising wail. The glass surface of
the lake has gone black and clear and then suddenly it's as if that glass
surface has vanished and the lake has become a vast, yawning gateway. The keening has seized my whole body now, I'm swaying with
its force as the sound tears through me, long, piercing wails rising out
endlessly to echo over the lake. I don't know how long I am keening.
Time seems to stop and all I can feel is this deep gateway that grief has
torn in the hollow of the lake, and the spirits pouring through it like a
mighty wind. I sing until I feel them rising free.

Eventually my voice slows and drops and then I'm just swaying in
the silence beside the water. My partner, who has been quietly beside
me through all this, taps me on the shoulder.

"Are you seeing this? Look at the water…"

I realize my eyes have been closed for a while. Opening them, I
see what he's pointing to. The lake's surface is no longer smooth and
glassy-still; waves are steadily crossing it, driving little crests straight
toward us, driven by a wind that had picked up while I was keening.
That wind I'd felt, but had thought was just the feeling of the spirits
in motion, is now moving across the whole of the lake surface stirring
it into waves.

I sit for a while longer, silently praying to the gods I walk with
and the gods in the land to help these spirits find their way safely, to
bless and heal the rift in the lake where the dead have been.

After this, I spend some time reading about keening traditions
and listening to the spirits. I begin performing keening sometimes
for ritual occasions or for people who have died. Each time I'm called
upon to keen for someone, I learn a little more about how the keening works to open a gateway to the Otherworld, so that spirits can
cross. It begins to make sense to me how it functions in a funerary
context, why professional keeners took on the practice, how it served
the living to facilitate grieving and at the same time opened the way

for the dead. I learn to shape my keening, to use my voice not just to open a gateway but to build a road for spirits, and to close the ways again after their crossing.

Ancestral Celebrations

Rich traditions of ancestor veneration abound within the Celtic cultures. The care of the dead does not end with funerary rites, but continues as living ancestor veneration. Beyond the initial transition stage represented by funerary ritual, devotional rites for the continuing care of the ancestral dead are reflected in archaeology, literature, and folk tradition.

These traditions reach back to the heritage of pre-Celtic civilizations, with their great Neolithic passage mounds. These are often spoken of as tombs, but it may be more accurate to think of them as ancestral temples. Archaeologists now believe these chambered mounds were built for continuing ritual engagement and would have been opened for ceremonial occasions.[221] Seasonal gatherings likely conducted at these sites would have served both to memorialize the ancestors as well as fulfill communal social functions for the living. Thus these temple mounds served not just as tombs, but as centers of community ritual life.

In Ireland as well as Britain and the Continent, most of these temple mounds were built in the pre-Celtic Neolithic to Bronze Age periods, but many of them show continued interment of the dead and ritual deposition of offerings (such as food, coins, tools, jewelry, and other valuables) into later periods.[222] The dead originally buried in these temples may or may not have been genetic ancestors of the Celtic peoples, but it's clear that these temple mounds were absorbed into the mythologies and ancestral veneration practices in the Celtic period. The megalithic mounds continued to function as centers of ritual and sacred community into the Iron Age and early medieval periods.

The royal fair or *óenach* was in many respects a rite of ancestor veneration, held within kingdoms annually or at longer intervals, and generally located at

---

221. Waddell, *Archaeology and Celtic Myth*, 15–19.

222. Swift, "The Gods of Newgrange in Irish Literature & Romano-Celtic Tradition," 58–60.

major ritual centers that contained temple mounds or grave sites. The name *óenach* means "funerary games" and most óenach sites had an important funerary legend about an ancestor or goddess. Feasting, games, and ritual performances at the *óenach* were dedicated to and felt to benefit the souls of the ancestral dead. Such a festival would have been a vibrant celebration of communal life. Its being convened in the sight of the ancestors in their ancient mounds meant that this vibrancy and richness could enliven those ancestors and help to uplift their memory.

Sorcerer's Toolkit
spirit shrines

I started making spirit shrines some years ago, as a kind of private analog to funerary temples and mounds. A spirit house gives a home to anchor ancestral spirits in our physical world, and a place to connect with them. A place to feed and honor them and listen for their voices. Here, I'll offer a simple template you can build on for creating spirit houses.

Preparation

There are three components that make up the spirit house that you will need to prepare ahead of your ritual.

Container: This can be made in all sorts of forms, but the simplest approach would be a jar, urn, or basin. From a historical perspective, you can think of objects like the carved stone vessels found in some Neolithic chambered tombs, in which the cremated ashes of ancestors had been stored. Similarly, in individual graves the cremated remains were often placed in urns. For this ritual template, we'll assume we are using an urn, but I have made spirit houses out of boxes, tins, birdhouses, and even lanterns.

Anchor material: A volume of soil, pebbles, or other natural material that is placed inside the container. This material serves as a kind of surrogate body for the spirit to occupy at will, giving it a home and helping to anchor it in the material world. Preferably, these materials should be gathered from places connected to the spirit whom the shrine is for, such as their home area, or a place they loved or spent time in. This helps the spirit identify the shrine as a home.

Objects connected to the ancestor: If you have access to them, cremated ashes or bone offer an ideal link. Objects that belonged to the ancestor are also helpful, particularly if they were worn on the body or handled often. In the absence of such close personal links, anything that is identified with the person may be of help: something from their house, a bit of handwriting, something inscribed with their name, or even a portrait.

Spirit Shrine Rite

For this rite, you'll need:

- Cleansing tools, such as blessing water.
- An urn or vessel.
- Anchor material.
- Objects connected to the ancestor.
- A candle.
- Food and drink favored by the ancestor.

First, cleanse the materials you'll be working with and yourself, by sprinkling some of the blessing water over everything.

Take up the urn and breathe a prayer over it, asking it to care for, house, and protect your ancestor who will be residing within it. Set it down in front of you.

Take up the anchor material (soil, pebbles, or whatever you have for this). Visualize the place it came from as clearly as you can, thinking of the ancestor's connection to that place. When you can see and sense that place clearly, begin pouring or placing this material into the urn. You are drawing the essence of that place into the spirit house so that the ancestor will feel at home.

Take up the objects or materials that link directly to the ancestor. Holding them in your hands, speak to them directly and from the heart, as if that person were sitting right in front of you. Invite the ancestor to take up residence in the spirit house. You can say something like this: "Beloved [Name], please be here with me. I have made this home for you, from the soil of [whatever you've used]. Be at home here, take rest here, be nourished and fed in the company of one who loves you," or similar words. When you can feel the ancestor with you, place their objects into the spirit house.

Light a candle beside the spirit house to give them light and warmth. Lay out offerings of food and drink that suit the ancestor, and invite them to eat and drink and be nourished. If you feel called to, you can eat some of the food yourself so you are sharing a meal together.

Spend some time in communion with the ancestor as they settle into their spirit house.

When you are ready to close your ritual, give thanks to the ancestors and remember to cleanse yourself again.

Story
An Ancestral Spirit Shrine Rite

After my uncle Rhett died, I wanted to make a spirit shrine for him. I didn't grow up having much contact with my Appalachian relatives. But I did have Rhett, an uncle who had moved out West and become part of my world. He brought a little bit of Appalachia to my very California life and I treasured that. Rhett loved to fish and spent a lot of time fishing in the McKenzie River where he lived at the end of his life. One evening in early July 2017, as my aunt Nancy described it, "He sat down in the grass by the prettiest river there is, on the most beautiful summer day you could ask for, and died." They found him in the morning looking just like he had fallen asleep there beside his beloved river. I like to picture him coming out of the river and sitting himself on the bank to watch the water turn to molten gold in the evening, his spirit slipping out into the radiant stream pouring down westward toward the setting sun. When I traveled up to Oregon to attend his memorial, I walked out along that riverbank and chose a smooth round black river stone to carry with me—a little piece of that beautiful place where his spirit left his body and went into the river.

It's a few years later and I've made the trip out to the Blue Ridge Mountains where my relatives were from. I've decided I'd like to strengthen my connection with my ancestors so I've located a little cemetery where some of them are buried. I visit on a breezy day in June, climbing up to the little hillside plot where there are a handful of graves with familiar names mostly from the nineteenth century. I sit beside one, looking out over the hills. I pour some fresh water on the roots of the tree that arches over me, for the spirits of the land, and a splash on the grave I'm sitting beside, for my ancestors. I talk to them about being their descendant, about being part of them and also different from them. I talk to them about how some of them were Confederate soldiers and participated in the system that enslaved Black people and tore Native people from the land here; I tell them that as their descendant, I'll spend my life striving to make that right. To put us back into right relationship with the land and the people we share it with.

The sun seems to glow a little brighter and the hill grows quiet around me for a moment, and I feel that an agreement has been accepted. I gather a small scoop of soil from beneath the tree and a little twig from its branches and carry them with me. Before we leave the mountains, we stop by a folk life center and watch a local artisan demonstrating pottery techniques, using local clay and a firing technique that uses horse hair from local farms to burn fantastical patterns into the surface. It's just the thing I need for my spirit shrine so I buy a beautiful little hipped vessel and wrap it carefully in layers of my clothing to protect it on the flight home.

At home in my shrine room, the candles are lit and I shake a bit of blessing water over myself and all the things I've gathered to make my ancestor spirit shrine. I pick up the little ceramic vessel and ask it to be a house for my ancestors, to hold and protect their space here, to serve as a liminal boundary that will contain them, opening to allow me to commune with them while holding them separate from the living. Pouring the grave earth into the vessel, I invite my ancestors to enter the shrine and make it their home, mindful of the agreements we have made. The bit of twig is tucked down into the soil so it stands like a little tree, a bridge between the worlds of the dead and the living for them to travel along. Last, I take the stone from Uncle Rhett's death place and hold it in my hands for a moment, breathing a whispered blessing into it, praying him into the vessel with the circle of our ancestors.

Setting the spirit house before me in its place, I ask my ancestors to share a meal with me. I put out water, coffee, and simple foods that I think they'd recognize and enjoy: smoked salmon and cheese, homemade cornbread with butter and honey. I offer some to them on a little plate and I sit and eat with them.

This spirit house looks very different from the chambered mounds and tomb temples we see in the places our spiritual traditions come from. To me it's not so different though; it's a house for the dead that can be ritually opened, where we can make offerings and spend time in communion with the ancestors, reestablishing the continuity of the living and the dead.

meeting the heroic ancestors

Among the countless dead who have gone before us, there are often those who are lifted up for special honors. I call these special ancestors who lead and guide us the Heroic Ancestors.

What do I mean by heroic? In modern popular culture the word "hero" tends to conjure caped superheroes, or a moralistic image of the hero as someone who is admired; a jumbled mix of role model, celebrity, and fantasy. However, in its original mythic context rooted in Iron Age warrior cultures and the myths and sagas memorializing them, a hero was understood rather differently. The defining features of heroes in this context were firstly that they were semidivine; sometimes through having one divine and one mortal parent, or as a reincarnation of a god in mortal form, or sometimes by being a mortal who is favored by gods or undergoes apotheosis to become divine. Secondly, heroes tend to be individuals whose lives are focused on the performance of rare or extraordinary deeds in order to be remembered after death, and especially through dying a hero's death.[223] There is a sense in which, by undergoing this specially charged kind of death, hero characters forge a link between the mortal and the divine, the worlds of humanity and the Otherworld domains of the gods and ancestors.

While the sagas of the Iron Age and medieval periods tend to focus on warrior heroes, hero cultus can focus on anyone who embodies these qualities: whose deeds are worthy of memorialization, who is especially touched by divinity, or who becomes in death a bridge between humans and gods. Ancestors of struggle can be Heroic Ancestors, such as great activists, liberators, or people of especial courage whose actions or ways of living their lives forge pathways that we walk in our own lives. Similarly, individuals who were especially devoted or close to a deity in life and who are felt to walk with that deity or become identified with them in death may be seen as a heroic ancestor.

---

223. Haeussler, "From Tomb to Temple: On the Rôle of Hero Cults in Local Religions in Gaul and Britain in the Iron Age and the Roman Period," 201–202.

While traveling in France and visiting Gallic archaeological sites in 2019, I spent a lot of time thinking about Heroic Ancestors and began developing the concept for their sigil. I witnessed some profoundly striking sculptural art from Iron Age Gallic sanctuaries, such as Roquepertuse and Entremont, which featured stunning, larger-than-life seated warrior statues. These statues are figured wearing armor, but rather than any martial posture they are seated in a cross-legged posture, which conveys a deeply meditative presence. One can imagine sitting in ritual meditation before these statues, communing with the Heroic Ancestors and listening to their voices. The sanctuaries also featured figures with two heads looking in opposite directions, suggesting beings who can see into both worlds at once, the human and the Otherworld, the mortal and the divine.

The Heroic Ancestors are a spirit collective who link us to the gathered wisdom of the many generations who have gone before. They are the mighty and heroic dead, those who were touched by the gods or who overcame great struggles in their time. They are a source of knowledge, guidance, and support from the Otherworld. Their sigil is built from the Gaulish letter-signs Orbion, for ancestral wisdom and memory; Ualos, for the elevated dead; and Dubnos, for the chthonic Otherworld; as well as the Irish letter-sign Onn, for its association with warrior bands, and Úr, for the grave and the dead. The sigil takes a circular shape with a stylized standing figure, a line representing a staff or spear, and two small circles for the two heads that look into both worlds.

heads and hero-cults

Out of the various Celtic traditions, a great many myths, tales, and rituals center around heads, a phenomenon that some scholars have referred to as "the cult of the severed head," though this term tends to obscure a great deal of variation in cultural expression. Head practices range from social status marker to religious veneration and tap into a rich vein of necromantic ritual.

It is an often-repeated trope that the Celts were fond of taking severed heads as trophies in warfare. Contemporaries of the Gauls describe how the heads of captured adversaries would be displayed on warrior gear, preserved in

Sigil Illustration for the Heroic Ancestors

cedar oil, or decorated and used as a cup. Recent archaeological work has been able to substantiate the preserving of heads in aromatic oil, so this appears to be more than just sensational propaganda.[224] Irish sagas also describe the collecting of heads as markers of status and domination over enemies, and that these heads might be displayed on a warrior's chariot or before the walls of a fortress. Trophies were also apparently made from the brains of an adversary, by extracting the brains, mixing them with lime, and drying to form a hardened cement-like ball that was kept as a trophy or could be used as a weapon.[225]

The interest in heads seems to be more complex than simply trophy collecting, however. It was not only the head of the adversary that was of interest for preservation. Ongoing religious veneration of the honored dead was often also performed through ritual treatment of the heads of honored individuals or Heroic Ancestors.[226] In Britain and Ireland, skulls have been found preserved beneath houses, in ritual pits, watery votive sites, and in burial sites of the Iron Age and medieval periods.[227] Several Gallic sanctuaries included structures with niches for displaying preserved heads, as well as figurative decoration centering on heads. Entremont and Roquepertuse, both stone-built Gallic sanctuaries in the vicinity of the Greek colony of Massilia, are notable for this motif. At Entremont, stones carved with niches for the display of heads were found alongside statuary of heroic warriors shown with clusters of severed heads.[228] At Roquepertuse, a massive stone portico also held niches for the display of severed heads, and its niches were carved specifically to fit a preexisting collection of heads, which clearly held great significance to the people of that place. Some of these skulls were found to have been decorated in a contiguous fashion with the masonry in which they

---

224. Ghezal, et al, "Embalmed Heads of the Celtic Iron Age in the South of France," 12.

225. Sayers, "Extraordinary Weapons, Heroic Ethics, and Royal Justice in Early Irish Literature," 10.

226. Aldhouse-Green, *Caesar's Druids*, 132–133.

227. Hoggard, *Magical House Protection*, 157; O'Sullivan, "Magic in Medieval Ireland," 109–110.

228. Armit, *Headhunting and the Body*, 145.

were embedded, making the heads part of the fabric of the sanctuary itself.[229] These sites also associate severed head motifs with horses and carrion birds, highlighting the concept of the transition of the dead, perhaps with the aid of psychopomp divinities in horse or bird form.

This broad pattern of the elevation and display of severed heads or skulls, varying in many details across cultures and locations, seems always to point toward facilitating contact between the living and the heroic dead. Mythologically, this motif is reflected in the ubiquitous mythic theme of the oracular severed head that continues speaking after death, which appears in texts of the Celtic-speaking world.

In many instances, severed heads of leaders or figures who hold some form of authority, whether social or spiritual, may speak after death. Brân, a Welsh chieftain divinity featured in the *Mabinogion*, is killed and his head is cut off while leading his people on an extended journey.[230] His head continues to speak afterward, so it is placed on a shield and carried along so that he might continue to guide his people in death. There is also a tale of Cú Chulainn's father, Súaltaim mac Roích, whose head was cut off while attempting to deliver warnings to rouse the Ulstermen from the curse of Macha in the *Táin Bó Cúailnge*; so urgent was his need to convey the message that his head continued to shout the warning until the Ulster warriors rose and came to battle.[231]

Another Irish text, *The Battle of Allen,* extends this motif with a detailed set of rituals for a head that speaks after death. Two parts of the story contain variations on this motif. First, a poet named Donn Bó who was killed in the battle is found to be speaking after death, because he had pledged to his king Fergal to sing for him that night after the battle, and he needs to fulfill that pledge.[232] The Leinster forces who have killed him bring Donn Bó's head into the feasting hall where they are celebrating their victory, and the head sings a

229. Armit, "Porticos, Pillars and Severed Heads: The Display and Curation of Human Remains in the Southern French Iron Age," 95.

230. Ross, *Pagan Celtic Britain*, 156.

231. O'Rahilly, "Táin Bó Cúalnge Recension 1," 217.

232. Stokes, "The Battle of Allen," 59–63.

mournful warrior chant, which makes all the warriors in the hall weep, thus fulfilling his promise to his lord. This motif is reminiscent of the tale of Sualtaim in that the head seems to retain its speech as part of a need to complete an unfulfilled commitment.

In *The Battle of Allen*'s second severed head vignette, the head of a chieftain named Fergal mac Maile Duin is gathered after the battle as a trophy by the victorious Leinster forces.[233] The head is carried by a contingent of warriors to the hall of their chieftain Cathal mac Finguini, where it receives what appear to be funerary honors. The head is washed, and its hair combed and plaited. It is draped in fine velvet cloth and set in the hall with a massive feast laid before it in offering. The head speaks, giving thanks for these honors, and then the food is distributed to the people, and the head is returned to Fergal's people to be buried. In the story's context, this appears to be an amends-making, as the battle was in breach of a peace agreement that Cathal had made, and so he orders this honoring of the head of Fergal apparently in an effort to mend the peace. At the same time, it demonstrates what the story's authors understood to be proper veneration of a dead hero.

This ritual reprises elements that appear in funerary ritual, accomplishing a number of important spiritual ends. It separates the dead from the violence and chaos of the battlefield, bringing him into a place of welcome with the living. It provides cleansing and beautification, showing reverence and elevating the dead hero. It provides for the feeding of his spirit by laying a feast before him. It is after all of these elements have been completed that the head opens its mouth to speak. These ritual elements—the transition from the battlefield to the place of honor, cleansing, beautification, and feeding—serve to establish communication between the living and the dead, elevating the dead person into their role as a Heroic Ancestor, and consecrating the head as an oracular mouthpiece.

---

233. Stokes, "The Battle of Allen," 63–65.

Sorcerer's Toolkit
oracular skull rite

Here, I'd like to offer some considerations and a ritual template for consecrating an oracular skull. First, any discussion about working with human bones needs to begin with some ethical considerations. Depending on where you live, there may be legal restrictions on obtaining and owning human remains. In the US, it is currently legal to purchase and own human bones, except for those covered by Native American graves and repatriation law; though some states do have restrictions on sales and shipping of bones. However, most of the human bones you might be able to access are extremely ethically problematic. Most commercial listings on online sales sites do not provide specific sourcing information, but they often come from looting, grave robbing, and other exploitative practices, often of Native American graves or from exploited countries overseas. Others may be sourced from vintage medical or educational skeletons or collections, and most of these were originally obtained in a highly colonialist, racist and exploitative fashion. A few companies do provide bones certified as designated for donation by a donor.

All of this illustrates the complex ethical issues around skull sourcing, and I think when it comes to an animist practice like this, the highest possible standards on ethical sourcing should apply. Reinforcing exploitation is a terrible way to start a spirit relationship. Thus for many practitioners, it will likely be more reasonable to substitute something else for a human skull. Ceramic, carved, cast, or otherwise crafted replicas can work. Depending on the spirits involved, an ethically sourced animal skull may serve. Whatever is used, it should at minimum have a discernible face; this becomes important in the ritual process of opening the mouth so it can speak.

Preparation

Once you have your skull vessel, it's advisable to prepare by performing divination to gain guidance from the spirits for your ritual.

If using a once-living skull, human or animal, the residing spirit must be respectfully asked for consent to engage with the skull as an oracle. You need this spirit to be an ally, and you may need to work to establish that trust. It's recommended to use divination tools to get clear answers about consent. Some questions to ask: Are you willing to be an oracle for me to communicate with the spirits? Are you willing to have another spirit or deity installed within who will speak with me? Do you wish to be released from this skull and go to the spirit world? How may I honor you and what kind of reciprocity can I offer you in thanks?

If using an artificial skull or head, it may or may not have a spirit in it, depending on its provenance. It's advisable to verify with divination.

The remaining phases of ritual presented here are modeled from the oracular head ritual in early Irish literature and the evidence from Gallic sanctuaries. This is intended as a template you can adapt and build upon to establish communication and open the mouth of the oracular skull.

Oracular Head Rite

For this rite, you will need:

- Cleansing tools, such as blessing water and sacred smoke.
- Candles.
- Offerings of food and drink.
- A shield or tray to carry the head.
- Items to beautify and inscribe the head, such as paint, pigments, or pens.
- Fine cloth.
- An aromatic oil, such as cedar.

Begin by cleansing yourself and your working space, sprinkling the blessing water.

Call upon the ancestors and gods you trust to aid in necromantic communication, with prayers of praise, asking them to support you in this rite and to guide the spirits involved in the ritual. Light candles for them and present some of the offerings.

Receive the head with honor. In the Irish story, the head is carried in procession to the feasting hall on a shield. Think creatively about how to create an honorific arrival for your ritual. Place the head on a shield, decorative tray, or even a fine pillow and carry it to the place where you will enshrine it. You may wish to sing or play music as you carry it to its place.

Washing and purification. Wash the skull with blessing water and pass it through incense smoke to cleanse away any unwanted influences it may have picked up on its journey to you. If there is a spirit in the skull who is staying with you, speak to it as you cleanse it, inviting it to stay and be purified, and reassuring it that you are not attempting to banish it. If there is a spirit in the skull who you believe prefers to be released, speak to it as you cleanse the skull, inviting it to find its way to a new home in the spirit world.

Beautification and blessing. You may wish to adorn the skull with painted ornamentation to add to its beauty. You may wish to inscribe it with sigils or inscriptions to help identify it with the spirits who will speak through it, and protect it from being accessed by unwanted spirits. For example, to consecrate it to the Heroic Ancestors, you could use the sigil given in this chapter for them. After decorating and inscribing the skull, anoint it with an aromatic oil such as cedar. Take a piece of fine cloth, folded like a shawl, and wrap it so that it cradles the skull but leaves the face visible.

Enshrinement and feeding. Settle the skull in its shrine place. Speak to it, inviting the spirit to be enshrined here and receive honor from you. Offer light and warmth by lighting candles beside it. Offer food and drink to feed the spirit. Consider singing honorific songs or chants to please the spirit.

Opening the mouth. Address the spirit and ask it to speak. You can say, "You are the voice of [the spirit's name]. Speak, speak, speak: I open your mouth to the power of speech. May you speak truth and fulfill this bond," or similar words. If it is a skull with a jaw that can open, this can be physically opened. Anoint the mouth or jaw with spirits such as whiskey, or you can use another dab of the aromatic oil.

Spend some time in communion with the spirits through the skull.

When you are finished, give thanks and close up the shrine space. You may wish to cover the skull when not actively consulting it by using a fold of the cloth, or covering. Remember to cleanse yourself again after completing ritual.

necromantic communication

The term *necromancy* can have spooky connotations but simply means divination through contact with the dead. Which is to say that any form of divination can be necromantic, in so far as it may be functional for communicating with the dead or is consecrated to them. Tradition and experience provide some particular approaches.

Irish tradition hints at a connection of ogham with the dead. Ogham is referred to as "the testimony of the dead" in *The Judgment of Cormac's Sword*. In the tale, an inheritance claim on an heirloom sword that once belonged to Cú Chulainn is overturned by means of ogham written on its blade. This written ogham evidence is framed in a poem as a way in which the voice or testimony of the dead can be heard among the living: "It is then that the dead corrected the living, in the pure testimony of ogam concerning them."[234] The story in context appears to be exploring tensions around the transition from a nonliterate society to one using writing; the idea that the written word itself can be seen as a kind of necromantic technology that preserves the voices of

---

234. Carey, "The Testimony of the Dead," 10.

the otherwise silent dead. John Carey, the prominent Celticist, suggests that the inscription on the sword appears to be taking the place of the ancient custom of spirits in swords being heard vocally.[235] More broadly, objects inscribed with ogham seem to be similarly seen as representing the testimony of the dead, possibly due to its presence on pillar-stones serving as boundary markers and funeral pillars, associated with the dead.

Divination methods using bones are also especially suited to necromantic communication. Contemporary methods of throwing the bones, in the form of divination using collections of different bones, generally seem to have their origins in New World conjure, Hoodoo, and African Diaspora traditions and do not appear to intersect much with Celtic traditions. However, the use of dice or "knucklebones" for divination was widespread across Europe, including in many of the Celtic-speaking countries, possibly as an inheritance from the influence of Rome.[236] This custom originates with the use of small astragali bones from the ankles of mammals, typically sheep, beginning in early Greece and spread throughout the European continent in the Iron Age by Roman legions. Knucklebones were used both for divination and in dice games, which have been inherited into the modern period as children's games. Oracle bone or "speal bone" divination is another mode that employs animal bones for divination; best known as practiced in Chinese cultures from ancient times, it is also documented in Scotland and some other European locations and typically uses a large mammal scapula or similar flat bone.[237]

Early sources also speak about the practice of cultivating necromantic dreams at graves or tombs. It seems to have been understood that the dreaming spirit may slip into the Otherworld, and there be able to access knowledge of future events or unseen realities through communication with the dead. In the second century BCE, the poet and physician Nicander of Colophon described the practice among Gallic people of dream incubation by sleeping at the tombs of family ancestors or heroes, in order to receive prophetic

---

235. Carey, "The Testimony of the Dead," 4.

236. Budd, "Knuckle-Bones: An Old Game of Skill," 10.

237. Campbell, *Superstitions of the Highlands & Islands of Scotland*, 263–266.

dreams.[238] A compatible practice is more fully described from medieval Ireland, as a method for retrieving lost cultural knowledge from ancestral memory. It is by by this method that the great heroic epic, the *Táin Bó Cúailnge*, was recovered after it had been lost to memory. A poet named Muirgen recovered it by performing a ritual at the grave of Fergus, one of the heroes of the *Táin*: "Muirgen chanted a poem to the gravestone as though it were Fergus himself."[239] From a mist, Fergus appears and recites the *Táin* for him so that he learns it and returns it to the memory of the living.

For contemporary practitioners, going to the tombs of the ancestors we might wish to contact for necromantic dreams may not always be feasible. However, to a certain extent we can bring them to us, through the use of spirit shrines as local conduits for the dead. Skulls, spirit vessels or shrines, icons, pictures, or other talismans keyed to necromantic veneration can be placed near where we sleep. Practices that aid in cultivation of prophetic dreams generally are also of help here, such as the use of herbs and trance practices before entering sleep.

---

238. Koch and Carey, *The Celtic Heroic Age*, 10.

239. Kinsella, *The Táin: Translated from the Irish Epic Táin Bó Cúailnge*, 1.

CHAPTER 7

bindinɡ maɡic, oaths, and ɡeis-prayers

Binding magics comprise a very large genre of sorcery. Their action illuminates and rests on a cultural and metaphysical framework about the functioning of fate and the methods of interacting with it. Binding magics are frequently associated with protection; equally often they are associated with cursing, either for justice or for malefic purposes. Beyond these functional uses, their study will open the way into the deeper cultural narratives about destiny and identity and the relationships between oaths, binding magics, and ritual prohibitions.

As we enter into the study of binding magics, it's important to recall the ethical framework that underpins all of these techniques, which I covered in the introduction. Before undertaking any working that binds, restrains, or infringes the agency of another person, remember to take some time to assess the ethical impacts and potential risks of the action you are considering. You can use the template presented in the introduction, or develop your own.

weaving and binding charms

Themes related to spinning, weaving, and fiber arts thread themselves throughout the lore of binding magic. People who have been in the presence of spinning and weaving readily observe an intuitive fate-fixing symbolism that is inherent in the textile arts. Raw fibers are transformed from a state of loose organic chaos; passing through the spinner's hands, their randomness gently spirals into a singular, smooth thread, which winds endlessly onto the spindle. At her discretion, it may be measured, cut, twisted, tied. Many ancient goddesses and a few gods have been envisioned winding the raw stuff of life into the threads that become the life histories of humankind, weaving these different human threads into a tapestry of destiny, and cutting the threads at the end of life. In stepping into this craft, the human practitioner was seen to take up the threads of life and access the power to bind fates. Traditional textile practices often included songs that were sung while the work was done; it is easy to see how this lends itself toward magical ritual.

Many of the artifacts of textile practices come into use in binding charms through the principle of sympathetic magic. The spindle whorl—the round weight attached to the shaft of a drop spindle—has frequently been associated with fate-weaving magics. Decorated spindle whorls from early Scotland and Ireland, including examples inscribed with blessings in ogham, attest to the belief in spiritual properties inherent in these objects.[240] Such blessings inscribed on the whorl can be understood to be activated each time it rotates—similar to the concept of a prayer wheel. Folk customs often employ such artifacts in magical rites. For example, a Scottish custom detailed in an early modern folklore collection describes a blessing charm in which a red woolen thread is passed through the hole of a spindle whorl, and this charm

---

240. Black, *Scottish Charms and Amulets*, 473–474; Forsyth, "The Ogham-Inscribed Spindle-Whorl from Buckquoy: Evidence for the Irish Language in Pre-Viking Orkney?" 679.

is dipped three times in water taken from a sacred well while a rhyme is said over it in Gaelic to consecrate it.[241]

Sympathetic magic also favors objects associated with the manipulation and control of animals as powerful vehicles for binding magic. Early Irish literature appears to associate items such as the horsewhip with binding power. In *The Wasting-Sickness of Cú Chulainn*, the fairy woman Fand lashes him with a horsewhip, which causes a wasting sickness, a binding of his vitality and abilities.[242] This has been read by some scholars, such as Bernard Mees, as deriving from a linguistic ambiguity similar to the way in which the English phrase "to lash" can mean both to whip and to tie with a cord.[243] In either case, the story illustrates the association of the whips and cords used to control animals with the magical power to bind and control someone's vitality.

Another early Irish tale, *The Adventures of Nera*, shows the warrior Nera placing a withe around the feet of an executed criminal hanging on a gibbet.[244] This occurs on Samhain, and appears to be an effort to prevent the corpse or its spirit from walking and endangering the living. (Spoiler ... it doesn't work out so well for Nera; he fumbles the closure on the withe and the dead man gets his arms around Nera's neck and forces him to carry him about the whole night.) Many charms appear among Irish and British customs employing such withes or spancels—various types of cuff or shackle, typically woven from wickerwork or leather and used to bind the feet of horses and cattle to prevent them from wandering. In the tale of Nera, the Irish word is *id*, defined as "a hoop-shaped object, a withe (bound around some object)," and also "a fetter, a chain, a spancel."[245]

A similar type of binding magic is used by Cú Chulainn in the *Táin Bó Cúailnge*, where he makes a wicker ring (again *id*, in Irish) from an oak sapling, carves an ogham inscription on it, and places it over a standing

---

241. Black, *Scottish Charms and Amulets*, 473.

242. O'Curry, "The Sick-Bed of Cuchulainn and the Only Jealousy of Emer," 3.

243. Mees, *Celtic Curses*, 4164.

244. Meyer, "The Adventures of Nera," 215.

245. Royal Irish Academy, "EDIL 2019, s.v. 1 *id* dil.ie/27166."

stone.[246] It serves to bind Cú Chulainn's adversaries against proceeding past the stone, under threat from his wrath. One version of this story provides the additional detail of how the withe is ritually prepared: he adopts the ritual posture of standing on one leg, using one hand, and looking through one eye while preparing it.[247]

The same word *id* appears in an early Irish law text on distraint, a practice whereby a plaintiff could seize the property of an accused person in order to force them to meet justice. In some cases of distraint, a fetter would be placed around the professional property of the accused to give notice that it had been distrained. For example, one could distrain a smith by binding a withe around their anvil; for a physician, their medicine bag, etc.[248] The withe itself doesn't physically prevent use; it is symbolic of the social and legal requirement to respect the act of distraint. This symbolic weight bears both social and magical power, which can be deployed to enforce the law, to control animals and people, or to bind the dead from walking. Naturally, such a powerful object does not escape the notice of folk custom. Many folk collections attest to the practice of using cattle withes for binding charms.

Sorcerer's Toolkit
withe binding

To make a binding withe, or *id*, there are a range of methods. Here, I'll offer three ways to make a withe, with a template withe binding ritual you can use as a starting place to explore and build your practice.

Preparing a Yarn Withe

For this type of withe, all you need is some yarn. Any yarn will do. A better choice would be a hand-spun natural fiber yarn, as this will

---

246. O'Rahilly, "Táin Recension 1," 131–132.

247. O'Rahilly, "Táin Leinster," 150.

248. Kelly, *Early Irish Law*, 181.

have passed through the hands of an expert spinner, and its fibers coaxed into their twist through the age-old technique of spinning. If you can spin your own yarn or get it from a magically skilled spinner, even better still. I recommend braiding or knotting several pieces of yarn together to make a cord that is stronger than a single strand of yarn would be.

Cut three lengths of yarn, about a third longer than the length you need the finished cord to be.

Take the three lengths and line them up together so the ends are even. Tie the three ends into a knot. As you tie the knot, blow a breath over it to enliven it, with an instruction to the cord about what you want it to do for you. "I make you a binding cord, with power to bind the fate of my enemy" or words to that effect.

Begin braiding by taking the strand on the right and passing it over the center strand, then take the strand on the left and pass it over the center strand. Continue in this fashion, right over center, left over center, alternating. You can continue whispering instruction to the cord as you do this. When you get near the end of the strands, tie all three together again with a final knot, completing your instruction to the cord with a breath blown over the knot.

Preparing a Livestock Withe

For this type of withe, you will be repurposing a piece of tack made for control of livestock. You can find these items at rural feed stores, livestock suppliers, and horse tack suppliers. Cow or horse hobbles can be put to use; these are often made from flexible nylon or leather strap, which passes through rings on each end to form cuffs for the animal's legs. You can also use horse reins, made from narrow lengths of leather. If you can get hold of used hobbles or horse tack, even better, as these have already been used to control an animal and will have that much more power as binding tools. In choosing what type of item to use, you'll want to think ahead about the physical limitations of the target object you'll be binding it around; heavy leather or wide nylon hobbles may not be flexible enough to use with a small target object. You may want to cut a piece from the tack if its original form is too bulky, wide, or long to make a binding from.

As you prepare the tack to make it into something you can use for a binding, blow breaths over it to enliven it, speaking your instructions to it about what you want it to do for you. "I make you a binding spancel, with the power to bind the limbs and actions of my enemy" or similar words.

Preparing a Wicker Withe

For this type of withe, you will need some twine, and a length of plant material that is flexible enough to tie and wind and tough enough not to break. The slender, flexible branches of weeping willow are ideal, as are lengths of vine. If the material is very fine and at risk of splitting or breaking, you can twist multiple lengths together. Gather a long enough section to wind several times around your target object, with a little extra length for binding off.

Since you are taking material from a living plant for this, make sure to give an offering in thanks when you collect the plant material.

Prepare the plant material by stripping away any leaves or side twigs that are attached. As you do, blow breaths over the plant material to enliven it, speaking your instructions to it. "I make you a binding withe, with the power to bind the will of my enemy" or similar words.

Preparing the Target Object

Since this approach to binding magic involves a physical withe that is wound and tied, you need something to wind it around—a target object. This target object will stand in for the person or group that you're binding, so that by sympathetic magic they are bound as the object is bound. It's helpful to think ahead about what you can use for a target object as you'll need to consider the physical interaction of withe and target. Here are some possible approaches to work from:

- An effigy or poppet made in human shape to represent the person. I will cover constructing poppets in more detail in the next chapter, as they can be made in a variety of ways.
- An object that belongs to the person or contains a link to their person in some way.
- An object that represents the specific aspect of the person that you're seeking to bind. For example, say you're seeking to bind someone who's done harm in a professional capacity; you could use an object with their business brand or professional logo on it.

Withe Binding Ritual

For this ritual you will need:

- Cleansing tools, such as blessing water.
- Offerings for your protective spirits and any other divinities whom you may be calling on.
- Your target object.
- Your prepared withe.
- Twine.

Begin by cleansing yourself and all of your materials by sprinkling with the blessing water.

Perform a shielding prayer, lorica, or caim to ensure your safety.

Call in your protective spirits and any other divinities you trust to aid you in this binding work. Present offerings as you ask for their aid and protection.

Take up the target object. Hold it and visualize the person whom you are binding. Speak to it, naming it for them so that it becomes that person spiritually: "I name you [Name], you are [Name] in body and spirit. Your body is the body of [Name]. Your deeds are the deeds of [Name]. What befalls you befalls [Name]. What binds and holds you binds and holds [Name]."

You may wish to also enumerate what deeds this person has done that merit being subjected to this binding, so that all the spirits know you are acting in alignment with *cóir*.

Take up the withe. Holding the target object in one hand, grasp the end of the withe against the target object, leaving an end you can tie off. Begin to wind the withe around the object. As you wind, speak the binding aloud. It's helpful to name each aspect of the person that is being bound, with especial focus on the capacities that they may have used to cause harm. You can be poetic, but also try to be specific. You can say something like, "I bind your limbs, I bind your body, I bind your spirit. I bind your hands against doing violence, I bind your feet against escape, I bind your mouth against speaking lies, I bind your heart against doing magic, I bind your power against doing all harm" or similar words as appropriate.

When you get toward the end of the withe, get ready to tie it off so it cannot unwind. If the withe is flexible enough, such as with braided yarn or narrow, flexible leather, you can simply knot it together with the first end. If it is too stiff to tie a knot in the withe material itself, you can use twine to tie the two ends of the withe together, or tie down the loose end of the withe against the object itself. This knot seals the binding—so make it tight and strong. You can even triple it for extra effect. While you're tying it, blow a breath into the knot and speak your final words of binding. "Thus are you bound and thus shall you remain bound, forever or unless I shall unbind you" or in whatever terms are appropriate for your working.

After it is completed, you can deploy the binding wherever it will have the most effect. If possible, you can hide it near the home or workplace of your target, or somewhere they will come near it. Alternately, you can deposit it in a place where the spirits who help you have their strongest presence. Graveyards, crossroads, and liminal spaces such as watery places are traditional sites for deploying magic.

Remember to always finish with a thorough cleansing of yourself and the space where you did the work.

Story
A witHe binding Ritual

I'm aiding a friend who has come to me for magical help with a court case. She's scared: in the midst of her divorce, the ex has petitioned to take full custody of their children and has tried to frame her as incapable of caring for the children because of a disability that limits her mobility. "Can you help me constrain him? At least, prevent lies from being used against me?" We've settled on a binding rite; she doesn't want to hurt her children's other parent, just to limit his power in court.

It's a good time to begin; the moon is dark. At dusk, I go to collect willow withes where the willows grow beside a local creek. Choosing my spot carefully, I walk along the bank seeking the most liminal space I can find: beside a crossroads, where the stream enters a culvert to traverse the road underground. Here. I lay out some offerings and speak to the willows: "Who will help me? I seek protective justice through binding; who will help me bind this aggressor?" Then I wait a little, listening meditatively. Sometimes the signs from the spirits are really subtle, but not today. A faint stirring in the evening air has whisked itself into a bit of a breeze that sets the willows swaying. I key in on the one that's moving the most, its branches seeming to wave like someone raising a hand, saying "I will help you." I cut a fine, flexible withe from the narrow end of a branch and take it home.

She's made a little effigy we can do the binding on. After we've blessed ourselves and called in and fed our spirit allies, and her gods and ancestors, we set to making. I strip away the leaves from the withe and bless it; then while speaking more prayers to its spirit I work it a bit in my hands, bending this way and that to make it still more flexible so it can be wound properly tightly on the effigy. Now we're ready to bind.

I invite my friend to speak the charm while I make the binding. She holds her hands out over mine, adding power to the binding as as I work and she begins to speak. Haltingly at first, and then more confidently as she roots into the injustice and fear and anger of her situation and the words begin to pour out of her. I press the withe along the effigy so the thick end stands free as and I wind around and around the little body, as tightly as the willow tension will let me, weaving under and around so the winding cannot uncoil. She is just about hissing with protective fury when I reach the end of the withe. Now I have her hold the whole winding in place while I grab a piece of twine to tie the ends off.

"Ready? Here's the twine." I take the effigy back and hand her the twine so she can tie this last binding knot herself.

"And so it shall be, by all the gods and spirits who stand here with me," she hisses, and yanks the knot fast.

She will carry the hidden effigy with her when she walks proudly with her cane into the court to defend her parenting, knowing she has the aid of her gods and spirits and the power of the binding to help her.

meeting mongach

Mongach is an Irish eel monster who appears in the medieval Irish tale called *The Siege of Knocklong*. I have already introduced her in the chapter on working with spirits. She is connected with binding and aggressive magics.

Her full name is Mongach Maoth Ramhar (meaning "long-maned, wet, sleek"). She is described as a giant female sea eel, large enough at least to coil nine times around the body of a man, strong enough to fling a man's body violently with a blow of her tail, delivering poison with the bite of her teeth.[249] The literature uses a variety of poetic metaphors for this spirit—a red water-snake, a sea eel, a vulture, an adder, a spear-headed reptile, a fiery dragon. She is allied with the druid Mug Roith, who teaches his student how

---

249. Ó Duinn, "The Siege of Knocklong," 82–87.

to conjure her to fight on their behalf in a war between the forces of Munster and those of the High King Cormac Mac Airt.

Mongach personifies a vein of somewhat obscure traditions about eels and eel magics. Her action in attacking, binding, and entangling is similar to the way that the Morrígan attacks in the form of an eel when she is challenging Cú Chulainn. There are some interesting linguistic connections between eels and language used about magical binding. Eels are also fascinating, strange predators that can seem like survivors from a primordial age: for example, some species have a secondary jaw, called the "pharyngeal jaw," that shoots out of their mouth like James Cameron's *Aliens* to snap at prey and drag it down their gullet.

Irish folklore traditions about eels also preserve a wealth of material about these mysterious, often frightening creatures, and her shape seems discernible within these tales. Mongach's name hearkens to folklore stories with large eels described as having a mane or sometimes called "hairy." These tales often resemble water-monster or water-horse legends; monstrous Otherworldly eels who dwell in lakes, and can be summoned by sinking a horse hair in water.[250] They are also said to aggressively leap and hurl themselves out of the water to attack people, and could cross land by forming themselves into a hoop, with their tails in their mouths, to travel like a wheel. Often there is said to be a "master eel" or "king of the eels," an especially mighty or large eel that could change its shape and could command all the other eels.[251] These story themes and many more seem to support the sense that a great eel spirit such as Mongach would lead a generalized retinue of eel spirits.

In my practice, I honor eels as one of the spirit retinues of the Morrígan, headed by Mongach. She and the eel spirits bring powers of binding, cursing, entangling, and devouring. She emerges from the watery Otherworld to attack, ensnare, and drag victims below. Her sigil incorporates a name-sign, that is to say her name written in ogham, with Celtic letter-signs Nemetos for eels, binding and holy power; Ratis for Otherworldliness and the Morrígan; and Lugion

---

250. Butler, "Water Monsters in Irish Folklore," 8.

251. National Folklore Collection UCD, "Dúchas, Volume 0095," 302–306; Volume 0200," 184–185.

Sigil Illustration for Mongach

for underwater realms. These are woven together into a shape that evokes the sinuous motion of the eel. She is illustrated as a muscular, maned eel in a fierce, coiled stance underwater and framed by watery plants.

oaths

The first thing that should be said about oaths is to differentiate them from promises or simple commitments. This is important in setting the lens through which oaths can be understood as a form of binding magic. Promises operate on a level of social and emotional commitment and are enforced through interpersonal and social mechanisms, such as personal honor, trustworthiness, and group status. Oaths, on the other hand, are magically charged bindings that operate on a spiritual level and are enforced by spirits or magical mechanisms. This spiritual aspect of oaths is not always visible in an ostensibly secular culture such as that of contemporary Western societies, but it is very apparent in animist and magical Celtic worldviews. Oaths, in this framework, are held by spiritual entities, enhanced through Otherworldly powers, and enforced by magical means.

The tradition sees oaths as invested with the spiritual agency of the Otherworld, which acts through them. This spiritual agency is vividly illustrated in examples from the Irish literature such as this description of warrior oaths in *The Wasting Sickness of Cú Chulainn*: "They laid their swords over their thighs when they declared the strifes, and their own swords used to turn against them when the strife that they declared was false."[252] Similarly, the poem *Reicne Fothad Canainne* mentions a shield "by which they used to swear binding oaths."[253] This practice with inspirited weapons was examined in more detail in chapter 3 on spirit work. Here I want to highlight the action of the oath, which is witnessed and held and enacted by a spirit being. In the words of Jacqueline Borsje: "The false oath calls forth a supernatural sanction. The sword as guarantee of the truth will be the instrument through which this sanction will be implemented. What we have here is a reference to the ordeal

---

252. Leahy, *Heroic Romances*, Vol I, 57.

253. Meyer, *Fianaigecht*, 15.

by battle: the next battle fought by the lying boaster will end in his defeat, for his sword will no longer serve him."[254]

A related anecdote in *The Judgment of Cormac's Sword* refers to an oath sworn over a sword and reinforced through the incantation of a spell (*bricht*): "The bond of the oath which the son of truthful Fithal bound, with a spell, around the sword which was in his hand."[255] It seems that the practice of ritualized oaths sworn in the presence of a sword that was understood to have spiritual agency to enforce the oath was widespread. In this respect, oaths and binding magics are connected; the power of the Otherworld is what gives them their force and is the agency acting within them.

Ritual Prohibitions

The spiritual agency of the oath is also reflected in the related lore of the *geis* (plural *gessi* or *geasa*). *Geasa* might be best be described as ritual prohibitions or injunctions and as such are closely related to oaths. As presented in early Irish tales, the term has often been translated as "taboo," though this is not an ideal term to use since it is inaccurate and lifted from Polynesian culture. The *geis* is a spiritually charged binding that typically requires a character to avoid doing certain prohibited things, at risk to life and strength. Although this negative, proscriptive binding is the more common type, there are examples of *geasa* that are prescriptive in nature—requiring the character to fulfill an action rather than avoid an action.

In some instances, *geasa* function as ritual boundary-marking behaviors that act to preserve the sanctity of holy things. This dimension is illustrated by an example of ritual observance around chariots from *The Wooing of Emer*: "A foal is the ruin of a chariot to the end of three weeks … And there is a gess on a chariot to the end of three weeks for any man to enter it after having last eaten horse-flesh. For it is the horse that sustains the chariot."[256] Here the *geis* acts to protect the chariot, clearly a very valuable and important item of war-

---

254. Borsje, "Omens, Ordeals and Oracles," 227.

255. Carey, "The Testimony of the Dead," 9–10.

256. Meyer, "Wooing of Emer," 152.

rior gear, from spiritual harm through contact with horsemeat. The horse is sacred to the chariot; so when horsemeat is eaten, this *geis* comes into force as a ritual boundary requiring three weeks time before the chariot can be entered without causing spiritual harm.

More commonly, the *geis* protects and sets boundaries upon individuals. Bernard Mees describes *geasa* as "fateful personal contracts"—that is to say, contracts with Otherworldly forces.[257] The bond grants benefit so long as the person is in right relationship with the spiritual contract. This right relationship is codified in the term *sogeis*, an archaic word denoting virtue, but that literally means *"geis*-good," i.e., to be good or in alignment with one's *geasa*.[258] It is used in *The Instructions of Cormac* in a list of proper qualities fitting for a king.[259]

The Irish mythic tradition suggests that such a spiritual contract, when one is *geis*-good and in right relationship, confers not only protection but certain gifts or powers. These powers are referred to in the tradition as *búada*, "gifts," particularly associated with powerful individuals in the mythic lexicon such as kings, druids, or heroes.[260] Thus while the most common representation of a *geis* in the literature is as a prohibition, these prohibitions are something like the tip of an iceberg. Underlying these visible injunctions at a deeper level is the spiritual contract or bond with its heroic gifts and protections, maintained through adherence to the terms of the bond. When the *geis* is broken, it withdraws the powers and protections it had granted, and typically unleashes itself as a curse.

One of the most well-detailed examples of *geasa* are those of the hero Cú Chulainn. As a heroic warrior, he is subject to several ritual injunctions. He may not touch or eat dogmeat, since the hound is his name-animal and therefore sacred to him.[261] He also has a *geis* that requires him to accept food from

257. Mees, *Celtic Curses*, 4057.

258. Mees, *Celtic Curses*, 4272.

259. Meyer, "The Instructions of King Cormac Mac Airt: Tecosca Cormaic," 12.

260. Charles-Edwards, "Geis, Prophecy, Omen, and Oath," 42.

261. Tymoczko, *Two Death Tales from the Ulster Cycle: The Death of Cu Roi & The Death of Cu Chulainn*, 49–50.

a hearth where he is invited. *Geasa* are a little like Chekhov's gun in the Irish literature—if a *geis* is mentioned in the story, you can be reasonably sure it's going to hurt someone before the end. Sure enough, they are his undoing. On his way to a battle, Cú Chulainn encounters three hags who have cooked a dog on rowan stakes and offer it to him. Since it is *geis* to him both to eat the meat, and to refuse to eat at their hearth, he cannot escape their curse. He does his best to accommodate both *geasa* by accepting the meat without eating it, but loses his strength simply by touching it. This enables his enemies to overcome him and brings about his death.

Here, his destruction is made possible by an inversion of the heroic powers granted to him by the *búada*, the gifts of his *geasa*. Cú Chulainn's story lays out the connection between the *geasa* and these heroic gifts quite plainly. The reason dog is *geis* to him is because it is sacred to him in his identity and role as a warrior. This canine identity was collective rather than personal, and was carried by warriors in Irish society generally, as reflected by the many warriors in the sagas with names relating to dogs or wolves (as was also true of other cultures of the time, such as the Norse). His heroic martial skills—the Hero's Light, the salmon leap, the special deadly spear feats—are the *búada* conferred by this canine identity.[262] They reflect the blessings of a spiritual bond undertaken in ritual at the time when he received his warrior name. Indeed, in the Irish source text, the name is formally placed on him by the druid Cathbad in a ritualized atmosphere shortly before the time when he takes up arms.[263] His role and its attending spiritual powers are what is tied up in the *geis*, and it is this relationship and the strength and protection it gives him that is undone by the breaking of the *geis*.

Another story that offers rich illustration of the working of *geasa* is the story of the king Conaire Mór, in *The Destruction of Dá Derga's Hostel*. Conaire has a *geis* pronounced for him at his birth against killing birds, because of his familial kinship with a tribe of Otherworld bird-people.[264] These same bird kinsmen

262. O'Rahilly, "Táin Bó Cúalnge from the Book of Leinster," 152.

263. O'Rahilly, "Táin Bó Cúalnge from the Book of Leinster," 163.

264. Stokes, "The Destruction of Da Derga's Hostel," 170.

are responsible for arranging his accession to kingship in a spiritual contract, which brings additional *geasa* into force. Here, the *búada* that are brought are the powers of kingship itself, and many of the *geasa* relate to the king's roles in justice, hospitality, and securing the land.[265] As with Cú Chulainn, these *geasa* were conferred in rites of accession to a new status—kingship, in Conaire's case. This illustrates the role of druids in ritually conferring a role and its accompanying *geasa*, reinforcing the idea that it requires a role of authority or a position of close relationship to be able to place a *geis* on someone. And similarly to the previous example, after making a false judgment and so violating his obligation, Conaire's Otherworld allies entrap him into further breaking his *geasa*, so that the powers granted to him through the spiritual contract are stripped from him.

An important element to highlight here is that these *geasa* come into force by way of ritual, which binds the participant to a spiritual contract with Otherworld powers. Studying this further will yield insights applicable to binding magics.

Geis-prayers and Fate-Binding

As historian Bernard Mees points out here, the *geis* has its origins as a type of incantation:

> Geases are clearly described in the earliest Irish tales in terms which connect them with fate—like Irish destinies, they are often expressed as if they were passive acquisitions of heroes and kings. It is not just the way in which geases were obviously felt to be binding that makes them so reminiscent of ancient Celtic curses, though: a geas seems literally to have been a 'prayer'—the term appears to be related to the verb uediiumi used in the Chamalières defixio.[266]

It is this root I am interested in following. The Irish tales tend to present the *geis* in terms of its consequences to characters in story plots—prohibi-

---

265. O'Connor, *Da Derga's Hostel*, 75–76.

266. Mees, *Celtic Curses*, 4264.

tions and the curses that cascade from breaking them. Underlying these consequences is a spiritual contract enacted through ritual magic. In addition to its usage as a prohibition, in both Old and Modern Irish, *geis* also retains the additional meaning of a spell or incantation.[267] The word *geis* arises from the same root as the Old Irish verb *guidid*, "to pray, to invoke," and it also appears in Gaulish in the verb *uediiu-* "to invoke," appearing in spell tablets.[268]

These etymological linkages relate *geasa* to the ancient tradition of versified ritual magic found throughout Celtic cultures and indicate that at the root it is a fateful binding charm applied through invocatory prayer. Thus the *geis* refers to both the contract with the Otherworld powers, and the binding ritual used to seal it. Such a *geis*-prayer likely would have been chanted in a metrical form. Irish ritual poetry provides models of what such a binding incantation might sound like.

One poem that vividly addresses binding is Mug Roith's incantation to invoke an eel to bind and constrict his enemy. The language and tenor of the incantation is reminiscent of this genre of binding prayers, describing the nooselike binding action of the eel:

> *Woe to him around whom it coils,*
> *Betwixt the swelling waves…*
> *Be it an adder of nine coils,*
> *Around the body of gigantic Colpa,*
> *from the ground to his head,*
> *The smooth spear-headed reptile…*
> *The bonds which it binds on,*
> *Are like the honey-suckle round the tree…*[269]

---

267. Royal Irish Academy, "EDIL 2019: An Electronic Dictionary of the Irish Language, Based on the Contributions to a Dictionary of the Irish Language,, s.v. *geis.*"

268. Royal Irish Academy, "EDIL 2019: An Electronic Dictionary of the Irish Language, Based on the Contributions to a Dictionary of the Irish Language, s.v. *guided.*"; Delamarre, *Dictionnaire Gauloise,* 309–310.

269. Ó Duinn, "The Siege of Knocklong," 77–79.

Notice the binding language: "the bonds which it binds on." The translator here has streamlined this part of the text down to one line. In the original this binding language becomes an emphatic rhymed incantation of its own, repeating the binding in three different ways:

> *in trascradh nos trascrann*
> *is fasdar no fastann*
> *is nascad nos nascann*

Each of these phrases presents another way of describing a binding: *trascrann* is "overthrows, knocks down, lays low"; *fastann* is "stops, holds back, detains, hinders"; and *nascann* is "binds, makes fast."[270] This part of the incantation, with its emphatic elaboration and alliterative repetition, comes straight out of the same tradition of metrical magic that produced the Gaulish binding charms. It is easy to imagine the passionate chanting of such a binding incantation in ritual.

Another important example of a binding or fating incantation is found in the justifiably famous Gaulish spell text known as the Chamalières *defixio*. A *defixio* is an ancient magical technology whereby magical prayers (often curses) were inscribed on objects such as lead tablets and deposited into magically charged locations. The Chamalières *defixio*, found in a hot spring in central France, dates to the Gallo-Roman period and its inscription scratched in tiny Latin cursive provides a rich vein of insight into magical practice of the period. I will examine it further in the chapter on cursing. For now, the key line I am interested in reads: *Etic segoui toncnaman toncsiiontio*, translated either as "it is the destiny of the victor to which they shall be destined," or alternately "it is the oath of the victor which they shall swear."[271]

The ambiguity as to whether this phrase *toncnaman toncsiiontio* should be read as "destining a destiny" or "swearing an oath" is not simply a matter of the translators disagreeing; this ambiguity points to a crucial concept

---

270. Royal Irish Academy, "EDIL 2019: An Electronic Dictionary of the Irish Language, Based on the Contributions to a Dictionary of the Irish Language, s.v. *trascrad*, s.v. *fostad*, s.v. *nascad*."

271. Koch and Carey, *The Celtic Heroic Age*, 2; Delamarre, *Dictionnaire Gauloise*, 298.

about the connection between fateful magic and oath-swearing. It is clear that this is pointing to something very deep indeed, because this ambiguity exists throughout the complex of phrases relating to fate, destiny, oaths, and binding magic across the different Celtic cultures. The cognate of the Gaulish phrase *toncnaman toncsiiontio* is found in Welsh myth in the phrase *tynghaf tynghet*, variously translated as "I doom a destiny," or "I swear an oath." This is, for example, used in the Fourth Branch of *The Mabinogion* by Arianrhod when binding a destiny onto her son: "I swear a destiny on him, that he may not get a name until he gets it from me." It is also found in cognate in the early Irish oath-formula *tongu a toingend*, typically appearing in oaths such as "I swear by the Gods my people swear by."[272]

The Indo-European root *tenk-* is at the root of each of these phrases, meaning "'to become solid, manifest, fixed."[273] This concept of fixing developed into phrases in the context of various rituals for the fixing of destiny, the swearing of oaths, or the laying of a *geis* or a binding curse. That this phrase appears intact across these different Celtic cultures, spanning the separation of Goidelic, Brittonic, and Continental languages, indicates that it comes from a very ancient cultural root, which bears its fruits in this complex of related words for prayer, invocation, binding, oaths, and spells. Each of these modes of fate-fixing magic seem to associate to a similar use of contractual language, similar to the incantatory language of "binding a bond."

Here is a window into a deep layer in the Celtic worldview on the conception of destiny: that it can be invoked and can be fixed or manipulated through incantatory ritual technologies, and that ritual mode and agency shape the form and impact of that binding. Each of these types of magic—oaths, *geasa*, fate-fixing, and binding curses—can be understood as a type of fateful invocation. The difference in these ritual modes and the type of fateful consequence they invoke appear to hinge on the agency of the invoker. To swear an oath is to undertake the binding of one's own fate autonomously. In

---

272. Koch, "Further to Tongu Do Dia Toinges Mo Thuath, &c," 249–250.

273. Koch, "Further to Tongu Do Dia," 256.

a case where the agency is exterior, where one person makes a fateful invocation upon another person, this would be understood as a *geis* or binding spell.

Sorcerer's Toolkit
Fateful Invocation

As mentioned in the previous section, *geasa* are traditionally performed by individuals who either have a position of spiritual authority, such as a druid or priest, or who have a bond of connection with the person receiving the *geis*, such as a family member or lover. In a more general sense, what this illustrates is that in order to successfully perform a fate-binding prayer, you need to position yourself in such a way that the spiritual world recognizes your authority to access that person's fate. Without needing to be acting in an official capacity, there are some ways that you can accomplish this access.

First, you may be able to speak from connection to your target. That can be personal connection, as of someone you know personally. The closer the bond, the more direct access you have to affect their fate.

Second, influence is also connection. To the extent that someone has the ability to impact the conditions of your life, you are within their sphere of influence. The same is true for any power relation—whether that is social, political, institutional, or spiritual power. Being a party to power relations means that your fates are already entangled, even if only slightly. These connections can be called upon to position you for access to fate-binding.

The third point of access I want to talk about is oaths of office and professional oaths. Where officials in public or institutional positions of power have sworn oaths, those oaths can become a point of access to fate-binding. We might not think of these oaths as *geasa*, but they are ritualized binding pacts and they are often sworn in the presence of images of divinities who hold their fulfillment. For example, these divinities may be ones relating to justice, in the case of governmental and legal institutions; or divinities of healing, in domains related to health care. The point is that even if undertaken in ostensibly secular contexts, oaths of office are still ritualized oaths and are upheld by certain powers. Such oaths can be instrumentalized to bind the individuals subject to them. Further, if these oaths are violated, this positions you to invoke the fateful consequences of the oath-breaking, and call on the authority of the powers who oversaw the oath in doing so.

Binding Invocation Rite

While this rite can take a myriad of forms depending on the situation, as a starting point I'll present this ritual template in the form you might use for a binding invocation taken against a public official. You can adapt this template and build upon it to suit other contexts for fate-binding.

This ritual does not require much material preparation, as it consists primarily of devotional petitions and spiritual action.

For this rite, you will need:

- Cleansing tools, such as blessing water.
- Offerings for your protecting spirits and for the powers and divinities you will be petitioning.

Begin by cleansing yourself and your place of working, using the blessing water or other cleansing tools.

Perform a shielding prayer, lorica, or caim to ensure your safety.

Call upon your protecting spirits; present offerings and ask them to see you through this safely.

Call upon the divinities you trust to aid with binding power and with justice; present offerings and ask them to lend their power to your action, to make the binding fast and to see justice done.

Call upon any powers that may be associated with the institution your target represents, or who would have overseen their oath (such as Lady Justice, etc). Speak your name and state your connection to the official whom you're targeting; identify what gives you standing to invoke this oath and bind the official to its fulfillment. Speak about how you are impacted by this official so that your right to bind their fate is clear.

Speak the terms of the binding against the official. It is helpful to name each aspect of the powers that they wield, focusing on their capacities or institutional powers that can impact you, and binding each of those in specific terms. You can also invoke the particulars of their oath of office so as to bind them to obey it in the way that you need them to.

For example, "I bind you that you must deal justly and rule fairly toward me. I bind your authority, I bind your word, I bind your speech, I bind your writing, I bind your hands, I bind your tongue, I bind your work, I bind your fate under oath. Your oath to deal equal justice to rich and poor alike binds you. Your oath under the scales of Justice binds you. The power of Justice binds you" or similar words that are adapted for your situation.

Continue speaking this binding until you feel you have stated all the terms clearly enough. If you feel you might forget something, you can also write all this out ahead of time and recite it from the page during your ritual.

Perform the binding incantation. Now that you have stated the terms of the binding, you will chant it into effect. For the incantation, choose something you can chant repeatedly as you enter into a spiritually activated state, to contact the Otherworld and gather the power of the spirits to the binding. I favor this incantation from the Chamalières *defixio*: *"luge dessumíis luge dessumíis luge dessumíis luge* ("I commit them to the oath."[274]).

As you chant your binding incantation, focus on the necessity of the binding. Let the chant become fierce and urgent with the need for this binding. As you chant, reach your heart and spirit between

---

274. Mees, *Celtic Curses*, 653.

the worlds, reaching out till you can sense and see your target in your mind's eye. Still chanting, see yourself taking hold of the strands of their fate, and with the aid of the divinities you have called, binding them to their oath.

When this feels complete, rest from your chanting and close your rite. Remember to give thanks to the spirits and divinities who helped you. Cleanse yourself and your space again.

You can adapt this approach to fateful binding invocation to the needs of your situation. This type of fateful invocation can also be combined with physical binding rites, such as withe binding charms (described earlier in this chapter), as well as with poppet magic or tablet curses, which are covered in the next chapter.

CHAPTER 8

Justice, Cursing, and Transgressive Magic

At the beginning of this book, I introduced the concept of *cóir*—rightness and justice. Justice magic in its fundamentals is magic directed toward a wrong that needs to be made right. More than this, it is empowered by the existence of a wrong. This moral imperative is the engine that powers the magic of justice.

In this chapter, I will explore the workings of *cóir* in more detail, particularly with respect to what happens when it is violated and in the magics of righting injustice. I will explore the ways in which power that has been abused can be inverted against the transgressor, and the techniques that allow us to take power back and actively bring justice to the powerful. This chapter also includes methods for aggressive curse magic, which are at their best when used for purposes of justice and liberation. As with any work that may entail interfering with the agency of another, it's imperative to situate these magics within a carefully considered ethical framework. I encourage the reader to make use of the ethics and risk assessment tools presented in the introduction as part of your preparation for any workings you undertake.

Cóir and Transgression

In the early Irish literature, one of the incarnations of Macha provides a teaching tale with rich lessons for the practice of justice magic. Macha, an Otherworldly woman, comes to be a wife to a farmer named Cruinn. Foolishly and against her warnings, he boasts in front of the king of Ulster that his wife can outrun the royal horses, and Macha is unjustly forced to race the king's horses while heavily pregnant to prove her husband's boast. She wins the race but dies in childbirth trauma at the finish line, bearing twins. With her dying screams, she curses the men of Ulster with the pain and weakness of childbirth whenever they are most needed to defend their province.

Macha's tale contains many layers of mythic and social narrative. For this study of justice magic, perhaps what is most significant is the way the story represents a conflict between the martial honor code and natural justice, or *cóir*. Macha has asked for compassion and fairness, that she be allowed to wait until she has given birth before having to race the horses, and this fair request is denied her by the king. In denying her what is just, he breaks his contract with the Otherworld and disrupts the justice of their society and the natural order of *cóir*. Macha's curse is the Otherworld's retribution for this transgression.

The curse itself seems to operate through the power of liminality, as well as the justice of her case. She is in a liminal state while giving birth, a condition that was understood to place her in contact with the Otherworld. This belief is reflected in *The Triads of Ireland*, where the oath of a birthing woman is described as one of three oaths that do not require counter-oaths (meaning such a person's word carries the force of truth and can stand alone as legal testimony, without requiring additional witnesses). These three oaths that are positioned as carrying the force of truth are "the oath of a woman in birth-pangs, the oath of a dead man, the oath of a landless man."[275] Each of these classes of people has a liminal or Otherworldly status, or both. Thus due to Macha's liminal state, her word and her curse carries the force of the Otherworld.

Macha's tale exists in multiple versions, and each offers slightly different insights into how the curse works. Some of these narratives indicate that the curse comes into force by way of her shame; that exposure to the shame being done to her brought a curse on the men who witnessed it (and who tacitly allowed it).[276] Some versions focus on the sound of Macha's birthing scream, or even the screams of the newborn twins, as the force that carries the curse, rather than her words; it is said that all the men who could hear the scream came under the curse.[277] This is a vivid, evocative picture: the force of *cóir*, the power and outrage of the Otherworld, is being channeled through her body and in her voice. In each of these versions, however the initial curse is received by the men of Ulster, it is passed on to their descendants to the ninth generation.

Macha's curse, in all its variations, is an example of transgressive magic. It is driven by a transgression. The injustice done to Macha, the violation of her right to fair treatment and safety, and the shame inflicted on her are the motive forces behind the curse. Her scream or verbal curse invocation can be thought of as the vehicle of deployment where the shame of the transgression is inflicted back onto those who brought it about. The curse inverts her shame and suffering against the transgressors. In doing so, the curse transgresses social divisions of gender identity, inflicting a form of suffering that was female-identified in Irish society onto the men who are held responsible for that suffering. Thus it transgresses the social order by stripping these men of the powers that are coupled to their male and martial identities, and this transgression redresses the original transgression.

---

275. Meyer,. *The Triads of Ireland*, 23.

276. Toner, "Macha and the Invention of Myth," 95.

277. Gwynn, "Metrical Dindshenchas Vol. 4," 308–311.

One way to think about this is that the transgression of *cóir* has created a tension in the natural order, and this tension is like a coiled spring or a drawn bow. This tension can be weaponized in order to redirect its power against those responsible for the transgression. By employing a matching transgression of the social order, and by channeling and vocalizing the outrage of that injustice, Macha's curse captures the tension of the transgression and redirects it against the king and the men of Ulster who stood by and allowed her suffering, thus restoring the balance of *cóir*.

This is highly instructive for thinking about justice magic. Macha's story demonstrates several features we can adapt into magical practice:

- The use of liminality to place yourself in contact with Otherworld forces.
- Focusing the emotive power of outrage through screaming, to viscerally channel power.
- Transgressing against the status of the curse target, equivalent to the injustice that motivated the curse, and so weaponizing *cóir*.

We will see some of these themes recur in other examples we will be studying.

The Rage of the Otherworld

Irish tradition articulates the concept of sacred obligations as *geasa*. I discussed *geasa* in chapter 7, covering how they function as both oaths and spiritual bindings. Because of their relationship with special powers such as the authority wielded by sovereigns, *geasa* have a strong intersection with justice magics.

In myth and literature, positions of power are often bounded by *geasa*. The *geasa* are the oath-bound ritualized prohibitions and requirements placed on someone who is elevated into a position of power, such as that of a sovereign or a warrior of especial martial strength. The connection between these powers (*búada*) and prohibitions (*geasa*) is not incidental—it is crucial. The *geasa* serve as controls and boundaries containing the potential impacts of the powers a person wields, and when needed, they can function as a kind of kill switch, removing those powers if they have been misused. It is the dissolution clause of a spiritual contract in which special powers can only be held within the bounds of responsibility.

What happens when *geasa* are broken? The spiritual agency of the Other-world activates them, and they become curses. This tends to be a cascading process with progressive stages of increasingly severe omens as the *geis*-curse comes into effect. This model can be particularly helpful in thinking about justice magics relating to abuses of power by people in positions of authority, particularly where there has been an oath of office, or other sworn legal or ethical commitments.

The Destruction of Dá Derga's Hostel illustrates this process vividly. Conaire breaks his central obligation to dispense justice, and the story follows the increasingly doomed king as the omens of his destruction mount. Once the first of his *geasa* has been violated, the rest seem to spring into action, actively hunting him to trap him in situations where he will break the rest of them. Conaire himself comments on this sense that his oaths have sprung to life: "All my *gessi* have seized me tonight."[278] First, a group of mysterious animals appear where he and his cohort are hunting; too late, he realizes that they are animals who are *geis* for him to hunt. Next, red riders who are *geis* to Conaire to follow on the road appear in front of his company while traveling. Finally, a hostile crone who calls herself Cailb ("Veiled"), but who is identified as the goddess Badb, personifies his *geasa* against refusing hospitality, or receiving a solitary woman in his company at night.[279] She thus entraps Conaire by means of a dilemma wherein no matter whether he receives or refuses her, he will break a *geis*. (As discussed in chapter 7, this motif of the dilemma is a classic one, appearing also in the death-tale of Cú Chulainn. A similar dilemma between conflicting moral imperatives often appears in classical tragedy, as well.)

This story illustrates the cascading sequence of the *geis*-curse. It centers on a person who held power through a spiritual contract. Once he violates that contract, the Otherworldly powers supporting it turn hostile, and its gifts

---

278. Stokes, "The Destruction of Da Derga's Hostel," 40.

279. O'Connor, *Da Derga's Hostel*, 208.

and protections are progressively stripped in order to bring about his end. The spiritual agency behind the oaths becomes progressively more personified throughout the story: first animals, then people, then a named woman identified with a hostile goddess. Each of the beings appearing in this sequence, the mysterious animals, the strange red riders, and finally Cailb herself, represent increasingly forceful manifestations of the Otherworld's malevolence, activated and furthered by the breaking of the *geasa*.

It is worth reflecting a little on the nature of the beings involved. In this story, Badb appears as a cursing crone who acts as a catalyst of *geis*-breaking, and agent of destruction for the removal of a king. Ralph O'Connor points out how her appearance is strongly couched in the mythic language of sovereignty, as many early Irish stories are concerned with this concept.[280] The notion of *fír flathemon*, the truth and justice of the ruler being reflected in the material reality of the land, appears here as spectral visions of devastation during his downfall. Ritual elements drawn from sovereignty myth appear in the story: Conaire's adversaries inflict him with a raging thirst in the midst of the final battle, but no water is to be found—the waters of Ireland hide themselves from him, reflecting the traditional symbolism of Irish kingship, the drink of sovereignty being refused to him.

In this setting rich with sovereignty symbolism, Badb can be seen as a hostile goddess protecting the land from this loss of prosperity that was believed to result from an unjust ruler. Indeed, the text strongly highlights her role as the malevolent face of sovereignty. She is intentionally mirrored and contrasted with Étaíne, the sovereignty goddess who granted kingship to Conaire's lineage. Where Étaíne is bright and fair, surrounded by imagery of natural fertility and beauty, Badb is black-clad, harsh, surrounded by frightful, gloomy, desolate imagery.

This association of Badb with the destructive consequences of oath-breaking is not unique to this story. A trio of crones very like Badb in description also appear in Cú Chulainn's death-tale as the ones who entrap him to geis-breaking.[281] Early

---

280. O'Connor, *Da Derga's Hostel*, 148–150.

281. Tymoczko, *Two Death Tales*, 49–50.

Irish scholars tended sometimes to equate Badb, and the Morrígan, with the Greek furies, or Erinyes. These were vengeful spirits or goddesses involved with the punishment of oath-breakers or perjurers; the name may derive from a root meaning "strife." The medieval Irish rendition of Lucan's *Civil War* calls her "The Badb of battle Erinys."[282] What this indicates is that for the medieval Irish, when contemplating a classical divinity active against oath-breakers, the native goddess they identified with such a role was Badb. For them, she seems to have been associated with the justice required of leaders, and the consequences that should fall upon those who perpetrated injustice or who violated oaths.

The description of Badb's *geis*-curse in *Dá Derga's Hostel* is rich with ritual elements that can provide inspiration in justice magic, so it is worth reproducing in detail:

> She came and leaned one shoulder against the doorpost of the house, casting the evil eye on the king and the youths who were about him in the house.
>
> He himself addressed her from the house: "Well then, woman, what do you see for us, if you are a seer?"
>
> "Indeed, I see for you," she said, "that neither wart nor flesh of you shall escape from the house where you have come but what the birds carry off in their claws."[283]

She is then asked her name, and she responds by chanting a litany of her names, while taking up a ritual posture: "She chanted all these to them from the doorway of the house, standing on one leg, and in one breath." The litany of her names is instructive as well:

> *Samain, Sinand, Seiscleand, Sodb, Saiglend, Samlocht, Caill,*
> *Coll, Díchoem, Dichuil, Dichim, Dichuimne, Díchuinne,*
> *Dairne, Dairine, Der Uaine, Egem, Agam, Ethamne, Gnim,*

---

282. Stokes, "In Cath Catharda: The Civil War of the Romans," 71.

283. O'Connor, *Da Derga's Hostel*, 135–138.

CIuichi, Cethardam, Nith, Nemain, Noenden, Badb, Blosc,
Bloar, Huaet, Mede, Mod.

Translation: Samhain (i.e. All Hallows), Stormy, Wasteland,
Bitch, Punishment, Blemish, Forest, Destruction, Ugly,
Neglect, Tributeless, Oblivion, Foolishness, Little Oakwood,
Little Oakwood (again), Green Girl, Outcry, Battle, Arable
Land, Deeds, Sport, Four Oxen, Conflict, Battle Fury, War,
Scaldcrow, Crash, Noise, Fear, Headless One, Surly.

She calls upon the same powers that were involved in granting his kingship, and thus also who hold his *geasa*. Conaire was granted these powers by
his Otherworldly bird-kindred and the sovereignty goddess Étaíne; both are
subtly invoked here. The bird people are alluded to in the reference to "what
the birds carry off in their claws." The sovereignty goddess is subtly invoked
through the names associating with fertile land: Little Oakwood, Green Girl,
Arable Land, etc. As Ralph O'Connor describes it:

> By the time Cailb appears, the smile has turned to an unmis-
> takable snarl. This change is reflected in the chaotic spurts of
> imagery in Cailb's chanted list of names: fine weather turns
> stormy (Sinand), beauty turns ugly (Díchoem), sweetness
> and music turn harsh and noisy (Blosc), a gentle, dignified
> voice becomes an outcry (Égem), cheerfulness becomes
> gloom (Mod), neighbourly love becomes the fury of battle
> (Níth, Noenden, Némain), and nature's fertility withers to a
> wasteland (Seiscleand).[284]

This act of cursing against an oath-breaker illustrates several features that
we can adapt into magical practice:

---

284. O'Connor, *Da Derga's Hostel*, 150.

- Invoking the powers through which the curse target held authority, in order to withdraw that authority when it has been abused.
- Use of liminal positioning (standing in the threshold) to access Otherworld power.
- Ritual posture and action of standing on one foot, with one hand, seeing through one eye, speaking the curse in one breath.

Notice the theme of liminality occurring again. In the next section, we'll study the ritual posture described here in more depth.

sharp wounding

This story also demonstrates features of a ritual cursing technique that is instructive for this practice. Badb delivers this prophecy in a ritual form that empowers it as a curse: "She chanted all these to them from the doorway of the house, standing on one leg, and in one breath." First, it is significant that she chants the whole curse litany in one breath. This references a traditional belief that what could be chanted in one breath was made to come true. It is a marker of ritual breath control and contributes to the power of the delivery.

A key element here is the ritual posture she adopts while chanting the litany. She leans in the doorway, neither in nor out, while standing on one leg, and looking through one eye, and chanting. In doing so, she is calling upon the power of liminality in at least three ways—being one-legged, half blind, and standing on a threshold. A similar ritual posture is used again by Badb while giving a death prophecy, in a similar story called *Dá Choca's Hostel*: "And then, standing on one foot, and with one eye closed, she chanted to them, saying: 'I wash the harness of a king who will perish…'"[285] It is also performed by Lugh while delivering a battle poem, in an act of war magic in *The Second Battle of Mag Tuired*.[286]

---

285. Stokes, "Da Choca's Hostel," *Revue Celtique* 21 (1900), 157.
286. Gray, "Cath Maige Tuired," 59.

This cursing technique is identified in the literature as *corrguinecht*, which means "sharp/pointed wounding" or "crane wounding."[287] While most descriptions of its use come from mythological stories, such as the one mentioned, *corrguinecht* also appears in legal texts about the practices used by poets in early Irish society, suggesting that it was a cultural practice and not simply a myth motif. It is defined in glossaries such as O'Davoran's: *"corrguinecht*, i.e. to be on one foot and [using] one hand and one eye while making the *glam dicinn* [a form of poetic satire]."[288] Its use of seeing through one eye links this practice with casting the evil eye, or with seeing in the Otherworld, faculties particularly associated in myth and folklore with one-eyed beings. The Irish phrases for the practice are illuminating: *leth-cois* or "half foot," for going on one foot; *leth-laimh*, "half-hand"; *lethsuil*, "half eye." This language emphasizes the liminal power in *corrguinecht* practice: you are half in the Otherworld and therefore channeling its power through the body.

In the lore of *corrguinecht*, it is performed both for cursing in war, and by poets acting in judicial capacity against someone who has authored an injustice. Poets, in this social system, held social standing nearly equivalent to that of kings, with a spiritual authority wherein they were understood to speak for and wield the power of the Otherworld in their word magic. This empowered them to act as a counter-force against abuses of power, even by a king, since the poets spoke for the Otherworldly source from which sovereigns drew their authority. Their poetic abilities were framed as both sacred and magically potent, and while these powers ordinarily served to protect the sovereign, they could equally be weaponized to cause wounding, blemishing, and destruction. The poetic blemish was a source of real social impact within a society structured around honor. In the case of a king, such an attack could delegitimize their authority, since according to tradition a blemished king could not continue to rule.[289] In this sense, the significance of being unblemished was that the person had a clean record of enacting justice and had not earned poetic attack.

---

287. Mees, *Celtic Curses*, 5330; Royal Irish Academy, "EDIL 2019, s.v. *corr*, https://dil.ie/12514."

288. Stokes, "O'Davoren's Glossary," 257.

289. Kelly, *Early Irish Law*, 19.

A full ritual to destroy an unjust king is described in Middle Irish law text on the roles and offices of poets. In this ritual, a group of seven poets would go to the top of a hill to chant the *glám dícenn*, a powerful satire.[290] *Glám dícenn* is often translated as "cry of extremity," referencing the severity of injustice that would motivate such a ritual, from *glám*, "satire, outcry, clamor," and *dícenn*, "end, extremity, culmination."[291] *Dícenn*, however, also means "headless," and in a figurative sense, "leaderless"; that is to say, *glám dícenn* was a rite to "make headless" the body politic by removal of the king or chief.[292] In this ritual, the seven poets chant in each of seven poetic meters, while using *corrguinecht* ritual cursing posture. Each poet holds a thorn from a whitethorn bush, and these are used to pierce and wound a clay effigy of the victim of the satire.

We can identify several layers of sorcerous practices in this ritual of justice against one who has abused their official power:

- The use of ritual posture to enter into a liminal state and call upon the powers of the Otherworld.
- The full wounding power of satire poetry brought to bear by way of the seven poets encompassing all seven poetic meters.
- The emotive power of the voice in performing the satire as an "outcry."
- The use of sympathetic magic in the stabbing of the clay figure.
- The use of whitethorn, a plant associated with dangerous Otherworldly powers.

This combination of verbal, metrical sorcery with sympathetic ritual involving stabbing a figurine comes to us from the Irish context, but it has been compared with practices surrounding the Continental and British use of curse tablets, which are covered further in a later section of this chapter.

---

290. O'Curry, *Manners and Customs*, Vol. II, 216–217.

291. Royal Irish Academy, "EDIL 2019, s.v. 1 *glám*, https://dil.ie/25963," and "s.v. 1 *dícenn*, https://dil .ie/16069."

292. Royal Irish Academy, "EDIL 2019, s.v. *dícennacht*, https://dil.ie/16072."

Sorcerer's Toolkit
Figure Magic

Figure magic, also sometimes called poppet, doll, or effigy magic, is a common form of sympathetic magic found in many folk cultures and with a well-documented history stretching to ancient times. Scholars sometimes call into question whether pagan rituals depicted in medieval literature, like the *glám dícenn*, represent real practices, but in the case of figure magic, there is abundant evidence for its use throughout Europe as well as the Mediterranean and beyond. Clay and wax are perhaps the most common materials, although there are examples of ancient figures made in other materials, such as lead.[293] This practice continues with a clear through-line into the premodern poppets described in the literature of witch trials, as well as eighteenth- and nineteenth-century folklore collections of western Europe, such as the *corp creadha*, "clay body," in Scotland, and similar practices elsewhere in the isles.[294]

The essence of figure magic lies in the creation of a small figurine in the form of a human body, and the identification of that figure with the target of magic, so that what is done to the figure manifests in the body of the target. This magic is sympathetic and animistic in nature. Usually, the figure is given life and identified with the target individual by being invested with something that can link it to the life force of that individual. This may be done through the use of "personal concerns" such as clippings of the hair or nails of the target, bodily fluids, bits of clothing, handwriting, or items touched by the person. Or, the figure can be spiritually linked to the individual sim-

293. Borsje, "Celtic Spells and Counterspells," 29–30; Mees, *Celtic Curses*, 1601; McKie, S. "The Social Significance of Curse Tablets in the North-Western Provinces of the Roman Empire," 69–70.

294. Campbell, *Witchcraft & Second Sight*, 46–47; Mees, *Celtic Curses*, 5797.

ply by naming it with their name, which may also be inscribed onto the figure.

Here, I offer a basic template for figure magic you can build upon in your own practice.

Poppet Curse Ritual

For this ritual, you will need:

- Cleansing tools, such as blessing water, sacred smoke, and milk.
- Offerings for your protective spirits and any other divinities you may call in for aid.
- Material to make your poppet, such as clay.
- Something to inscribe the poppet.
- Personal concerns of your target if you have them.
- Sharp instruments, such as nails.

Begin by cleansing yourself, your materials, and your space by sprinkling with blessing water and/or burning sacred smoke.

Perform a shielding prayer, lorica, or caim to ensure your safety.

Call in your protective spirits and any other divinities you trust to aid your work. Present offerings and ask them for protection as you do this work; especially, to turn away any harm that might come toward you from protections that your target may have.

Make the poppet. Take your clay and begin to shape it into the form of a person (or if making in wax, begin to carve, etc). As you shape the poppet, focus on your target, seeing them so that their identity is invested into the figure. It does not need to look like their likeness—a rough human shape is fine because you will be identifying it with them through magical means. If you have personal concerns or items connecting to your target, press or insert them into the clay body.

Name and enliven the poppet. Inscribe the target's name into the poppet. Speak the target's name aloud and invest the poppet with their identity. For example: "I name you [Name]. You are [Name]. You live and breathe as [Name]. Your limbs are the limbs of [Name], your body is the body of [Name], your senses are the senses of [Name], etc. What hurts you hurts [Name], what wounds you wounds [Name], what binds you binds [Name], etc." You may also wish to enumerate what wrongs your target has done that are the reason for the curse.

Curse the poppet. Take the poppet in one hand and the nail in the other. Speak aloud the form of justice you are invoking onto your target, such as: "May you wither and grow weak, and may your life force ebb and drain away, so that you can never hurt anyone again. May you know the pain you have caused others, so you never seek to do harm again." For additional potency, try standing on one leg, closing one eye, and speaking your curse in a single breath. As you complete the recitation of the curse, pierce the poppet with the nails, focusing on the area of its body that corresponds most closely to the effect you are invoking. Leave the nails in the figure.

Deploy the figure in an appropriate location. Try to position it near the target's home or workplace, if you can do so without detection. Alternately, take it to a liminal place such as a crossroads, graveyard, or watery place. Burial in the ground or depositing in water also brings the sympathetic magic of dissolution, as the figure dissolves or decays, the well-being of the target declines.

Cleanse yourself and your working space carefully. You may wish to use multiple forms of cleansing to ensure you are clear of any lingering effects from curse work. I favor a sequence of three cleansings, such as blessing water, sacred smoke, and milk blessing.

While figure magic is more known for its use in cursing, it can and has been used for benefic magics, such as healing, shielding, fertility, or just about anything else. In fact, the effigies often deposited into holy springs to seek healing are also a form of figure magic. I've constructed this template as for cursing, where the target would be pierced; however, you can adapt this for other approaches. For example, if you're seeking to bind or constrain your target rather than hurt them, you could tie cords around the figure, or seal it inside a container. For healing, you could apply medicine, inscribe blessings, or deposit the figure at a site of healing. The possibilities for this animistic sympathetic magical practice are broad.

curse tablets and judicial prayers

Celtic curse tablets as found in Britain and the Continent bring together many of the same elements appearing in Irish justice curse rituals: poetic incantation, a judicial orientation to the act, binding or fate-fixing language, and piercing and wounding actions.

The curse tablet, often referred to by its Latin nomenclature *defixio* (plural *defixiones*), is a magical practice originating in ancient Greece and Egypt, adopted across the Iron Age Mediterranean world and imported into Gaul and Britain by Roman influence.[295] In its most basic form, it consists of a magical charm or petition inscribed on an object, deposited into a spiritually potent place for action by associated spirits. The typical material was small pieces of thin-hammered lead sheet, in part since the softness of lead lends itself to easy inscription with a hand tool, and in part due to the associations of lead with chthonic, underworld powers, and the dead.

While tablet curses are clearly Mediterranean in origin, where the practice was imported into Celtic regions it seems to have been adopted enthusiastically and localized. Many vivid examples of curse tablets have been unearthed from Roman-era sites in both Gaul and Britain, some from sites that yielded an abundance of such tablets, evidence of active use in cult centers at these sites. These tablets, when translated, show that the practice was not simply passively absorbed. Rather, it was actively reinterpreted within the framework of local custom within these Celtic-speaking cultures.[296] Evidence shows native concepts and ritual contexts being woven into the practice, with

---

295. McKie, "Significance of Curse Tablets," 13–14.

296. Adams, "The Social and Cultural Implications of Curse Tablets [Defixiones] in Britain and on the Continent," 10–13.

inscriptions in local Celtic languages and using poetic incantation forms recognizable in later insular written materials.[297]

A frequent feature of these tablet curses is the use of a recurring prayer structure or formula in the inscriptions. Scholars of the practice often refer to this as "judicial prayer."[298] This judicial prayer structure is found in some variation in much of the corpus of curse tablets that have been uncovered from Celtic regions, particularly the British examples. It seeks to address the spirits and establish the validity of the petition for magical justice using a regular sequence of appeals. Typically, the judicial prayer formula begins with an invocation of gods or Otherworld powers. This opening invocation is usually followed by a petition for redress of grievances in which the identity and claim of the invoker are stated, along with the nature of the wrong, establishing the spiritual grounds for justice. The target is also named, often using contractual language binding their fate and specifying the consequences of the grievance. Finally, most judicial prayers close with a final invocation, handing the target over to the powers that have been invoked; sometimes including mention of offerings or sacrifices that have been made to seal the curse.

The language that appears in some of these petitions is particularly interesting in its similarity to the kind of fate-binding language seen in oaths and bindings in the Irish and Welsh contexts. One famous example, the Gaulish Chamalières *defixio,* inscribed in lead and deposited in the spring at a sanctuary, uses the phrase *toncnaman toncsiiontio,* examined earlier in the chapter on binding magics, and that is exactly cognate with a phrase found across many Celtic cultural contexts including Irish and Welsh literatures, meaning to "destine a destiny, bind a bond, or swear an oath."

The Chamalières *defixio* is worth examining in full as an example of judicial prayer and a very effective curse format. Here is its inscription in Gaulish, followed by English translation:

> *andedíon uediíumí*
> *diíiuion ri sunartiu*

---

297. Mees establishes this throughout *Celtic Curses;* see for example, 5876.

298. Versnel, "Beyond Cursing: The Appeal to Justice in Judicial Prayers," 117–118.

Mapon(on) Arueriiatin

lopites snieθθic

sos brixtia anderon

C. Lucion Floron Nigrinon adgarion Aemilion Paterin(on)

Claudion Legitumon Caelion Pelign(on)

Claudio(n) Pelign(on) Marcion Victorin(on) Asiaticon Aθθedilli

etic Secoui toncnaman toncsiiontio

meion ponc sesit

buetid ollon

reguc cambion

exsops pissiumi

isoc canti rissu

ison son bissiet

luge dessumiis

luge dessumiis

luge dessumiis luxe[299]

Translation: before the powers of the infernal gods,

I invoke Maponos Arveriatis

quicken and spin

with magic these below

[names of the invoker and targets]

and also the Secovi [infernal spirits] who will destine a destiny

what is little, when sowed,

may it thus become great,

I straighten what is crooked

blind I shall see it so happen through this charm

I prepare them for the oath, I prepare them for the oath,

I prepare them for the oath, for the oath![300]

---

299. Mees, *Celtic Curses*, 414, 542, 653

300. Translation compiled from the work of Koch and Carey, *The Celtic Heroic Age*, 2; Koch, "Further to Tongu Do Dia Toinges Mo Thuath, &c.," 255; Mees, *Celtic Curses*, ch 2.

To set this out clearly, there is a patterned structure to the invocation:

- A petition to a deity and associated spirits (Maponos, and associated chthonic powers) to quicken the magic.
- The identity of whom is invoking these powers, and the identities of the targets.
- Binding language reminiscent of a *geis*-prayer ("who will destine a destiny").
- A litany of terms describing the outcome being contracted.
- Final incantation and binding charm.

Beyond their ritual content and structured language, the metrical and rhythmic modes of many such curses show evidence of their origin as curse-poems that were sung or chanted. Bernard Mees analyzes these curses written in Celtic languages and identifies features that align with the poetic charm patterns seen in later Irish tradition, such as the use of rhythmic incantatory metrics, alliteration, and emphatic language patterning. Indeed, the names used within curse texts to reference the procedure of casting often point toward being not just inscribed but sung or incanted: these curses refer to themselves in musical terms, such as *duscelinata*, "malevolent death song," and *ison canti*, "curse song."[301] These spells can be seen as expressions of a common and very ancient Celtic tradition of weaponized judicial poetry, refracted differently into the Mediterranean-influenced Gallic and British cursing traditions, as well as the Irish and Welsh literary traditions.

The conditions in which these curse tablets have been found also reveals something of the ritual practices surrounding their deployment. Some of them, along with the written inscription, feature drawings of the deities invoked for aid, or symbols representing them. For example, a curse tablet from Bologna includes a drawing of a snake-haired Hecate, who is invoked in the curse.[302] Other tablets feature incised drawings of the spell's target, sometimes wound in binding cords to indicate the target's fate being entangled, bound, and handed

---

301. Mees, *Celtic Curses*, 5497–5504.

302. Urbanová, *Latin Curse Tablets of the Roman Empire*, 232.

over to the chthonic powers.[303] The letters of the inscriptions are sometimes manipulated to enhance the form of the curse: lines of text may encircle and wind around the tablet, like the winding of a binding cord. Others twist or reverse, perhaps imitating the twisting of the attack.[304] This example from Cologne states its reason for using reversed text: "You act perversely, even as this writing is perverse."[305]

The sheets have usually been manipulated after being inscribed; they are often found folded multiple times or rolled, and frequently have been pierced with nails—a detail that recalls the wounding and piercing actions found in the Irish poetic curse ritual.[306] Sometimes the nails have been carefully situated so as to pierce directly through the inscribed name of the target; others have been stabbed repeatedly with force in what appears to have been frenzied or cathartic actions in the curse ritual.[307]

The tablets have then been deposited, usually in a chthonic Otherworld location, such as a well, spring, bog, cave, or tomb. The Mediterranean practice seems to have favored grave sites, whereas Celtic examples of these curses are more typically found in wet sites, highlighting the Celtic cultural habit of making votive pacts by depositing objects in water. There are also some examples where evidence of offerings or sacrifices has been preserved along with the curse.[308] Tablets have been found with seeds, coins, or bones indicating offerings; or in some examples the offerings are described in the curse inscription as part of the magic. In some instances, effigies or figurines, pierced with nails as part of the ritual, have been found with curse tablets as well.[309]

Taken together, these evidences portray a full picture of the ritual practice. The spell is composed in verse so as to be sung, and this is inscribed on the tablet, along with the identifying details that will allow it to find its

---

303. Adams, "Implications of Curse Tablets," 3.

304. McKie, "Significance of Curse Tablets," 108.

305. McKie, "Significance of Curse Tablets," 109.

306. Versnel, "Beyond Cursing," 1991.

307. McKie, "Significance of Curse Tablets," 109, 112.

308. Mees, *Celtic Curses*, 2020.

309. McKie, "Significance of Curse Tablets," 70.

target. The tablet itself seems then to be consecrated to the invoked powers through the making of offerings or sacrifices, and the charm itself would likely be chanted aloud to invoke the attention of these powers. The spell is sealed through closure of the tablet by folding or rolling, and the invoker might charge it for the attack by stabbing it through with a nail or other sharp instrument. Finally, it is deployed in a spiritually potent place into the hands of the Otherworld powers.

Sorcerer's Toolkit
curse Tablets

What exactly is a lead tablet—what are these archaeological reports describing? It is simply a small, flat sheet of lead. In ancient times, these were usually produced by hammering a soft piece of lead until it flattened out into roughly sheet form. On some of the artifacts, you can still see hammer marks and the rough-shaped edges that come from being hammered flat. Others are more refined in their manufacture and look like a cut sheet. Traditionally, *defixiones* are often quite small—just a few inches—as the intention was for them to be easily secreted away. Today, it is usually easy to source manufactured sheet lead, which is used commercially for radiation shielding and a variety of other uses. You can source it from sheet metal suppliers, though you may get strange looks and questions when you ask for such a small quantity.

There are some safety issues to consider with tablet cursing. First, lead is toxic, so it's important to think about controlling your exposure. This is for the same reason that you see warnings about lead paint used in houses. Prolonged or repeated exposure to lead can cause all kinds of health issues. This exposure can happen via absorption through the skin, breathing dust coming off the surface of the lead, or if you have residues on your hands, from touching lead and then touching your mouth, eyes, or other absorbent areas. You are unlikely to get enough exposure to notice any ill effects from any one time using a lead tablet, but it is wise to take precautions. I recommend handling the lead with gloves, and washing hands afterward (the latter is advisable for spiritual hygiene anyway).

I am often asked about the environmental impact of using lead in curses; if it's toxic to us, wouldn't it also be toxic to wildlife and the environment? It's true that depositing lead into natural environments does contribute a little bit of toxicity. This would be quite a small effect, however. Where lead causes significant problems is when water flows into a waterway continually through lead piping, leading to a constant contribution of lead residue; or when it is put into the environment in small enough form to be ingested by wildlife and build up in their bodies, as is the case with lead shot used by hunters. So, while it is true that the amount of lead in a tablet deposited in nature would still contribute micro-amounts of toxin into the soil or water, the impact would be very small in the scale of things.

It is possible to do tablet magic without using lead. There are quite a few alternatives; any material that provides a surface soft enough to etch into can really be made to work. Copper is a little harder to inscribe on than lead, but is workable. Leather can be inscribed with a small sharp blade and is readily biodegradable. Clay tablets have been used since ancient times; air-dried, unfired clay takes on a leatherlike consistency that is very easy to inscribe on. With the right tool, bone and wood can also be inscribed. One traditional writing surface popular in ancient times was wood with a flat layer of wax that could easily be etched upon. Your creativity and ingenuity can be your guides here.

Preparation

It is advisable to compose the written portion of your spell in advance. This will allow you to carefully frame how its terms are phrased, as well as checking the size of tablet it needs.

Here is a template you can use as a basis to develop your curse text:

*By the power of [deities and spirits] the binding of this spell is
enacted.*

It is [your name] who invokes.

*Against [name of the transgressor and the nature of their
transgression],*

*It is the destiny I doom on you: I curse your will, I curse your
words, I curse your actions. I curse your eyes, mouth, hands.
I curse your heart, health, body. That any transgression
whether in thought, in word, or in act shall bind you more
tightly under this curse.*

If you wish, you can add a clause that offers release from the curse
should they make amends or right the wrong.

You may also wish to practice the incantation ahead of time that
you will use to charge the curse. Here are a few example incantations
you can try:

- For a binding curse: *luge dessumíis luge dessumíis luge dessumíis luge* ("I commit them to the oath"[310]).
- For an expelling curse: *celete celete, coudate coudate* ("leave
  leave, begone begone"[311]).
- For any kind of justice curse: *fercurib fristongarar* ("your
  violations are renounced"[312]).

Use metal-cutting shears to cut your sheet lead to size for your
spell. It should be as small as possible while still allowing your inscription to fit, but not so tiny that it will be terribly hard to fold or roll.

Curse Tablet Rite

For this rite, you will need:

---

310. Mees, *Celtic Curses*, 653.

311. From an unpublished incantation by Gallic reconstructionist Bellouesos Isarnos.

312. Carmody, "Thesis, Antithesis, Synthesis: An Examination of Three Rosc Passages from Cath Maige
Tuired."

- Tools for cleansing, such as blessing water, sacred smoke, and milk.
- Candles.
- Offerings for the divinities who will aid your work, such as wine or spirits, food, and incense.
- Gloves.
- Lead sheet, precut to size.
- A sharp tool, such as a nail.
- Cloth to wrap the spell.

Begin by cleansing yourself, your materials, and your space using blessing water or sacred smoke.

Light candles and call upon your protective spirits and any other divinities whose aid you are seeking. Present the offerings, asking them to guide and protect you, and especially to turn aside any malevolent forces that may react to the curse.

Inscribe the tablet. Put on gloves and place the lead sheet on a firm working surface, and etch the text of your curse into the tablet with the point of the nail. As you inscribe, speak the terms of the curse aloud. Focus and visualize your target as you do so, seeing the impacts of the curse being realized. When it is fully inscribed, pour some of the liquid offerings over it, with a renewed prayer asking the divinities to see it made real. Fold or roll the lead to seal the tablet.

To charge the curse, begin your curse chant. As you do so, rise into curse posture, standing on one foot, looking through one eye. Take your time, gathering your power with the tension of the pose, so that you are like a coiled serpent or a crane ready to strike. When you feel ready, unleash yourself and stab the nail into the tablet. Work it through so that it fully pierces.

To close, wrap the tablet in cloth so that you are not contaminated when you handle it further. Give thanks to your spirits and divinities with a final offering, and snuff the candles. Deposit the tablet into a liminal site, such as a watery place, crossroads, graveyard, or as near to your target as you can do undetected. Perform a thorough spiritual cleansing. It's recommended after work of this kind to employ multiple kinds of cleansing, such as a water blessing followed by sacred smoke and a milk blessing.

Story
A Tablet Curse Ritual

The last light of sunset has washed away and twilight is deepening over the wooded valley where we're camped, while we gather the implements of ritual and prepare ourselves. We're preparing to curse a man who's assaulted a friend, and we're vibrating with grim readiness. We've cleansed ourselves and all the tools. We pick up our things and walk in silence into the dark.

Down at a liminal crossroads where the path fords a stream, we find our spot for the working, a level area along the sandy bank. We set out candles around our working space, encased in glass to protect their flames from the breeze. By their dim, flickering light we begin our invocation prayers to the spirit guardians whom we're asking for protection while we do this work, and to the spirit allies under whose power we seek to do this work. She-wolves for protection, Badb and the Legion for justice, Mongach and the eels for binding power. Speaking prayers to each, we recite their names, scribe their sigils into the sand, and pour a libation into the sigil.

I unwrap the flexible sheet of lead from its cover and lay it out on the unfolded cloth. I breathe the power of the spirits we've conjured into the iron nail and then begin to inscribe the curse, scratching the letters into its soft leaden surface slowly by the low light of the curse candles. As the nail carves, it cuts through the dull, dark gray oxidized surface of the lead, making letters that shine and glitter eerily in the candlelight. Speaking the terms of the curse as I inscribe them,

I call a binding on this man who has committed assault against the bodily sovereignty of another: "It is the bond I bind on you, and it is the destiny I doom on you: I bind your will, I bind your aggression, I bind your words, I bind your actions, I bind your body, I bind your breath, I bind your life."

I can hear the whispers of the group who have joined me, echoing the binding as I speak it. Voices growing rougher with the fierceness that we feel against this transgressor: "And the bonds I bind on you shall bind ever more tightly, so that every transgression against the sovereignty of women whether in thought, in word, or in act shall bind these bonds more tightly, as a noose that strangles."

I scratch a figure marked with his name, drawing cords winding tightly around it while I entreat the spirits of eels to bind and strangle. When the inscription is finished we pour more offerings over it and then fold the lead, once, twice, three times.

Now I gather myself for the last attack. We begin the chant, "*Dessummiis luge, dessummiis luge, dessummiis luge*," as I rise over the curse altar. Carefully, balancing weight onto my right leg, gripping the nail in my right hand, I close my left eye, let the left hand drop behind me, lift my left foot from the ground. My left side slides into the Otherworld and I balance there, letting the tension of holding this posture gather in my body till I feel like a coiled serpent or a tightened spring—and then I drop, fist first onto the curse altar, stabbing with the nail again and again into the folded tablet. At the last time, I push the nail through and leave it in.

We wrap the tablet in the cloth it had been laid out on, and then another layer of clean cloth tied with a string. Later, it will be dropped into a wet bog from the bridge of a road crossing.

For now, it's time to attend to our spiritual hygiene, so we first thank all of our spirits and then gather all our things. We wash our hands and faces in the cold water of the stream and make our way back to camp where our comrade greets us with a second layer of cleansing by circling each of us with the fire of a candle lantern, and a third by sprinkling us with blessed milk.

meeting boudica and the legion

An ancestor I honor as a spirit of resistance and the drive for justice is Boudica. She will be familiar to many readers as the British Celtic queen from the first century BCE, who led a militant uprising against the Roman occupation of Britain, burning several Roman cities including London and Colchester.

The root of her name, *boud-*, means "victory" in Brittonic, and her name can be read as "Victorious One."[313] This name links her to a group of inscriptions of goddesses of victory with similar names found from the period, such as Boudiga, Boudina, and Boudena.[314] Boudica may represent an example of a cultural pattern wherein a female spiritual leader carries the title of a tutelary goddess, and may have served to represent that goddess in war and in political or religious leadership.[315] This would square with Boudica's relationship with the goddess she invoked on the battlefield, Andraste, whose name seems to mean "the Invincible" or "the Unconquerable."[316]

In my practice, I honor Boudica among a group of spirits that are known as the Legion. The Legion are a collective of spirits whose lives and deaths were impacted by gendered violence, particularly those of women, femme-coded, and queer individuals. I became aware of the Legion starting in about 2018, arising from rituals of grief conducted by a small group of polytheists including myself, to honor a friend who had been murdered by a male partner. As a collective, the Legion isn't specifically part of any Celtic tradition and in fact includes spirits from all over the world and throughout history. What they share with Boudica are the experience of gendered violence and a spirit of resistance against the sources of such violence. For me therefore, Boudica takes a place as one of the ancestors of resistance who stands among the Legion.

---

313. Delamarre, *Dictionnaire Gauloise*, 83.

314. Olmsted, *The Gods of the Celts and the Indo-Europeans*, 411.

315. Koch and Carey, *The Celtic Heroic Age*, 45.

316. Beck, "Goddesses in Celtic Religion," 184.

Relationship with the Legion spirit collective can bring solidarity and strength to resist injustice, to find support in the strength of comrades, and to heal through fighting to right wrongs. Their sigil design is oriented around solidarity and is intended to visually convey the weaving of collective strength through mutual care and defense. Its component parts are made up of the Celtic letter-signs Corios (for the strength of the collective; it actually means "troop or army," which is pretty close to "legion"), Touta (for the bonds of community), Nemetos (for sacredness, and transformative ordeals), and the ogham letter-signs Fearn (for the protection of the heart), Nin (for communication and bonds, especially among women), and Getal (for the healing of wounds). In the illustration, the sigil is inscribed on a shield, carried by one of two warriors who support each other, their spear arms interlinked.

cursing bones

A theme that emerges in this material is the relationship of cursing with Otherworld powers of an infernal or chthonic character. The chthonic Otherworld can be understood as those Otherworld powers and spaces associated particularly with the dead or divine powers dwelling under the earth, and with caves, tombs, or watery sites. The Gaulish and British curse tablets deposited in tombs and springs provide a clear example of this type of chthonic cursing.

Another cursing practice that vividly illustrates this relationship to chthonic powers is the phenomenon of the "cursing bone." Extant examples of this practice come from Scotland and England, and are of nineteenth- and twentieth-century date, representing folkloric witchcraft practices that are modern but appear to draw upon similar cosmological and spiritual principles to that found in earlier Celtic traditions.

The Scottish cursing bone is a composite magical instrument collected from Glen Shira in Argyll, consisting of a section of thigh bone (identified as deer or sheep by National Museums Scotland), which has been fixed into a naturally occurring knothole in a diamond-shaped piece of bog oak so that the hollow of the bone transits through the hollow of the wood. According to the folklore collected with this item, its use was as follows: "When the 'witch' wanted to 'ill-will' one of her neighbours, she went out with her bone

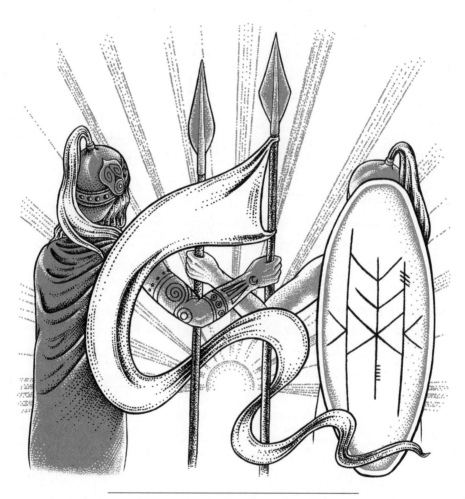

Sigil Illustration for Boudica and the Legion

between sunset and cock-crow and made for the neighbour's croft. She did not go to the dwelling-house, however, but to the henhouse, and seized the hen that sat next the rooster (his favourite), thrawed its neck, and poured its blood through the cursing-bone, uttering her curses the while."[317]

A similar item was found in West Dorset, England, and resides in the collection of the Museum of Witchcraft and Magic. This example lacks the bone and consists of only a similarly shaped piece of darkened wood, thought to be yew; it has been supposed by curators that it may have originally been part of a composite tool constructed in the same way as the Glen Shira cursing bone. Its folklore details indicate an oral family tradition that it had been used for bewitching cattle and possibly for cursing.[318]

The cursing bone displays clever and very powerful ways of engaging with chthonic Otherworld powers for magical purposes. Each aspect of its design and use and reveals layers of potency. First, its material construction is both liminal and chthonic. The wood is bog oak—ancient wood preserved beneath the surface in a bog for thousands of years, stained dark by its tannic waters. Bogs are liminal in multiple dimensions: as places where land and water interpenetrate, they are geographically and ecologically liminal; and as places where the decay of death is suspended and objects from the ancient past are preserved, they are also liminal in terms of time. Thus, the use of bog wood as material connects the tool with the bog as a liminal gateway to the chthonic Otherworld, existing in deep time and populated by the dead and all the other mysteries held in its dark waters, allowing its user to access and call upon all these powers.

Next, the bone, whether of wild deer or domestic sheep, would provide connection with the spirits of the land and the world of the living, bringing in another domain of spirit allies to the work. These two materials are cleverly interlocked so as to invoke and open a space of liminality. The two realms have been brought together, as they are at the margin between dry land and dark waters. The bone representing the living world passes through a hole

---

317. Society of Antiquaries of Scotland, "Donations to and Purchases for the Museum, 1943–44," 141.

318. Museum of Witchcraft and Magic, "3079 Cursing Stick: Ill-Wishing Stick."

into the bog wood representing the chthonic Otherworld, so that the whole structure of the tool represents the opening of a doorway between worlds.

This doorway is then activated and instrumentalized in the act of cursing. In the example of its use recorded with the object, the killing of the hen appears to be a form of sympathetic magic. Here, the hen is a favored animal that would therefore provide a close connection to the target of the curse, its life force standing in for theirs. The killing of this hen sympathetically targets the owner, appropriating and redirecting their life force, sending it through the hollow bone, which channels it into that open doorway into the Otherworld where it can be bound and held by the chthonic powers represented by the bog wood.

We're told that the witch would be reciting verbal magic while this cursing bone is deployed, and while the verses or charms used are not recorded here, one can imagine that they would help the witch to invoke the various powers and effect that sending of the target's life into the Otherworld. This curse and the instrument designed to carry it out represent an excellent example of the way in which mythic, cosmological principles can be at work within an act of magic.

CHAPTER 9

war and
conflict magic

War magic is the domain of magical practices used in war and conflict. In war magic, the focus is political, and the action is collective. In a sense, many of the techniques already covered here can be used in conflict, and may have political aims, but they are designed to act on an individual basis, such as the binding or removal of a harmful individual. This chapter will focus on conflict magic in the wider sphere, the magics that we can use in collective struggle and conflict, drawing inspiration from the ritual and magical techniques found on battlefields in myth and folklore, as well as historical sources.

Some readers may wonder how magical practices created for warfare would be relevant to your own practice, if you are not part of a military force. Without delving into an extensive tangent on the nature of warriorship, what I'd like to point out is that battle magics can be adapted to support any kind of struggle where we face conflict and risk, whether or not that struggle is physical or takes place in an arena with lethal violence. Activists, antifascists, revolutionaries, community safety organizers, and anyone involved in a struggle against hostile social forces, groups, or organizations can find these practices helpful.

My study of this domain of magic arose from my experience as a dedicant of the Morrígan. As a war goddess with a profound interest in justice and social change, she has inspired my involvement in justice activism and my interest in developing magical practices that could be of help in collective struggles. My approach to conflict magic emerges from street activism in support of communities fighting for justice, where we have often had to confront very real violence coming from police, paramilitary forces, and white supremacist gangs and militias. Second, my relationship with the Morrígan has also inspired an involvement in the sport of medieval armored field combat, where there is collective violence of a consensual and managed kind, and the risk of harm is primarily due to accident or excessive force. The personal narratives I share in this chapter will be drawn from both of these types of conflict experiences.

It should be said that this is not beginner magical work. Any adversarial force, group, or institution will have emergent spiritual forces surrounding it, even without accounting for any intentional magics or protections they may have in place. It is crucial to be fully prepared when undertaking work of this kind, and to approach it in as strong a coalition of solidarity as you can muster. Remember that it's strongly advisable to undertake an ethical and risk assessment before beginning any adversarial magical work, and to take the time to ensure that all of your protections and spirit alliances are as strong as possible before stepping on the battlefield. Battles aren't won by individuals acting alone.

THE battle sian

Spells of consecration, blessing, and protection for the battlefield are found throughout folk tradition. Folklore collections from Scotland contain many mentions of *sian* charms (also spelled *seun*). As *sian* charms are part of a broad genre of protection magics, they are related to material covered in the earlier chapter on protection magics. Many of the examples of these charms are specifically for protection in the field of battle and to provide safety in an environment of mass conflict, and this will be my focus here in this section.

Folklorist Alexander Carmichael describes the *sian* as follows: "'Sian' or 'seun' is occult agency, supernatural power used to ward away injury, and to protect invisibly."[319] *Sian* charms were often said to turn away blades and bullets or to prevent them piercing the carrier of the blessing. This passage exemplifies the genre, here describing a charm used during the battle of Culloden:

> A woman at Bearnasdale, in Skye, put such a charm on
> Macleod of Bearnaray, Harris, when on his way to join
> Prince Charlie in 1745. At Culloden the bullets showered
> upon him like hail, but they had no effect. When all was
> lost, Macleod threw off his coat to facilitate his flight. His
> faithful foster-brother Murdoch Macaskail was close beind
> him and took up the coat. When examined it was found to
> be riddled with bullet-holes. But not one of these bullets had
> hurt Macleod![320]

This feature where the carrier of the charm is struck by weapons, but the weapons cannot pierce and wound, is typical of the folklore about *sian* charms. In one instance recorded by the Scottish folklorist John Gregorson Campbell, the carrier of the charm is said to have been so bruised he wished he had been pierced by the bullets instead![321]

The folklore collections contain many examples of verbal *sian* charms. In part, their text often echoes the lorica or poetic armor style of charm, enumerating the parts of the body to be protected and the divine powers shielding them, such as this excerpt from an example recorded by Gaelic scholar Norman Macleod:

---

319. Carmichael, *Carmina Gadelica*, Vol. II, 26.

320. Carmichael, *Carmina Gadelica*, Vol. II, 26.

321. Campbell, *Witchcraft & Second Sight*, 76.

St Michael's sword by his side;
St Michael's shield on his shoulder-blades.
There is nothing between heaven and earth
Which will overcome the King of grace.
No blades shall cleave you,
Sea shall not drown you.
The mantle of Christ about you,
The shadow of Christ over you.
From the top of your head to the sole of your foot,
The seun of luck is now on you...[322]

The battle *sian* charms are often specific toward protection from violence and invocation of success in battle, such as these lines from the same charm:

You shall stand amidst the slaughter;
Your shall run through five hundred,
And your enemy shall be caught in distress.

They often include a recitation of types of wounding that the wearer is protected against:

A charm art thou against arrow,
A charm art thou against sword,
A charm against the red-tracked bullet...[323]

The folklore about battle *sian* charms also points to an operative magic component that is deployed along with the verbal charm. Campbell mentions the use of physical items that might be hung around the neck or sewn into the clothing of the person receiving the charm; these items might include colored threads or even plant material.[324] The noted example from the battle of Culloden suggests the charm may have been applied to the soldier's

---

322. Macleod, (Caraid nan Gaidheal), *Cuairtear Nan Gleann*, 309–12.

323. Campbell, *Witchcraft & Second Sight*, 75.

324. Campbell, *Witchcraft & Second Sight*, 73.

coat. Macleod is a little more specific in his description: "A sort of verse put [or set] up in fragments of linen, and sometimes [with] a fairy-arrow, sewn tightly into a single piece of cloth. This was carried under the shirt, close to the heart."[325]

This verbal charm from the Macleod collection also alludes to the ritual of its usage within the lines of the charm: "I will make the charm on Monday, In a narrow, sharp, thorny space."[326] The instruction to make the charm in a narrow, thorny place seems to be a form of sympathetic magic: as the charm is intended to enable its bearer to come safely through an environment where they will be beset all around by piercing weapons, so to invoke the safe path through these dangers, the charm is prepared in such a place. I picture a loving family member going to some narrow, thorny place to stitch the charm into clothing in colored thread, perhaps gathering a bit of sacred plant or other protective items too, while chanting the spell.

It seems also that battle *sian* charms might sometimes be aggressive rather than simply protective. The *Carmina Gadelica* collection gives a story where a mother sends a *sian* charm in the form of a cursed crooked sixpence coin, with which to curse the lord who forced her son into military service:

> 'Here, my son, is a sixpence seven times cursed. Use it
> in battle against Little Allan and earn the blessing of thy
> mother, or refrain and earn her cursing.' … When the strife
> was hottest and the contest doubtful, the son of the widow
> of Staonabrig remembered his mother's injunction, and
> that it was better to fight with her blessing than fall with
> her cursing, and he put the crooked sixpence in his gun. He
> aimed, and Clanranald fell.[327]

Her curse is carried by this crooked sixpence coin, which the son delivers by using it in place of a bullet.

---

325. University of Edinburgh, "Gaelic Battle Charms."

326. University of Edinburgh, "Gaelic Battle Charms."

327. Carmichael, *Carmina Gadelica*, Vol. II, 26.

Story
A stitched battle charm

Something's not right. My partner and I are fighters in a medieval combat society, where we put on armor and fight our friends with rattan weapons. Injuries are not uncommon, but I'm noticing that he's taking injuries almost every time he fights, and that's not normal. We've checked over all of his armor pieces but it's not a consistent type of injury and it's happening no matter whom he fights or where.

"The last time you fought and didn't get hurt, were you wearing different armor?" I ask.

"No," he answers, then continues "But now that I think of it, I forgot my tunic that day and had to borrow one."

"Your tunic? Hmmm, where did that tunic come from anyway?" I ask.

"Ah, my ex made it for me, actually," he says.

"Were you getting along at the time?" I ask.

"We were not," he says, and continues, "she was pretty unhappy with me and didn't want me spending time with the medieval society, but said she was gonna finish the tunic anyway because she'd promised to."

"So you're saying this tunic was made by someone who was angry at you while they sewed it, for an activity they resented you doing? Wow, no wonder you're getting injured. This thing is cursed!" I say.

We burn the tunic, musing about how readily a miserable person's feelings can throw a curse without them even intending to.

Now, I sit myself down to make a new one, and this one will have blessings instead of curses stitched in. After cutting the fabric pieces, I make sure to sprinkle them with blessing water and a prayer before sewing. I spend a few moments composing a little verbal charm that is alliterative and easy to remember. *Nerton, ualon, segos, slanos.* "Strength, power, victory, health."

As I begin to sew, I whisper the little charm into each stitch. *Nerton*; the needle finds its place to begin the stitch. *Ualon*; the needle pierces and I pull it through. *Segos*; I turn the needle and pierce it back again. *Slanos*; I pull the thread and finish the stitch. At first I'm slow and clumsy with it and I contemplate whether or not I was a fool to think of getting through this whole project with a prayer into every stitch. But I keep going. *Nerton, ualon, segos, slanos.* It starts to flow a little easier and I don't have to try so hard to fit the charm to the movements of my hands. Over and over, the needle slips in and through, the whispered prayers roll along and are stitched in. Eventually, I am reciting the charm silently and in rhythm with my stitching without even thinking about it, without missing a beat and even with conversations swirling around me.

I'll finish the tunic with the words of the charm also embroidered in Gaulish Lepontic script along the hem and sleeves. It will be a while before I stop hearing the charm repeating itself in my head while I'm falling asleep. But he looks good in his bold new fighting tunic and most importantly, he's no longer getting injured whenever he fights.

battle blessings and invocations

A theme that appears throughout many sources is the use of prayer and invocation to deities and spirits, to gain their support for the petitioner's success in a conflict. These invocations can be thought of as a type of religious or theurgic magic where devotion is employed specifically to focus the support of the gods toward a successful outcome in conflict. They may take the form of invocatory prayers to tutelary gods of a place or tribe, to secure a victory; or prayers to deities and spirits who oversee conflict, to attack the adversary on their behalf. There are also many examples of votive pacts and exchanges where offerings or sacrifices are vowed in exchange for the support of the divinities. Sometimes divinatory omens are taken as part of these invocations, and these omens may be used for strategic guidance in battle.

Classical histories provide several examples of battlefield invocations in conflicts involving the Celts. Historians wrote about Queen Boudica giving an invocatory prayer to a war goddess called Andraste (Unconquered) on the battlefield before her confrontation with the Romans. Accounts of this event may have been embroidered by their authors, as Boudica's story was heavily propagandized in classical accounts. However, some aspects of the description do sound compellingly like what a genuine practice of invocatory prayer might look like: "She climbed up onto a raised platform, which had been built of turf in the Roman manner...Raising her hand to the sky, Boudica said: 'I thank you, Andrasta [the 'Unconquered' goddess], and call out to you as one woman to another...I implore and pray to you for victory and to maintain life and freedom against arrogant, unjust, insatiable, and profane men.'"[328]

Notice here the invocatory posture she adopts, raising hands to sky to implore the goddess for aid. This invocatory posture is mentioned again in Tacitus's account of battle invocations by the British defenders during the Roman invasion of Mona (Anglesey): "On the shore stood the opposing army with its dense array of armed warriors, while between the ranks dashed women, in black attire like the Furies, with hair dishevelled, waving brands. All around, the Druids, lifting up their hands to heaven, and pouring forth dreadful imprecations, scared our soldiers by the unfamiliar sight."[329]

Some similar invocation practices are vividly illustrated in early Irish literature. In *The Siege of Knocklong*, druids turn toward the sky while calling upon their gods for aid in conflict: "Placing his confidence in his gods he directed a druidic breath into the sky and the firmament."[330] In another passage, a druid

---

328. Koch and Carey, *The Celtic Heroic Age*, 43.

329. Tacitus, *Complete Works of Tacitus*, 14,30.

330. Ó Duinn, "The Siege of Knocklong," 36.

seeks aid for victory by "gathering together the full force of his magic powers and invoking his god."[331]

The idea that a tutelary deity could be called upon to aid in battle continues into medieval Irish histories. *The Annals of Ireland* relate that the forces of Leinster "fervently prayed to St. Brighit that they might kill their enemies"; St. Brigit being a patroness of Leinster especially.[332] In that battle and others, she was seen hovering over the field and terrifying the adversaries of Leinster in answer to these prayers. This parallels the classical sources' descriptions of tutelary deities called on for protection and aid in battle.

The Second Battle of Mag Tuired offers an intriguing suggestion for a battle blessing ritual in the Irish tradition. The Morrígan meets and unites with the Dagda before the battle and relates prophetic information relating to battle strategy. She promises to kill Indech, the king of their Fomoiri adversaries, and to take "the blood of his heart and the kidneys of his valour." Then she gives "her two handfuls of that blood to the hosts."[333] To my eye, this sequence has the look and feel of a battle blessing ritual and I can't help wondering whether the saga's authors constructed this mythological scene in part from remnants of folk memory of such ritual. This seems plausible in so far as the use of battle ritual, such as the invocation to St. Brigit, appears to have continued into medieval times in a Christianized form. Whether or not this passage of text reflects historical custom, it can provide inspiration toward constructing rituals of blessing for those facing conflict.

As I reimagine this type of ritual, the Morrígan is being petitioned as war goddess through prayer and a symbolic forging of ties with a person representing the group preparing for battle, which would serve to align the fighters with her power and presence. After this bond is effected, she is asked for a blessing of victory, and this blessing is given with the oracular information on points of strategy in the battle. The detail of the two handfuls of blood suggests to my mind a priest with hands dipped in an offering—perhaps from

---

331. Ó Duinn, "The Siege of Knocklong," 46.

332. Mac Firbisigh, *Annals of Ireland: Three Fragments*, 191.

333. Gray, "Cath Maige Tuired: The Second Battle of Mag Tuired," 46.

sacrifices made to ensure victory, or a substitution such as wine—sprinkling that over the warriors or otherwise marking them with the blood as a victory blessing. Perhaps such bloody marks might represent the "warrior's mark" referenced in some of the lore about Irish warrior customs.[334]

Sorcerer's Toolkit
battle blessiηg rite

Here, I'd like to offer a ritual template loosely inspired by the battle blessings discussed in the previous section. It is a framework for invoking divine aid ahead of conflict, through invocatory prayer, offerings, and a blessing charm received in the form of a mark on the head. This can also be extended to bless the arena in which the conflict will take place, so as to prepare the ground, so to speak, for victory. In my medieval armored combat group, we usually perform a ritual like this one to seek blessing and protection from injury during the fighting. It can also be adapted for the arena of social struggle; for example, prior to a street protest or direct action where there is a risk of violence. Participants in the action can receive the blessing before going out into the street, and if the location of the action is known ahead of time, that battlefield can be surreptitiously blessed with some of the offerings. This ritual template is written for an invocation of Cathubodua, a Gallic war goddess who is related to the Irish Badb Catha; however, you can readily adapt the template to petition whichever gods you trust to call on for aid in conflict. You can recite the Gaulish or the English version of the incantation, or create your own, as you are inclined.

For this rite, you will need:

---

334. Macquarrie, "Insular Celtic Tattooing," 159.

- Tools for cleansing, such as blessing water or sacred smoke.
- Liquid offerings, such as wine, spirits, or another liquid, preferably red.
- Optionally, other offerings for your gods and spirits, such as food or incense.

Begin with cleansing by sprinkling yourself and your space with the blessing water.

Call upon your protective spirits with praise, and asking them to aid in the magic of protection and victory.

Call upon Cathubodua (or whichever gods you trust to aid you in this). Lift your arms to the heavens, and at the same time lift your heart as you pray aloud. Offer praise, speaking reverently and highlighting her powers that you seek to invoke on your behalf. Lift the offerings and consecrate them to her; pour the liquid offerings into a cup or bowl, light the incense, and present any other offerings you have prepared.

Perform the victory blessing. Taking up the cup of liquid offerings, speak this charm over it, visualizing and feeling the deity's power flowing into the cup:

In anuani Cathubodua
Âwûmi umê
Brixtom uritt anxton
Brixtom uritt aglon
Brixtom uritt trougon
Boudion wer suos bieto
In anuani Deuin Cathon
In anuani Rigana Cingeton
In anuani Rigana Toncnamnus
In anuani Cathubodua

Translation: In the name of Cathubodua
I make for you

Spell against pain
Spell against wound
Spell against suffering
Victory be on you
In the name of the The Goddess of Battles
In the name of the Queen of Warriors
In the name of the Queen of Fates
In the name of Cathubodua.[335]

Anoint each participant who wishes to receive the blessing, dipping a finger into the liquid and anointing them on the forehead. You can also bless equipment that you'll use in the field in the same way.

To close, give thanks to Cathubodua and any other spirits who have aided you. Pour out the remaining liquid offerings on the arena where the conflict will take place, to sanctify and prepare it for your cohort. Remember to cleanse yourself again after finishing your ritual.

votive pacts and the evocatio

One of the popular ways to reinforce a battle prayer was to include a votive pact, in which special offerings, gifts, or sacrifices would be promised, to be fulfilled only when the petition was granted with a successful outcome. The votive pact is a form of transactional devotion common in the ancient world, in which a devotee would vow some offering to be made to the deity in the event of a successful outcome or fulfillment of a wish.

Evidence of these votive pacts persists in the many ex-voto artifacts found in excavations—objects marked with inscriptions recording the fulfillment of the devotional pact. The term "ex-voto" comes from the Latin phrase *ex voto suscepto*, meaning "from the vow made" and is more commonly known in the present from Catholic practice, but originates in ancient Rome.[336] Ancient votive inscriptions also commonly included the phrase *votum solvit libens*

---

335. Gaulish text and English translation courtesy of Segomâros Widugeni, personal email communication, April 7, 2015.

336. Derks, "The Ritual of the Vow in Gallo-Roman Religion," 111–114.

merito, often abbreviated *VSLM*, and meaning that the dedicator "has willingly and deservedly fulfilled their vow"—that is to say, the requested blessing had been received, so the offering is earned and is freely given.[337] Variations on this type of inscription sometimes focus less on the vow and more on the offering, such as *SACRUM FLM*, for *sacrum fecit libens merito*, usually referring to a sacrifice and meaning the dedicator "made this sacred offering willingly and deservedly."[338] These dedication formulae are Latin and come from Roman practice, appearing in Gallo-Roman and Romano-British contexts after the conquest. However, the practice of votive pacts and dedications was described as being practiced by the Celts prior to conquest.

It was common to vow that portions or all the captured spoils of a battle would be promised to the gods in the event of a victory. This seems to have been understood as a way to persuade the gods to join the battle on one's side. These offerings could include captured treasure, weapons and armor, war horses and food animals, and even the sacrifice of prisoners as religious offerings. Votive war tributes might sometimes be burned, deposited into lakes, rivers, or bogs, or deposited in temple precincts. Gallic and British sanctuaries contained heaps of deposited treasures, both inside and displayed on palisades and gates.[339]

Authors contemporary with the Gauls note that these hoards of tributes were considered sacred and were displayed without fear of theft, as everyone knew that violation of the sanctuary would bring on a terrible curse. Caesar recorded the practice of votive battle pacts among the Continental Gauls in *The Gallic War*:

> To Mars, when they have determined on a decisive battle,
> they dedicate as a rule whatever spoil they may take. After a
> victory they sacrifice such living things as they have taken,
> and all the other effects they gather into one place. In
> many states heaps of such objects are to be seen piled up in

---

337. Beck, "Goddesses in Celtic Religion," 23.

338. Szabó, "The Reason and Background of the Vota and the Different Formulae," 111–112.

339. Brunaux, *The Celtic Gauls*, 25–33.

hallowed spots, and it has not often happened that a man,
in defiance of religious scruple, has dared to conceal such
spoils in his house or to remove them from their place, and
the most grievous punishment, with torture, is ordained for
such an offence.[340]

Here "Mars" is perhaps a reference to an indigenous god connected with
warfare, who has been syncretized to or identified with the Roman Mars.
Sopater, a Greek philosopher writing in the third century BCE, also mentions
similar practices of dedicating both prisoners and looted treasure as offerings
to the gods in return for victory.[341] The archaeological record in Gaul does
reveal temple sites where treasures had been stored, many showing evidence
of having been captured in battle, just as Caesar states.

To modern polytheist eyes, this type of votive practice can look oddly
transactional or even commodifying. However, it was an extremely common
form of devotional magic in the ancient world. In fact it was so common that
one could ruin an enemy's luck by making their sacrifices fail, as seen in a
Gallo-Roman curse tablet from Rom, in what is now France, which cursed
its target that "He must not be able to sacrifice."[342] That is to say, his votive
offerings would fail to bring him success.

Another way to think about the votive pact is in terms of mitigating risk.
It was a way of seeking to secure committed support from the gods at a time
of need, while at the same time acting as a focused expression of the dedicator's faith and commitment to their relationship with the god. Few things
strengthen trust in a relationship like the mutual fulfillment of a promise; in
this way, a completed votive pact can greatly strengthen the devotional bond.
This type of devotional magic was much emphasized in warfare, as a high-risk
endeavor on which great consequences turned, and that needed the secure
support of the gods. It's also worth remembering that in many instances, one's
adversaries might be expected to be making devotions to the same gods, so it

340. Caesar, *The Gallic War*, 43.

341. Koch and Carey, *The Celtic Heroic Age*, 7.

342. Adams, "Implications of Curse Tablets," 4.

was felt that a great offering might need to be vowed in order persuade the gods to show favor to one's side.

This approach to war magic by votive persuasion of the gods finds some interesting forms in the ancient world. The Romans practiced a variation on votive ritual wherein they would petition the tutelary or tribal gods of an adversary, promising special offerings and devotions should the god abandon the defense of the place or group, and instead support the Romans in battle. This type of votive prayer was called *evocatio*, meaning "calling away."[343] The Roman literature includes several notable instances of this ritual being employed successfully. It presents in some respects as a means of ritually undermining the sovereignty of a people by removing the support of gods whose powers upheld that sovereignty—as when the the Etruscan Uni (a tutelary goddess with a role in the sovereignty of the city) was evoked away from the Veii in 396 BCE.[344] Some scholars indicate that this practice did not originate with the Romans, but in fact was adopted by them from Etruscan religion, or may be part of a more common Indo-European religious inheritance.[345]

It's not clear that *evocatio* was ever employed by the Celtic peoples as such, but its frequency of use by the same Romans they interacted with often in the Continent and Britain suggests they would have been aware of it. Some scholars suggest that ancient peoples of the region were concerned with keeping the true names of their tribal and tutelary deities secret, as a form of protection against *evocatio* being performed against them by adversaries.[346] It is interesting to consider this in light of the cultural habit of some peoples to use indirect epithets to refer to their gods, in what may amount to a prohibition on speaking their names directly. Scholarship has pointed to examples of deity names that may actually be euphemisms, such as Toutatis, which roughly means "the god of our people," and Lugus, which can be interpreted

---

343. Kennedy, "Celts and Romans: The Transformation from Natural to Civic Religion," 23–24.

344. Bruun, "Evocatio Deorum: Some Notes on the Romanization of Etruria," 24.

345. Bruun, "Evocatio Deorum," 109.

346. Bruun, "Evocatio Deorum," 115.

as "the god of the oath."[347] Similarly, the Irish phrase "I swear by the gods my people swear by," may be evidence of a similar prohibition on directly naming the gods of one's tribe. There might be many reasons for such ritual secrecy, but protection against the common war practice of evocation by one's enemies is certainly one of the possibilities.

The Roman historian Livy records an interesting story in which, from the Roman perspective, a Celtic battle deity appears to switch sides to favor the Romans. A splendidly armored Gallic warrior approaches a Roman camp to challenge any soldier there in single combat, a challenge that is taken up by a tribune named Marcus Valerius:

> Just as they were engaging a crow settled all of a sudden on
> the Roman's helmet with its head towards his antagonist.
> The tribune gladly accepted this as a divinely-sent augury,
> and prayed that whether it were god or goddess who had
> sent the auspicious bird that deity would be gracious to him
> and help him. Wonderful to relate, not only did the bird
> keep its place on the helmet, but every time they encoun-
> tered it rose on its wings and attacked the Gaul's face and
> eyes with beak and talon, until, terrified at the sight of so
> dire a portent and bewildered in eyes and mind alike, he was
> slain by Valerius. Then, soaring away eastwards, the crow
> passed out of sight.[348]

Of course, such accounts, written from the perspective of the conquering Romans, can be taken as a type of propaganda; whatever took place there might have been described very differently from the perspectives of the Celts. Given the persistent importance of omens to Celtic peoples, it is clear that they were concerned that the favor of the gods could be turned.

---

347. Delamarre, *Dictionnaire Gauloise*, 295; Koch, "Further to Tongu Do Dia," 254.

348. Livius, *The History of Rome: English Translation*, book 7, s 26.

Story
A Shield Blessing Rite

It's another street action against police brutality. For some years I've been going out with a volunteer street medic crew, supporting the community's public demonstrations with first aid kits, water, and protective gear. Waves of protest activity come and go, increasing whenever there has been a new name added to the list of people murdered by the police without due process—usually Black, Brown or Indigenous folks.

It's 2020 and even in the midst of the uprising sparked by the murder of George Floyd, police here in Oakland are still shooting people. The streets are full of grief and rage. Attacks on protesters with military weapons like tear gas, rubber munitions, concussion grenades, and sound cannons have escalated. We are out almost daily, just trying to support and help keep people safe. Some activists have begun to use shields in the street, to try to fend off police weapons. We've made a set of light wood shields with a strap that a medic's buddy can use to shield them while they try to care for people. I'm painting and preparing them for the street—white with a bold red cross and "MEDIC" inscription. After they're painted we stand them up in the yard to dry and prepare offerings to bless them.

We call on the Morrígan, Badb, and the Badba spirits, pouring offerings into a fire:

> *We ask you to stand with the people as we rise in protest, Great*
> *Queen; watch over all who walk these streets in the pursuit of*
> *justice, grant your protection and your armor to the people,*
> *let them be safe from police violence, shine the Hero's Light on*
> *them. May the munitions of the police fail, may their arms*
> *weaken, may their resolve falter, may they scatter.*

From a previous encounter with the cops, I've collected a spent munition, a foam-covered hard projectile that was shot into a crowd. I hold it now and pour another offering. I speak now to the ancestors and associated spirits of those working in the police force. I speak about the violence, injustice, and murder done by the hands of their descendants; the dishonor and stain to their legacy. I challenge and invite these ancestors to act on the side of justice by standing with the people. It is a kind of *evocatio*: I am calling the spirit allies of the police forces to remove their support and place it behind the protesters.

When I'm done speaking to the spirits, I lay the projectile down on a stack of papers and sprinkle them with drops from the offerings to seal the magic. The papers are copies of a letter addressed to the police, which urges them to see the violent wrong they are participating in, to take the side of justice and quit their jobs. "How did it come to be that instead of keeping people safe you have been used as the instrument of state violence against your own people? Is this what you wanted or what your ancestors wanted for you?" We know that most officers who see this will discard it without thought, but it is a means of delivering the magic of the *evocatio*, and perhaps for a few it might plant a seed of doubt that may grow with time.

Since we know the shields are frequently confiscated during street confrontations, each shield gets a copy of the letter pasted to the back, and so the ancestral magic is also sealed into the shield, which will both protect us and deliver it into their hands. The spent projectile will be slowly dissolved with acids and then left to weather outdoors, with a prayer that the morale and power of the police dissolve with it.

meeting the baḋba

Here I wish to introduce a group of spirits called the Badba, associated with conflict, battlefields, chaos, and prophecy. Badba is the plural form of *badb*, a word from early Irish that can mean a variety of things. It means "crow," but it also can mean "witch," or a generally dangerous, malevolent person or spirit; it's also the name of the war goddess Badb.[349]

Badba are mentioned a number of times in Irish tales about battlefield environments where it's often not clear whether it's describing a flock of crows or a group of spirits or unearthly witchlike beings. Descriptive passages like this one are common: "The scald-crows and the sprites and the wild things of the glen raised hideous, fearful cries…"[350] Or "that band which was wont to accompany Cúchulainn, to wit war-goddesses and sprites and ravenous, red-clawed carrions…"[351] These passages are both from a tale called *The Pursuit of Gruaidh*, but there are many other colorful examples in the corpus of tales.

I understand the Badba as a collective of spirits who are associated with places of conflict; with the war goddesses such as Badb, Cathubodua, and the Morrígan; and with flocks of carrion crows and other beings who are drawn to battlefields. They're also associated with phenomena like battle ardor, the Hero's Light, trauma and madness, and the unquiet dead. They have the power of prophecy and their voices, sounding like the cawing of crows or frightful Otherworldly shrieks, can foretell the outcome of battles and conflicts. They are part of a diverse collective of Otherworldly battle spirits who make up the spirit retinue of Badb and the other war goddesses.

The Badba are powerful allies in war magic and when facing conflict. They can create chaos and noise, and terrify and disrupt enemies. Some of my personal work with them is in connection with my own experiences as a survivor with C-PTSD. These spirits respond to sound, like the noise of clashing weapons, the thrumming of bullroarers, and the blaring of war horns. Their sigil is built from the Celtic letter-signs Corios (for battle, and the beings of the battlefield) and Pritios (for madness and the Hero's Light) and the ogham *fid*, hÚath (for terror and battle spirits). Its shape suggests three crowlike beings spinning or flying through the air. The illustration envisions the Badba

---

349. Royal Irish Academy, "EDIL 2019, s.v. *badb*, dil.ie/5114."

350. O'Rahilly, *Tóruigheacht Gruaidhe Griansholus: The Pursuit of Gruaidh Ghriansholus*, 47.

351. O'Rahilly, *The Pursuit of Gruaidh*, 125.

Sigil Illustration for the Badba

as they're described in the texts, airborne, unmoored from the earth and gravity, dancing and leaping over tips of spears on the battlefield.

THE Clamor of war

The power of sound in warfare has been recognized and exploited by many cultures. In the traditions of the Celtic cultures are many illustrations of how this has been used, both for psychological impact and as part of spiritual and magical practices in the battlefield.

Medieval Irish texts describe the music and war chants of the Fianna—a music called the *dord fianna*. *Dord* means a buzzing, humming, droning, or intonation.[352] Some instances where this music is mentioned it seems to describe chanting:

> *In the pleasant Cruachan assembly,*
> *We sang the chant as we went to the house.*
> *Sweet were the voices of the Fenians;*
> *Everyone was delighted to listen.*[353]

There are also references to something called *crann-dord*, "tree/wood sound," which might refer to low thundering produced by the pounding of wood spear handles: "And we came to the court, and we performed the Dord-Fiansa with the trees (or handles) of our beautiful gold-socketed spears."[354] This wood-song seems to have been performed as an accompaniment or rhythm for vocal music made by warriors: "We chanted with the trees of our spears/ A Dord-Fiansa, with the voice of our men…"[355] In other instances, it seems more linked to the sounds of instruments, droning or hornlike, and in fact the word *dord* is still used in Irish for a large horn with a low droning sound, or for instruments in general that produce sound in the bass range.

---

352. Royal Irish Academy, "EDIL 2019, s.v. 1 *dord*, dil.ie/18319."

353. Pennington, "The Little Colloquy," 103.

354. O'Curry, *On the Manners and Customs of the Ancient Irish*, Vol. III, 409.

355. O'Curry, On the *Manners and Customs of the Ancient Irish*, Vol. III, 380.

It is a music performed by companies of warriors, both in public assemblies and on battlefields, which might include chants blending many voices, punctuated with the clashing of spear shafts and various horns and trumpets. Similar practices are recorded for many other ancient warrior cultures throughout the Iron Age and into historic times. The Greek historian Polybius described an enormous, terrifying roaring noise created by Continental Celtic tribes gathering for battle: "For there were among them countless horns and trumpets which were being blown simultaneously from every part of the army. The sound was so loud and piercing that the clamor didn't seem to come from trumpets and human voices, but from the whole countryside at once."[356] Similarly, Tacitus reported battle music used by Germanic tribes: "The war-song of the men, and the shrill cries of the women, rose from the whole line…"[357]

These musics and soundscapes were used to raise the morale of troops, while attempting also to frighten opponents. In addition to this psychological effect, I would argue that the instruments, songs, and noise also employed a spiritual component that amounts to a form of battle magic. These peoples were highly animistic and would have understood much of their war gear to be inspirited. Many of the horns used in these soundscapes were crafted with animal heads, as with the serpent- and boar-headed carnyces from Tintignac, France, and the boar-headed carnyx from Deskford, Scotland; similar instruments with boar heads are also depicted on the Gundestrup cauldron.[358] As with the anthropomorphic swords and other regalia given faces, it is likely that these animate forms were intended to enshrine and represent the spirits resident in the objects.

It is interesting to note in the medieval Irish sources a recognition of this animate quality of war gear. Weapons are said to produce *armgrith*, "clamor of arms," but this phenomenon is not simply sound.[359] *Grith* means shaking,

---

356. Koch and Carey, *The Celtic Heroic Age*, 9.

357. Beck, "Goddesses in Celtic Religion," 289.

358. Aldhouse-Green, *Caesar's Druids*, 62–63.

359. Borsje, "Omens, Ordeals and Oracles," 239–240.

shuddering, vibration, agitation, or frenzy; specifically of a kind that inspires terror.[360] This effect can be produced by warriors shaking and clashing their weapons, but also weapons are said to leap about of their own as well, indicating that there is a spiritual phenomenon happening here. The shuddering and leaping of these weapons often occurs in association with the appearance of battle spirits and the deities of war, as though their presence stirs up the weapons and armor to shudder and crash, or as if the sound of weapon clamor raised these spirits. It seems to me that these stories reflect a continuing sense that the spirits of battle animated these weapons and the regalia of war, and could be stirred to agitation through the creation of sound, to add their voices and powers to the forces being brought to bear on the battlefield. The rituals to enshrine spirits into these weapons have already been presented in chapter 3, and it's likely that similar spells would be applied to the musical instruments used in the field as well.

When played, the carnyx and similar instruments can create sounds from a low drone, to a thundering roar, to a high shrieking or clear trumpet call, and are shaped so that they tower above the troops and their voices carry across the field. I imagine that in lifting these instruments to sound, they would have been understood to also be raising the spirits of battle who would aid them on the field. One can hardly be in the presence of a singing carnyx without feeling the vibrating presence of such spirits. Similarly, the clashing or pounding of weapons would have the effect of waking the spirits housed in them. No wonder this landscape of sound was terrifying to those who experienced it—it would have been felt as the roaring of a host of spirits accompanying the army that you faced across the field. I have felt something like this at times in the clamor and noise of street protests, sensing in the roar of thousands of voices and noisemakers the presence of the myriad spirits supporting the struggle.

---

360. Royal Irish Academy, "EDIL 2019, s.v. 1 *grith*, dil.ie/26682."

Feats of Intimidation

Early medieval literatures from Ireland and Wales provide a wealth of descriptions of battlefield sorceries. Of course, these stories are mythological, and many scholars would view them as colorful storytelling rather than as reflections of actual historical practices. Still, they provide a rich vein of inspiration for sorcery practices. These accounts frequently dwell on the powerful, intimidating presence of druids or other magic workers at battles. On this point there are both historical and mythological accounts. For example, the Greek historian Diodorus Siculus wrote of their ability to still armies with the spiritual authority of their presence: "Not only during peacetime but also in war, the Gauls obey with great care these Druids and singing poets, both friend and enemy alike. Often when two armies have come together with swords drawn these men have stepped between the battlelines and stopped the conflict, as if they held wild animals spell-bound."[361]

Other accounts speak of terrifying vocal magical performances, such as Tacitus's account of the screaming and chanting of the druids during the invasion of Mona described earlier. Irish mythological accounts seem to draw on a similar cultural memory, describing druids, seers, and other magical operators in action on battlefields, such as at Mag Tuired where "seers and wise men stationed themselves on pillars and points of vantage, plying their sorcery."[362]

Accounts of battlefield customs among the Celts also frequently mention displays of martial performance, a feature shared by both classical descriptions of the Iron Age Gauls and Britons and early medieval accounts of ancient Irish warfare. These accounts describe showy chariot maneuvers, usually followed by spectacular feats of martial athleticism involving running, leaping, and balancing on the yoke or chariot pole as well as displays involving weapons. Of these customs, medieval scholar William Sayers observes:

> On the battlefield as well as in the hall, the element of
> honour-enhancing ostentation is essential in both appear-

361. Koch and Carey, *The Celtic Heroic Age*, 14.
362. Fraser, "The First Battle of Moytura," 43.

ance and behaviour. The exercise of the feats may also have had a ritualistic, hence magical dimension. The feats would complement the boasts, taunts and challenges, these too intended as self-fulfilling. All this evidence meshes well with classical authors' accounts of the Celts' emphasis on personal appearance and showy pre-battle tactics.[363]

Irish tradition refers to these specialized martial feats as *clessa* (singular *cles*), a word that also "had connotations of magic, shape-shifting, artifice, stratagems, deception and trickery."[364] These martial displays are also associated with spiritual phenomena such as the Hero's Light and related transformations.

Thus, while one might be inclined to overlook these martial performances as unmagical, on a closer look they can be recognized as a form of ritualized display that, within an animist culture, would be associated with the performance of battle magic and conjuration of spiritual allies. It would be at the same time both a form of psychological intimidation and spiritual warfare, summoning power and presence, raising spirits, and displaying martial power. To imagine what such a practice might have looked like, consider the Māori war *haka*, a specialized form of ceremonial *haka* dance traditionally performed in advance of combat and made familiar to global audiences through performances before football matches by teams from New Zealand. Indeed, some of the individual Irish *clessa* seem to describe shouting or roaring vocalizations as well as physical maneuvers that sound similar to this Indigenous custom.

Fire, Storm, and Phantom

A recurring theme in war magic is the conjuration of terrifying atmospheric effects. For example, in *The First Battle of Mag Tuired*, the war goddesses Badb, Macha, and the Morrígan attack the Fir Bolg with "magic showers of sorcery and compact clouds of mist and a furious rain of fire, with a downpour of red blood from the air on the warriors' heads," continuing for three days and

---

363. Sayers, "Martial Feats in the Old Irish Ulster Cycle," 68.

364. Sayers, "Martial Feats in the Old Irish Ulster Cycle," 46.

nights.[365] Similar phenomena are conjured by the legendary druid Mug Roith in *The Siege of Knocklong*: attacks of druidic fire, obscuring clouds, and showers of blood. The Mug Roith account is interesting in that it describes the particulars of a ritual. In this ritual, a druidic fire is made against the adversary, by gathering wood from special places in the landscape, which is used to build a magical fire. To this is added shavings from the wood of their spear shafts, and then Mug Roith chants a spell over it:

> *I knead a fire, powerful, strong;*
> *it will level the wood, it will dry up grass;*
> *an angry flame, great its speed*
> *it will rush up, to the heavens above;*
> *it will destroy forests, the forests of the earth,*
> *it will subdue in battle the people of Conn.*[366]

The smoke and flame of this druidic fire is sent up into the sky to turn the omens against their adversaries. It is aided by Mug Roith blowing his magic breath over it, which causes the smoke of the magical fire to rise up and form a dark cloud, from which a rain of blood descends that burns and terrifies them. The effects conjured in these rituals seem to combine both magical and psychological attacks, aiming both to weaken the adversary magically and to terrify them and break morale. This theme continues in the phantom army genre of battle magics.

The phantom army is a host of spectral creatures sent against enemies to confuse and terrify them. Some instances suggest illusions that are conjured simply to confuse an enemy force into turning on each other, or to undermine morale through fear. Others imply spirits have been conjured that may actively attack. From an animist perspective, the distinction is somewhat moot, as anything that can be conjured is animated by a spirit of some kind; the difference is one of effect rather than agency. Many examples of this type of attack exist in the literature. During the twelfth-century Norman conquest,

---

365. Fraser, "The First Battle of Moytura," 27.

366. Ó Duinn, "The Siege of Knocklong," 97–99.

Gerald of Wales recorded a phantom army attack that had a similar effect of terrifying, breaking morale, and shattering the cohesion of the army:

> On one occasion the army was spending the night encamped
> in and around an old fortification in Osraige, and these two
> were sleeping beside each other as was their usual custom.
> Suddenly there were, as it seemed, countless thousands of
> troops rushing upon them from all sides and engulfing all
> before them in the ferocity of their attack. This was accom-
> panied by no small din of arms and clashing of axes, and a
> fearsome shouting which filled the heavens. Apparitions of
> this sort used to occur frequently in Ireland around military
> expeditions. At this terrifying spectacle the greater part of
> the army took to flight and hid, some in the woods, others
> in the bogs.[367]

It is interesting that here the way of invoking this attack is not described, but he seems to recognize it as an example of a known and repeated tactic. Most of Gerald's work is intended as anti-Irish propaganda, and here he is drawing on a recognized folklore tradition to frame Ireland as a place of terrifying supernatural events. The tradition itself, however, seems to run quite deep.

This is vividly illustrated by a phantom army conjured by the daughters of Calatín in a late version of Cú Chulainn's death-tale: "Calatin's offspring therefore gathering hooded sharp-spiked thistles, the light wee puff-balls and the wood's withered fluttering leaves, made of them numerous warriors armour-clad, and of fighting-men bearing battle-weapons, so that around the glen was no hill nor hillock nor whole district but was filled with battalions, with companies of an hundred, and with marshalled bands."[368] This terrifies everyone around and succeeds in its intention to manipulate Cú Chulainn into rushing out into battle unprepared. Similarly, in *The Second Battle of Mag Tuired*, two Túatha Dé sorceresses, Bé Chuille and Díanann, conjure a phantom host

---

367. Mullally, "The Phantom Army," 89.
368. O'Grady, "The Great Defeat on the Plain of Muirthemne Before Cuchullin's Death," 240.

from "the trees and the stones and the sods of the earth," to create terror and scatter the Fomoire adversary.[369] Again in the *Lebor Gabála Érenn*, the sovereignty goddesses Ériu, Fodla, and Banba conjure phantom hosts from sods of the mountain peat against the Sons of Míl.[370] A possibly related account in the medieval Welsh poem *Kat Godeu* describes the enchanter Gwydion conjuring an army of trees to march and attack an adversary.[371]

A running theme throughout many of these examples is of a practitioner who, using incantation, animates elements of the natural world, such as sods of earth, stones, leaves, thistles, or trees, to become a force that moves with the presence, sound, and intimidation of an army. From an animist perspective, these natural elements are already alive, so what the magic here accomplishes is to increase the agency and physicality of the spirits inhabiting these natural materials. There is also a theme of creating noise, chaos, and overwhelming sensory experiences in which psychological intimidation and terror are aligned with spiritual conjuration and magical attack.

Sorcerer's Toolkit
war storm conjuration

In this section, I'll present a ritual template that combines some of the magics in the previous sections. It makes use of the techniques of storm-raising to send a storm fueled by battle spirits to spread confusion and chaos in an adversary. It then directs this chaos to sow division between the members of an adversarial group so that they attack each other. This kind of working can help even the playing field when facing adversaries with greater access to the levers of power. For example, antifascists often speak of the "three way fight," in which advocates of liberation have to contend against two adversaries at

---

369. Gray, "Cath Maige Tuired," 55.

370. Macalister, *Lebor Gabála Érenn*, Part V, 79.

371. Skene, *The Four Ancient Books of Wales*, Volume I, 276–284.

once: the forces of reactionary violence such as militias, paramilitary groups, and fascist gangs; and the forces of state oppression such as the police. This type of magic can help direct those adversarial forces against each other, weakening or dispersing the power of both. It can also be used to cause an adversarial group to turn on itself, wasting its energies and resources tearing itself apart and thereby bringing relief to those who might otherwise be its targets.

The elements of this ritual consist of invoking the divinities and spirits of battle; creating an enchanted fire whose smoke forms the basis for an enchanted storm that is sent against the adversary; and creating a war-vessel in which the adversaries are entrapped with phantoms and caused to attack each other in confusion. It is also possible to employ these different techniques separately. This ritual template is written for working with the Badba, battle spirits, and the Irish war goddess Badb Catha; however, you can adapt a version of this rite that works with other divinities you trust. As with all the rituals in this book, this is intended as a template for you to work from in developing your own practice, and I invite you to make it your own.

Preparations

Location: You will need access to a space where you can have fire. Outdoors is preferable, so that the smoke and the spiritual chaos conjured by the enchanted fire are not brought into your home space. You will also need to be somewhere you can safely make noise as you'll employ sound clamor in the invocation of the battle spirits.

Enchanted fire: The Irish source material describes a fire made with wood gathered from sacred places, and shavings from spear handles. You'll need to prepare these materials in advance of your ritual. In my experience, the wood can be from any place you have established a spiritual connection with; it does not need to be from an ancient or specifically Celtic sacred site. It is about having a rapport with the spirits of place so that the wood carries the strength of the spirits of the land. I also feel that the shavings don't need to be literally from spears—the purpose here is to make a fire of war, so what you need is material taken from a weapon that has been used in conflict. That can be shavings from a spear shaft, or it could be a martial arts practice sword, a protest shield, a bat used against fascists, etc. Prepare before your ritual by laying the firewood in a structure that is ready to light, setting aside the weapon shavings to be added during your ritual.

War-vessel: You will need to prepare a jar or other vessel with a lid that can close. You will also need something to represent your adversaries inside the vessel. If you have an object that carries a personal link to members of the group, or has organizational links such as a logo, insignia, that is ideal. Alternately, you can simply make a little effigy to represent them collectively, similar to what you might use for a curse poppet. You'll also need natural items that will be used to create phantoms that cause confusion. These can be stones, sticks, thistles—natural objects with some resemblance to a figure are ideal. They also should come from a place where you have a spiritual connection and rapport with the land. You'll also need sharp, piercing, and aggravating objects such as nails, thorns, broken glass, and the like; just as you would use in a witch bottle to harass the spirits you entrap in them.

War Storm Ritual

For this ritual, you will need:

- Tools for cleansing, such as blessing water, sacred smoke, and milk.
- Offerings to your protecting spirits, as well as the battle spirits and divinities you will be calling on.
- Noisemakers, such as a bullroarer, weapons to clash together, or other instruments of sound.
- Lighter or matches.

- Wood for the fire.
- Weapon shavings.
- Butter to feed the fire.
- Optional whiskey or other spirits for the fire.
- A jar or vessel with a lid for your war-vessel.
- Objects to represent your adversaries.
- Your phantom figures.
- Sharp, piercing, and aggravating materials.

Begin by cleansing yourself and your tools and working space.

Perform a shield charm over yourself, such as a lorica or caim prayer.

Next, perform invocations. Call on your protecting spirits, with offerings and prayers to gather close and activate their protections over you. Call upon Badb Catha, the war goddess, raising your hands to the sky with prayers of praise, speaking of her battle powers that you seek to call upon, and present your offerings. Call upon the Badba and the host of battle spirits, speaking of their powers to create fear, chaos, and confusion, and raise a clamor of noise to conjure them. Present offerings to them as well.

The next step is to enchant the fire. Standing before the fire pit where your firewood is laid ready to light, address the spirits and conjure them into the fire. You can use an incantation like these lines from Mug Roith's (or write your own):

I knead a fire, powerful, strong;
an angry flame, great its speed
it will rush up, to the heavens above;
it will subdue in battle the people of [your adversaries].

Light the fire, and continue conjuring over it as it catches the wood and builds. Holding the weapon shavings, conjure the battle spirits into them, inviting them to send their powers in to the fire as you sprinkle the shavings into the strengthening fire. Feed the spirit of the fire with offerings of a few pieces of butter placed into the fire. Continue until the fire is going strong and has a good column of smoke.

Send the storm against your enemies. Name them and, if you know it, the place where the spirits will find them. Let yourself be passionate in this, raise your voice, call out against them and why they must be destroyed. Blow your rage into the fire with your breath (taking care to turn away from it when you need to breathe in, so you don't give yourself a smoke inhalation attack). Visualize the smoke of the fire growing into a storm that traverses the sky to rain chaos against your adversary. Optionally, you can take a mouthful of whiskey or other alcoholic spirits and blow it into the fire, which will cause a big flare-up in the fire as you send the storm.

Then it is time to make the war-vessel. Take the vessel and place the effigy or objects representing your adversaries inside it. Name them and instruct them, as you would with charging a curse poppet. You could say, "I name you [Group name], you are all the members of [Group name], you are in the power of the battlefield spirits" or similar words.

Take up the phantom figures, and pass them through the smoke of the enchanted fire. Offer them to the battle spirits, and invite them to take possession of them and inspirit them: "Let these be phantoms to fall upon the people of [Group name], so they are surrounded by terrifying specters and seized by dread and confusion, they know not friend from foe and turn upon each other in chaos and confusion."

Add all the sharp and aggravating things you've gathered, like nails, thorns, broken glass, and anything else aggravating: "Let the people of [Group name] be set upon from all sides, wounded, pierced, terrified, hurt, confused, and in their confusion let them hurt and wound each other so they fall together and fail."

You can also take cooled twigs or ashes from the fire and add them into the vessel too, so that you are including the chaos from the enchanted storm. Just be sure they are fully cooled so that the contents of your vessel don't ignite. When you feel the magic is ready, and you can sense your enemies surrounded and entrapped by the chaos of the storm and phantoms, close the vessel and place it somewhere safe.

To close, thank all the spirits and deities whom you called on for aid. Ask the spirits of the battlefield to go in peace and friendship, so that they aren't hanging around you inviting chaos into your own life. Cleanse yourself and all your tools thoroughly. After rituals like this one, a three-stage cleansing is ideal, such as blessing water followed by sacred smoke and a milk blessing.

After completing this, you can hide or bury the war-vessel somewhere your adversaries will come near it, or you can deposit it in a liminal location such as a crossroads, graveyard, underground site, or in water. On the other hand, if you anticipate doing ongoing work against these adversaries, you can maintain the war vessel and periodically agitate it by adding more aggravating materials, or even add additional enemies into it. If you are keeping it for this purpose, you may wish to wrap it in cloth or place it inside another container, so that it will not bring spiritual contamination into your space.

closing

I thank the reader for joining me on this journey through some of the magics that have both fascinated me and formed the backbone of my sorcery practice. It's my hope that every reader, whether seasoned or new to these practices, might have found something of value in these pages to bring to life in your own practice.

I've said in the opening of this book that Celtic magics are like a bottomless well, which never runs dry and in which there is always another, deeper dimension to explore. Part of what makes this true is that these practices will look different in the hands and heart of each individual sorcerer. In sharing some of the personal stories that are included in this book, I've tried to offer glimpses of what's possible, and hoped to inspire you to think creatively about what these practices might look like for you.

More than any of the specific techniques I've shared here, what I most wanted to pass on is that sense of curiosity—the creative, experimental approach that I've taken to building magical practices rooted in Celtic traditions. To help empower you with the confidence to make this material your own, here I'd like to emphasize a few key working principles that can help you along your way:

Mastering the basics: It's in having mastery of the core practices and safeguards that it becomes possible to experiment in the unpredictable world of spirits and sorcery. So the first principle is to build a strong enough base of practice so you can afford to take risks in trying new things. These core practices are the ones that I began with in the opening chapters of this book—spiritual hygiene and boundaries, protection magic, and basic spirit work. The time you spend developing your habits around these practices is an investment in your own core strength and the strength of your relationships with the spirit world, which will open up the horizons of what is possible for you.

The wellspring of lore: To build a practice rooted in Celtic traditions, you need to drink deeply from the reservoirs of those traditions. I do this not in the pursuit of reconstructing any historical practice, but in order to immerse myself in the worldview and cultural lexicon, so that what I create is shaped by that immersion and carries its imprint. So the principle here is to study and drink deeply from the sources of lore: the early texts, archaeological and historical records, and the living folklore. As you do, look for what lights up for you— what sparks a moment of revelation or imaginal richness, or feels like a sudden glimpse into living ritual in a way that has meaning for you. Find those gleaming golden threads and follow them, seeking ways to weave them into your practice.

A magic of relationship: Animist and polytheist magics are magics of relationship. I spoke about this in the chapter on spirit work and spirit alliances, but I want to emphasize it again here. It's in building your skills in communication with spirits, and in cultivating a strong community of spirit relationships, that it becomes possible to learn magic directly from the spirits and to be guided by them intimately. This is important in a couple of ways. Robust spirit relationships give us greater protection within which we can take risks, and they can also grant us visibility in places we otherwise could not see. And since a great volume of lore and culture of the pagan Celtic world has been lost to history, many things can only be learned from the spirits, who remember it all.

Giving back: It is a gift to be able to learn from and be inspired by the heritage of the Celtic cultures. It's important to respect these gifts by giving something back to the living cultures and peoples who have inherited these traditions, especially if you are in the diaspora and coming to these traditions as an outsider (like myself). This is particularly important when it comes to traditions in the western islands, Ireland, Scotland, and Wales, all of which are living Celtic cultures that have been impacted by imperialism and colonialism. I believe it's important to practice reciprocity and respect by seeking out and materially supporting authors and practitioners of these traditions in their homelands, so that their voices are supported and are never drowned out by those from outside.

Lastly, the reader may have noticed that there are many domains of magic I haven't addressed at all in this book: healing, fertility and the magic of growing things, birth and family magics, hearth magics, wealth magics—the list could go on. It's never been my intention to suggest that these areas of practice don't matter or are less important. The material making up this book is built from my own affinities and areas of focus as a practitioner. No one specializes in everything, and my areas of special focus are certainly shaped by being an activist and lifelong dedicant of a war goddess. I look forward to reading the work of the many other skilled practitioners in Celtic magics who can offer what I cannot. Perhaps that's you, reader, and I hope one day I'll have an opportunity to learn from you.

Glossary of
Non-English Terms

apotropaios: Greek, "to turn away"; having protective power or pertaining to protection magic.

armgrith: Irish, "clamor of arms"; a sound produced by warriors clashing and banging weapons and shields for intimidation; also, a phenomenon where weapons and other war gear were believed to leap about of their own accord when seized by spirits.

aspergillum: Latin, "sprinkler"; an implement for sprinkling holy water.

atchíu: Irish, "I see"; a phrase that appears in mantic poetry and often indicates the start of a prophecy.

awenyddion: Welsh, "inspired people"; referring to people who perform prophecy while in a state of trance possession.

badb (pl. badba): Irish, can refer to a crow, a witch or sorceress, or any generally malevolent person or spirit. When capitalized as Badb, a war goddess. In the plural as badba, generally refers to groups of spirits associated with the battlefield.

bna: Gaulish, "woman"; prefixed in phrases to indicate a female role or quality, such as bnanom brictom, "the magic of women."

ban (also bean): Irish, "woman"; prefixed in phrases to indicate a female role or quality, such as banfaíth, "prophetess"; banfili, "woman-poet."

bean chaointe: Irish, "keening-woman"; a professional mourner who would keen and sing at funerals.

beansidhe (or ban síd): Irish, "fairy woman"; may refer to a female spirit who wails to warn of an impending death; also may refer broadly to any female Otherworldly spirit.

bó: Irish, "cow."

bodhbh chaointe: Irish, "keening crow"; a spectral or Otherworldly crow whose appearance is linked to omens of death; related to the beansidhe.

bricht: Irish, "magic, spell, bewitchment"; also appearing in phrases such as brichtu ban, "the magic of women."

brictom: Gaulish, "magic, enchantment, charm"; also appearing in phrases such as bnanom brictom, "the magic of women"; andernados brictom, "the magic of the underworld."

brídeog: Irish, a woven figure made of grain stalks, husks, or reeds and used as a devotional effigy or magical talisman. Often made in the figure of a woman or girl, the name may refer to the goddess Bríd/Brigid, or to St. Brigit.

búad (pl. búada): Irish, "gift"; in the sense of a special talent, skill, or spiritual power.

búadris: Irish, "victory-tale"; refers to a type of inspired poetry performed after emerging from trance.

caim: Scottish Gaelic, "loop, circle"; a type of shield prayer performed by encircling the body with the hand while praying for protection.

cáintecht: Irish, "satire"; a mode of magical attack through weaponized poetry that was believed to be able to wound, blemish, or harm.

caoineadh: Irish, "keening"; wailing or singing performed for the dead in a funerary context and believed to aid in the spirit's crossing to the Otherworld.

carnyx (pl. carnyces): Gaulish, "trumpet"; a type of long war trumpet used in ceremony and on the battlefield, often made of highly decorated metalwork or with a head shaped like an animal's.

clairín búirthe: Irish, "little roaring stick"; a bullroarer.

cles (pl. clessa): Irish, "feat, performance of feats"; usually describes a display of martial prowess through spectacular feats of athleticism or weapon skill.

coelbren: Welsh, "omen stick"; wooden staves used for divination.

cóir: Irish, "rightness, order, justice"; used in contemporary practice to refer to a spiritual worldview that sees the existence of a right order oriented around justice, in which actions in the service of justice have the support of the spiritual powers that animate the cosmos.

corrguinecht: Irish, "sharp wounding," or "crane wounding"; a poetic technique and ritual practice for cursing, in which poetic satire is performed while standing on one foot, using one hand, and looking through one eye.

crandchur: Irish, "casting in wood"; divination through drawing of lots, usually using inscribed wands of wood.

defixio (pl. defixiones): Latin, a curse tablet; from a verb meaning "to bind, to fasten down." Refers to the tradition of performing binding curses by inscribing them on small tablets, usually of soft metal such as lead.

deiseal: Irish, "direction of the sun, right-hand-wise"; movement in a right-turning or clockwise direction, aligned with the direction of the sun's movement in the sky; associated with luck-bringing, and the blessings of numinous powers.

dord: Irish, "drone, intonation, low sound"; used to describe chanting, droning music made by low horns, or the instruments used to make such sounds. As in dord fianna, the war chants or droning music made by the warrior bands.

erinyes: Greek, "furies"; vengeful spirits involved with the punishment of oath-breakers or perjurers.

evocatio: Latin, "calling away"; a ritual developed by Rome using votive prayer in which special offerings or devotional commitments were made to the gods of an adversary in war, in order to persuade those gods to remove divine support for the adversary and instead give victory to those performing the ritual.

fiachairecht: Irish, "raven-lore"; a form of divination by augury through observing and interpreting the behavior of ravens.

fid (pl. feda): Irish, "wood, stave, letter of an alphabet"; refers to the individual letters of the ogham script, which are often inscribed on wood staves.

fidlanna: Irish, "wood-divination"; a divination practice using inscribed staves of wood.

fili (pl. filid): Irish, "poet, seer"; an expert in poetry, also refers to the official role of poet-seer who served chieftains and kings.

fír flathemon: Irish, "truth of a sovereign, justice of a ruler"; a phrase describing both the obligation of a ruler to deliver justice, and the belief that the justice of the ruler would be reflected in the condition of the land. An unjust king would result in famine and loss of prosperity, showing the "truth" of their rulership in the land itself.

galdrastafir: Icelandic, "spell stave"; a style of medieval magical sigils found in Icelandic grimoires and incorporating runic and possibly ogham influences.

geis (pl. geasa): Irish, "prohibition, injunction"; a ritualized prohibition or injunction that binds a person from certain actions or obligates them to other actions; associated with oaths and binding prayers and, when broken, could lead to a person's destruction.

glam dicenn: Irish, "outcry of extremity"; refers to a form of severe poetic satire that could cause blemishing, harm, or destruction.

id: Irish, "fetter, withe, hoop"; a fetter that could be made from leather, chain, or wickerwork and used to bind the feet of livestock; also can used as a symbolic binding in legal distraint and in binding spells.

imbas forosnai: Irish, "knowledge that illuminates"; refers to the pinnacle of poetic mastery in which the practitioner could enter an inspired state and perform spontaneous poetry in perfect meter; associated with prophetic ability.

lorica: Latin, "breastplate"; in folk magic, refers to a type of protection prayer in which spiritual protection is invoked across the parts of the body like armor.

nemed: Irish, "sacred, holy"; designates sacred places as well as the privileged social class and religious functions associated with them.

óenach: Irish, "funerary games"; annual or periodic festivals typically held at royal sites or other major ritual centers from ancient times into the medieval period.

ogham: Irish; a script used in Ireland and Britain from the late Iron Age into the medieval period, consisting of horizontal and diagonal strokes crossing a foundation line; in modern times, also a divination system using these letters.

prinnos (pl. prinni): Gaulish, "tree, wood, stave"; also used of the lots cast in divination by sortilege. In this book, also refers to individual letters of the Viduveletia divination system.

ráth: Irish, "earthen rampart"; a protective boundary, usually circular, composed of a ditch and bank.

rosc: Irish, "poem, chant," also "eye"; usually refers to a poetic metrical form charaterized by short lines of alliterative, unrhymed poetry, considered to be a very ancient poetic form and associated with both prophecy and legal authority.

sian: Scottish Gaelic; a charm, usually protective, which may involve a spoken blessing as well as talismanic objects worn on the body.

bullaun: Irish; stones usually of a cobble size, which traditionally sit in hollows of larger stones at holy sites, and are associated with folk magic customs.

tarb feis: Irish, "bull feast"; a divination ritual involving the sacrifice of a bull and consumption of its meat in preparation for incubation of prophetic dreams.

vates: Gaulish, a ritual office associated with the druids and concerned with divination and the making of sacrifices.

viduveletia: Gaulish, "wood-seeing"; a modern divination system using staves inscribed with Gaulish Lepontic letters for divination by sortilege.

bibliography

Adams, Geoff W. "The Social and Cultural Implications of Curse Tablets [Defixiones] in Britain and on the Continent." *Studia Humaniora Tartuensia* 7, no. A.5 (2006): 1–15.

Aldhouse-Green, Miranda. *Caesar's Druids: Story of an Ancient Priesthood.* New Haven: Yale University Press, 2010.

Armao, Frédéric. "Cathair Crobh Dearg: From Ancient Beliefs to the Rounds 2017." *Estudios Irlandeses* 12, no. 2 Special Issue (2017): 8–31.

Armit, Ian. *Headhunting and the Body in Iron Age Europe.* Cambridge: Cambridge University Press, 2012.

———. "Porticos, Pillars and Severed Heads: The Display and Curation of Human Remains in the Southern French Iron Age." In *Body Parts and Bodies Whole: Changing Relations and Meanings*, edited by Katharina Rebay-Salisbury, Marie Louise Stig Sørensen, and Jessica Hughes, 88–99. Oxford: Oxbow Books, 2010.

Beck, Noémie. "Goddesses in Celtic Religion—Cult and Mythology: A Comparative Study of Ancient Ireland, Britain and Gaul." PhD thesis, Université Lumière Lyon, 2009.

Bernhardt-House, Phillip A. "Imbolc: A New Interpretation." *Cosmos* 18 (2002): 57–76.

Best, R. I. "Prognostications from the Raven and the Wren." *Ériu* 8 (1916): 120–26.

Black, George Fraser. *Scottish Charms and Amulets. Proceedings of the Society of Antiquaries of Scotland*. Edinburgh: Neill and Company, 1894.

Black, Ronald, ed. *The Gaelic Otherworld*. Edinburgh: Birlinn, 2005.

———. "A Scottish Gaelic Charm in the North Carolina State Archives." *The North Carolina Historical Review* 84, no. 1 (2007): 37–58.

Borsje, Jacqueline. "Celtic Spells and Counterspells." In *Understanding Celtic Religion: Revisiting the Pagan Past*, edited by Katja Ritari and Alexandra Bergholm, 9–50. Cardiff: University of Wales Press, 2015.

———. "'The Evil Eye' in Early Irish Literature and Law." *Celtica* 24 (2003): 1–39.

———. "Omens, Ordeals and Oracles: On Demons and Weapons in Early Irish Texts." *Peritia: Journal of the Medieval Academy of Ireland* 13 (1999): 224–48.

———. "Supernatural Threats to Kings: Exploration of a Motif in the Ulster Cycle and in Other Medieval Irish Tales." *Ulidia* 2 (2009): 173–94.

Boyle, Elizabeth. "On the Wonders of Ireland: Translation and Adaptation." In *Authorities and Adaptations: The Reworking and Transmission of Textual Sources in Medieval Ireland*, 233–61. Dublin: Dublin Institute for Advanced Studies, 2014.

Brunaux, Jean-Louis. *The Celtic Gauls: Gods, Rites and Sanctuaries*. Translated by Daphne Nash. London: Seaby, 1988.

Bruun, Patrick. "Evocatio Deorum: Some Notes on the Romanization of Etruria." *Scripta Instituti Donneriani Aboensis* 6 (1972): 109–120.

Budd, Elsie G., and Leslie F. Newman. "Knuckle-Bones: An Old Game of Skill." *Folklore* 52, no. 1 (1941): 8–17.

Butler, Jenny. "Water Monsters in Irish Folklore." *Journal of the Cork Folklore Project*, no. 19 (2015): 8–9.

Caesar, Julius. *The Gallic War*. Edited by H. J. Edwards. Cambridge: Harvard University Press, 1958.

Campbell, John Gregorson. *Superstitions of the Highlands & Islands of Scotland*. Glasgow: James MacLehose and Sons, 1900.

———. *Witchcraft & Second Sight in the Highlands & Islands of Scotland*. Glasgow: James MacLehose and Sons, 1902.

Carey, John. "Charms in Medieval Irish Tales: Tradition, Adaptation, Invention." In *Charms, Charmers and Charming in Ireland: From the Medieval to the Modern*, edited by Ilona Tuomi, John Carey, Barbara Hillers, and Ciarán Ó Gealbháin, 17–37. Cardiff: University of Wales Press, 2019.

———. "The Encounter at the Ford: Warriors, Water and Women." *Eigse: A Journal of Irish Studies* 34 (2004): 10–24.

———. "Ogmios and the Eternal Word." *Cosmos* 30 (2014): 1–36.

———. "The Testimony of the Dead." *Eigse: A Journal of Irish Studies* 26 (1992): 1–12.

———. "The Three Things Required of a Poet." *Ériu* 48 (1997): 41–58.

Carmichael, Alexander. *Carmina Gadelica, Vol. II*. Edinburgh: T. & A. Constable, 1900.

———. *Carmina Gadelica, Vol. III*. Edinburgh: Oliver and Boyd, 1940.

Carmody, Isolde. "Poems of the Morrigan." Story Archaeology Podcast, 2013.

———. "Thesis, Antithesis, Synthesis: An Examination of Three Rosc Passages from Cath Maige Tuired." M. Phil. thesis, Trinity College Dublin, 2004.

Carmody, Isolde, and Chris Thompson, "Some questions answered by the Story Archaeologists," November 25, 2018, on *Story Archaeology Podcast*,

https://storyarchaeology.com/some-questions-answered-by-the-story
-archaeologists/.http://storyarchaeology.com/poems-of-the-morrigan/.

Chadbourne, Kathryn. "Giant Women and Flying Machines." *Proceedings of the Harvard Celtic Colloquium* 14 (1994): 106–14.

Chadwick, Nora K. "Imbas Forosnai." *Scottish Gaelic Studies* 4, no. 2 (1935): 97–135.

Charles-Edwards, T. M. "Geis, Prophecy, Omen, and Oath." *Celtica* 23 (1999): 38–59.

Corthals, Johan. "Early Irish Retoirics and Their Late Antique Background." *Cambrian Medieval Celtic Studies* 31 (1996): 17–36.

Coyne, Frank. *Islands in the Clouds: An Upland Archaeological Study on Mount Brandon and the Paps, County Kerry.* Kerry County Council, 2006.

Delamarre, Xavier. *Dictionnaire de La Langue Gauloise.* Paris: Éditions Errance, 2003.

Derks, Ton. "The Ritual of the Vow in Gallo-Roman Religion." In *Integration in the Early Roman West: The Role of Culture and Ideology*, edited by Jeannot Metzler, 111–27. Luxembourg: Musée national d'histoire et d'art, 1997.

Discovery Programme—Centre for Archaeology and Innovation Ireland. "Ogham in 3D," 2021. Accessed December 12, 2021. https://ogham .celt.dias.ie/.

Dobbs, M E. "The Battle of Findchorad." *Zeitschrift Für Celtische Philologie* 14 (1923): 395–420.

Dolan, Brian. "Mysterious Waifs of Time: Some Thoughts on the Functions of Irish Bullaun Stones." *The Journal of the Royal Society of Antiquaries of Ireland* 142/143 (2012): 42–58.

Dowd, Marion. *The Archaeology of Caves in Ireland.* Oxford: Oxbow Books, 2015.

Duff, J. D. *Silius Italicus: Punica.* London: William Heinemann Ltd., 1961.

Enright, Michael J. *Lady with a Mead Cup: Ritual, Prophecy and Lordship in the European Warband from La Tène to the Viking Age.* Dublin: Four Courts Press, 2013.

Forsyth, Katherine. "The Ogham-Inscribed Spindle-Whorl from Buckquoy: Evidence for the Irish Language in Pre-Viking Orkney?" *Proceedings of the Society of Antiquaries of Scotland* 125 (1995): 677–96.

Fraser, J. "The First Battle of Moytura." *Ériu* 8 (1916): 1–63.

Ghezal, Salma, Elsa Ciesielski, Benjamin Girard, Aurélien Creuzieux, Peter Gosnell, Carole Mathe, Cathy Vieillescazes, and Réjane Roure. "Embalmed Heads of the Celtic Iron Age in the South of France." *Journal of Archaeological Science* 101 (January 1, 2019): 181–88.

Gilchrist, Roberta. "Magic for the Dead? The Archaeology of Magic in Later Medieval Burials." *Medieval Archaeology* 52 (2008): 119–59.

Grant, Kenneth. "Austin Osman Spare: An Introduction to His Psycho-Magical Philosophy." *Pastelegram* 8 (2014).

Gray, Elizabeth A. "Cath Maige Tuired: The Second Battle of Mag Tuired." *CELT: Corpus of Electronic Texts*, 2003. http://www.ucc.ie/celt/published/T300010.html.

Gwynn, Edward. "The Metrical Dindshenchas Volume 3." *CELT: Corpus of Electronic Texts*, 2008. http://www.ucc.ie/celt/published/T106500C/index.html.

———. "The Metrical Dindshenchas Volume 4." *CELT: Corpus of Electronic Texts*, 2008.Accessed April 16, 2014. https://celt.ucc.ie/published/T106500D/index.html.

Haeussler, Ralph. "From Tomb to Temple: On the Role of Hero Cults in Local Religions in Gaul and Britain in the Iron Age and the Roman Period." In *Celtic Religion across Space and Time*, edited by J. Alberto Arenas-Esteban, 201–26. Toledo: Junta de Comunidades de Castilla-La Mancha, 2010.

Henry, P. L. "The Goblin Group." *Études Celtiques* 8 (1959): 404–16.

———. "Verba Scathaige." *Celtica* 21 (1990): 191–207.

Hernández, Diego González. "The Apotropaic Function of Celtic Knotwork in the Book of Kells." Universidad de Valladolid, 2015.

Hickey, Kieran. *Wolves in Ireland: A Natural and Cultural History*. Dublin: Open Air, 2013.

Hillers, Barbara. "Towards a Typology of European Narrative Charms in Irish Oral Tradition." In *Charms, Charmers and Charming in Ireland: From the Medieval to the Modern*, edited by Ilona Tuomi, John Carey, Barbara Hillers, and Ciarán Ó Gealbháin, 79–102. Cardiff: University of Wales Press, 2019.

Hoggard, Brian. *Magical House Protection: The Archaeology of Counter-Witchcraft*. Berghahn Books, 2019.

Institute of Archaeology—University College London. "Celtic Inscribed Stones Project." Celtic Inscribed Stones: Language, Location and Environment, 1999. https://www.ucl.ac.uk/archaeology/cisp/database/.

Katla UNESCO Global Geopark. "Paradísarhellir." Katla Geopark, 2021. https://www.katlageopark.com/geosites/paradisarhellir/.

Kelly, Eamonn P. "An Archaeological Interpretation of Irish Iron Age Bog Bodies." In *The Archaeology of Violence: Interdisciplinary Approaches*, edited by Sarah Ralph, 232–40. Albany: State University of New York, 2012.

Kelly, Fergus. *A Guide to Early Irish Law*. Dublin: Dublin Institute for Advanced Studies, 2003.

Kennedy, Matthew Taylor. "Celts and Romans: The Transformation from Natural to Civic Religion." James Madison University, 2012.

Kinsella, Thomas. *The Táin: Translated from the Irish Epic Táin Bó Cúailnge*. Oxford: Oxford University Press, 1969.

Koch, John T. "Further to Tongu Do Dia Toinges Mo Thuath, &c." *Études Celtiques* 29 (1992): 249–261.

Koch, John T., and John Carey. *The Celtic Heroic Age: Literary Sources for Ancient Celtic Europe and Early Ireland & Wales*. Aberystwyth: Celtic Studies Publications, 2003.

Lambert, Pierre-Yves. "Celtic Loricae and Ancient Magical Charms." In *Magical Practice in the Latin West*, 629–47. Leiden: Brill, 2010.

Leahy, A. H. *Heroic Romances of Ireland, Vol I*. Edinburgh & London: Ballantyne, Hanson & Co., 1905.

———. *Heroic Romances of Ireland, Vol II*. Edinburgh & London: Ballantyne, Hanson & Co., 1906.

Lennon, John. "Fairs and Assemblies in Ireland." *Before I Forget: Poyntzpass and District Local History Society* 2 (1988): 55–62.

Lincoln, Bruce. "The Druids and Human Sacrifice." In *Languages and Cultures: Studies in Honor of Edgar C. Polome*, edited by Mohammad Ali Jazayery and Werner Winter, 381–96. Berlin: Mouton de Gruyter, 1988.

Livesay, Nora, and John D. Nichols. "The Ojibwe People's Dictionary," 2012. Accessed August 12, 2021. https://ojibwe.lib.umn.edu/.

Livius, Titus (Livy). *The History of Rome: English Translation*. Edited by Canon Roberts. New York: E. P. Dutton and Co, 1912.

Lysaght, Patricia. "Aspects of the Earth-Goddess in the Traditions of the Banshee in Ireland." In *The Concept of the Goddess*, edited by Sandra Billington and Miranda Green, 152–65. London: Routledge, 1996.

Mac Coitir, Niall. *Ireland's Wild Plants*. Cork: The Collins Press, 2015.

Mac Firbisigh, Dubhaltach. *Annals of Ireland: Three Fragments*. Dublin: Irish Archaeological and Celtic Society, 1860.

Macalister, R. A. S. *Lebor Gabála Érenn: The Book of the Taking of Ireland, Part V*. Dublin: Irish Texts Society, 1956.

———. "Temair Breg: A Study of the Remains and Traditions of Tara." *Proceedings of the Royal Irish Academy* 34 (1919): 231–404.

Macleod, Norman (Caraid nan Gaidheal). *Cuairtear Nan Gleann*. Glasgow: J. & P. Campbell, 1842.

Macquarrie, Charles. "Insular Celtic Tattooing: History, Myth and Metaphor." *Etudes Celtiques* 33 (1997): 159–89.

Mallory, J.P. *In Search of the Irish Dreamtime*. London: Thames & Hudson, 2016.

McCoy, Narelle. "Madwoman, Banshee, Shaman: Gender, Changing Performance Contexts and the Irish Wake Ritual." In *Musical Islands:*

Exploring Connections Between Music, Place and Research, edited by Elizabeth Mackinlay, Brydie-Leigh Bartleet, and Katelyn Barney, 207–20. Newcastle: Cambridge Scholars, 2009.

McKie, S. "The Social Significance of Curse Tablets in the North-Western Provinces of the Roman Empire." PhD thesis, The Open University, 2017.

McNeill, F. Marian. *Silver Bough Volume 1*. eBook Partnership, 2013.

Mees, Bernard. *Celtic Curses*. Kindle. Woodbridge: The Boydell Press, 2009.

Merriam-Webster. "Merriam-Webster.Com Dictionary." Accessed December 16, 2021. https://www.merriam-webster.com.

Meyer, Kuno. "The Adventures of Nera." *Revue Celtique* 10 (1889): 212–28.

———. *Cath Finntraga*. Oxford: Clarendon Press, 1885.

———. *Fianaigecht*. Dublin: Hodges, Figgis & Co. Ltd., 1910.

———. *Hibernica Minora*. Oxford: Clarendon Press, 1894.

———. "The Instructions of King Cormac Mac Airt: Tecosca Cormaic." *CELT: Corpus of Electronic Texts*, 2017. https://celt.ucc.ie/published /T503001/.

———. "An Old Irish Prayer for Long Life." In *A Miscellany Presented to John Macdonald Mackay, LL.D., July, 1914*, edited by Oliver Elton, 226–232. Liverpool: University Press, 1914.

———. *The Triads of Ireland*. Dublin: Hodges, Figgis, & Co., Ltd., 1906.

———. "The Wooing of Emer." *Archaeological Review* 1 (1888): 68–75; 150–155; 231–235; 298–307.

Moriarty, Colm. "An Unusual Ogham and Runic Inscription from Killaloe, Co. Clare." Irish Archaeology, 2019. http://irisharchaeology.ie/2019/02 /an-unusual-ogham-and-runic-inscription-from-killaloe-co-clare/.

Mullally, Evelyn. "The Phantom Army of 1169: An Anglo-Norman View." *Eigse: A Journal of Irish Studies* 31 (1999): 89–101.

Museum of Cultural History—University of Oslo. "The Origin and Development of Runes." Kiss me – the world of runes, 2021. https://www .khm.uio.no/english/visit-us/historical-museum/exhibitions-archive /kiss-me-the-world-of-runes/the-origin-and-development-of-runes/.

Museum of Icelandic Sorcery and Witchcraft. "Magical Staves." Galdrasyning.is, 2021. https://galdrasyning.is/en/galdrastafir/.

Museum of Witchcraft and Magic. "3079 Cursing Stick: Ill-Wishing Stick." Museum of Witchcraft and Magic, 2021. https://museumofwitchcraftandmagic.co.uk/object/cursing-stick-ill-wishing-stick/.

National Folklore Collection UCD. "The Schools' Collection." Dúchas, 2021. Accessed Aug 12, 2021. https://www.duchas.ie/en.

National Museum of Ireland. "A New Theory of Sacrifice." Kingship & Sacrifice, 2020. Accessed August 12, 2021. https://www.museum.ie/en-IE/Collections-Research/Irish-Antiquities-Division-Collections/Collections-List-(1)/Iron-Age/Kingship-Sacrifice-A-New-Theory-of-Sacrifice.

Nelson, Max. *The Barbarian's Beverage: A History of Beer in Ancient Europe.* London: Routledge, 2005.

Ó Duinn, Sean. "The Siege of Knocklong." *CELT: Corpus of Electronic Texts,* 2014. http://www.ucc.ie/celt/published/T301044/.

Ó hÓgáin, Dáithí. *The Celts: A History.* Cork: The Collins Press, 2002.

———. *The Sacred Isle: Belief and Religion in Pre-Christian Ireland.* Woodbridge: The Boydell Press, 1999.

O'Connor, Ralph. *The Destruction of Da Derga's Hostel: Kingship and Narrative Artistry in a Mediaeval Irish Saga.* Oxford: Oxford University Press, 2013.

O'Curry, Eugene. *On the Manners and Customs of the Ancient Irish, Vol. II.* Dublin: Williams and Norgate, 1873.

———. *On the Manners and Customs of the Ancient Irish, Vol. III.* Dublin: Williams and Norgate, 1873.

———. "The Sick-Bed of Cuchulainn and the Only Jealousy of Emer." *Atlantis* 1–2 (1858): 362–369, 98–124.

O'Grady, Standish Hayes. "The Great Defeat on the Plain of Muirthemne Before Cuchullin's Death." In *The Cuchullin Saga in Irish Literature,* edited by Eleanor Hull, 237–49. London: David Nutt, 1898.

———. *Silva Gadelica (I–XXXI): A Collection of Tales in Irish, Vol. 2: Translation and Notes*. London: Williams and Norgate, 1892.

Olmsted, Garrett. *The Gods of the Celts and the Indo-Europeans*. Budapest: Innsbruck, 1994.

O'Rahilly, Cecile. "Táin Bó Cúalnge from the Book of Leinster." *CELT: Corpus of Electronic Texts*, 2010. https://celt.ucc.ie/published/T301035/.

———. "Táin Bó Cúalnge Recension 1." *CELT: Corpus of Electronic Texts*, 2011. Accessed December 3, 2014. http://www.ucc.ie/celt/published /T301012/index.html.

———. *Tóruigheacht Gruaidhe Griansholus: The Pursuit of Gruaidh Ghriansholus*. London: Irish Texts Society, 1924.

O'Sullivan, Aidan. "Magic in Early Medieval Ireland." *Ulster Journal of Archaeology* 74 (2017): 107–17.

Pennington, Walter. "The Little Colloquy." *Philological Quarterly* IX, no. 2 (1930): 97–110.

Pliny the Elder. "Book XXXIV: The Natural History of Metals." In *The Natural History*, edited by John Bostock. London: Taylor and Francis, 1855.

Polson, Alexander. *Scottish Witchcraft Lore*. W. Alexander & Son, 1932.

Powell, Eric A. "Wolf Rites of Winter." *Archaeology*, September 2013.

Richardson-Read, Scott. "Skyrie Stanes." The Cailleach's Herbarium, 2018.

Ronan, Laurel. "Daily Purification." Unfettered Wood, Jauary 7, 2019. https://unfetteredwood.blogspot.com/2019/01 /daily-purification-and-some.html.

Ross, Anne. *Pagan Celtic Britain: Studies in Iconography and Tradition*. Chicago: Academy Chicago Publishers, 1996.

Royal Irish Academy. "EDIL 2019: An Electronic Dictionary of the Irish Language, Based on the Contributions to a Dictionary of the Irish Language." 2019. www.dil.ie.

Royal Irish Academy. "The Book of Ballymote." *Irish Script on Screen*, 2003. https://www.isos.dias.ie/libraries/RIA/RIA_MS_23_P_12/english /catalogue.html.

———. "Tírechán's Text in English (Transl. L. Bieler)." Saint Patrick's Confessio, accessed 3 11, 20212011. https://www.confessio.ie/more/tirechan_english#.

Sayers, William. "Extraordinary Weapons, Heroic Ethics, and Royal Justice in Early Irish Literature." *Preternature: Critical and Historical Studies on the Preternatural* 2, no. 1 (2013): 1–18.

———. "Martial Feats in the Old Irish Ulster Cycle." *Canadian Journal of Irish Studies* 9, no. 1 (1983): 45–80.

Serjeantson, D., and J. Morris. "Ravens and Crows in Iron Age and Roman Britain." *Oxford Journal of Archaeology* 30, no. 1 (2011): 85–107.

Sherwood, Amy. "An Bó Bheannaithe: Cattle Symbolism in Traditional Irish Folklore, Myth, and Archaeology." *PSU McNair Scholars Online Journal* 3, no. 1 (2009): 189–225.

Skene, William F. *The Four Ancient Books of Wales, Volume I.* Edinburgh: Edmonston and Douglas, 1868.

Smithsonian Institution. "Native American Relationships to Animals: Not Your 'Spirit Animal.'" Native Knowledge 360°, 2021. Accessed August 12, 2021. https://americanindian.si.edu/nk360/informational/native-american-spirit-animal.

Society of Antiquaries of Scotland. "Donations to and Purchases for the Museum, 1943-44." *Proceedings of the Society of Antiquaries of Scotland* 78, no. 9 (1943): 139–44.

Stacey, Robin Chapman. *Dark Speech: The Performance of Law in Early Ireland.* Philadelphia: University of Pennsylvania Press, 2007.

Stifter, David. "Ancient Celtic Epigraphy and Its Interface with Classical Epigraphy." In *Sprachen – Schriftkulturen – Identitäten Der Antike. Beiträge Des XV Internationalen Kongresses Für Griechische Und Lateinische Epigraphik*, edited by Petra Amann, Thomas Corsten, Fritz Mitthof, and Hans Taeuber, Nr. 10:97–123. Wien: Holzhausen, 2019.

———. *Sengoídelc: Old Irish for Beginners.* Syracuse, New York: Syracuse University Press, 2006.

Stokes, Whitley. *Acallamh Na Senórach*. Edited by W.H. Stokes and E. Windisch. Leipzig: Verlag Von S. Hirzel, 1900.

———. "The Battle of Allen." *Revue Celtique* 24 (1903): 41–67.

———. "Cóir Anmann (Fitness of Names)." In *Irische Text Mit Wörterbuch*, 288–411. Leipzig: Verlag Von S. Hirzel, 1897.

———. "Da Choca's Hostel." *Revue Celtique* 21 (1900): 149–75, 312–28, 388–404.

———. "The Destruction of Da Derga's Hostel." *CELT: Corpus of Electronic Texts*, Feb 19 2014 accessed 2009. http://www.ucc.ie/celt/published /T301017A/index.html.

———. "The Destruction of Dind Rig." *Zeitschrift Für Celtische Philologie* 3 (1901): 1–14.

———. "The Edinburgh Dinnshenchas." *Thesaurus Linguae Hibernicae*, 2007. Accessed Aug 12, 2021. https://www.ucd.ie/tlh/trans/ws.fl.4.001 .t.text.html.

———. "In Cath Catharda: The Civil War of the Romans." *CELT: Corpus of Electronic Texts*, 2010. http://www.ucc.ie/celt/published/T305001 /index.html.

———. "The Irish Ordeals, Cormac's Adventure in the Land of Promise, and the Decision as to Cormac's Sword." *CELT: Corpus of Electronic Texts*, 2015. https://celt.ucc.ie/published/T302000/.

———. "O'Davoren's Glossary." *Archiv Fur Celtische Lexikographie* II (1901): 197–504.

———. "The Prose Tales in the Rennes Dindshenchas." *Thesaurus Linguae Hibernicae*, 2008. Accessed Jan, 8, 2013.https://www.ucd.ie/tlh/trans /ws.rc.16.001.t.text.html.

———. *Three Irish Glossaries*. London: Williams and Norgate, 1862.

Swift, Catherine. "The Gods of Newgrange in Irish Literature & Romano-Celtic Tradition." In *Stones and Bones: Formal Disposal of the Dead in Atlantic Europe during the Mesolithic-Neolithic Interface 6000-3000 BC*, edited by Goran Burenhult and Susanne Westergaard. Sligo, Ireland: Archaeopress, 2002.

Szabó, Ádám. "The Reason and Background of the Vota and the Different Formulae." *Carnuntum Jahrbuch*, 2017, 109–14.

Tacitus. *Complete Works of Tacitus*. Edited by Alfred John Church, William Jackson Brodribb, and Sara Bryant. New York: Random House, 1942.

Toner, Gregory. "Macha and the Invention of Myth." *Ériu* 60 (2010): 81–109.

Towrie, Sigurd. "Orcadian Childbirth Traditions." *Orkneyjar: The Heritage of the Orkney Islands*, 2013. Accessed Aug, 12, 2021. http://www.orkneyjar.com/tradition/childbirth.htm.

Tuomi, Ilona. "Parchment, Praxis and Performance of Charms in Early Medieval Ireland." *Incantatio: An International Journal on Charms, Charmers and Charming* 3 (2013): 60–85. https://doi.org/10.7592/Incantatio2013.

Tymoczko, Maria. *Two Death Tales from the Ulster Cycle: The Death of Cu Roi & The Death of Cu Chulainn*. Dublin: The Dolmen Press, 1981.

University of Edinburgh Centre for Research Collections. "Gaelic Battle Charms—1." *The Carmichael Watson Project*, 2012. http://carmichaelwatson.blogspot.com/2012/02/gaelic-battle-charms-1.html.

Urbanová, Daniela. *Latin Curse Tablets of the Roman Empire*. Innsbruck: Innsbrucker Beiträge zur Kulturwissenschaft, 2018.

Versnel, Henk. "Beyond Cursing: The Appeal to Justice in Judicial Prayers." In *Magika Hiera: Ancient Greek Magic and Religion*, edited by C.A. Faraone and D. Obbink, 117–33. New York: Oxford University Press, 1991.

Volmering, Nicole. "The Second Vision of Adomnán." In *The End and Beyond: Medieval Irish Eschatology*, edited by John Carey, Emma Nic Cárthaigh, and Caitríona Ó Dochartaigh, II:647–81. Aberystwyth: Celtic Studies Publications, 2014.

Waddell, John. *Archaeology and Celtic Myth*. Dublin: Four Courts Press, 2014.

———. "Celts, Celticisation and the Irish Bronze Age." In *Ireland in the Bronze Age: Proceedings of the Dublin Conference, April 1995*, edited by

John Waddell and Elizabeth Shee Twohig, 158–69. Dublin: The Stationery Office, 1995.

———. "Rathcroghan—A Royal Site in Connacht." *Journal of Irish Archaeology* 1 (1983): 21–46.

Webster, Jane. "A Dirty Window on the Iron Age? Recent Developments in the Archaeology of Pre-Roman Celtic Religion." In *Understanding Celtic Religion: Revisiting the Pagan Past*, edited by Katja Ritari and Alexandra Bergholm, 121–54. Cardiff: University of Wales Press, 2015.

Wilde, Lady. *Ancient Legends Mystic Charms & Superstitions of Ireland*. London: Chatto & Windus, 1919.

Williams, Mark. *Ireland's Immortals: A History of the Gods of Irish Myth*. Princeton, New Jersey: Princeton University Press, 2016.

Wood-Martin, W.G. *Traces of the Elder Faiths of Ireland, Vol. I*. London: Longmans, Green, and Co., 1902.

———. *Traces of the Elder Faiths of Ireland, Vol. II*. London: Longmans, Green, and Co., 1902.

Wright, Thomas, Richard Colt Hoare, and Thomas Forester. *The Historical Works of Giraldus Cambrensis*. London: George Bell & Sons, 1863.

Zeidler, Jürgen. "Cults of the 'Celts': A New Approach to the Interpretation of the Religion of Iron Age Cultures." In *Interpretierte Eisenzeiten: Fallstudien, Methoden, Theorie*, edited by Raimund Karl and Jutta Leskovar, 171–79. Linz, 2005.

INDEX

b

C

d

Є

F

J

K

L

m

P

R

S

Y

TO WRITE TO THE AUTHOR

If you wish to contact the author or would like more information about this book, please write to the author in care of Llewellyn Worldwide Ltd. and we will forward your request. Both the author and publisher appreciate hearing from you and learning of your enjoyment of this book and how it has helped you. Llewellyn Worldwide Ltd. cannot guarantee that every letter written to the author can be answered, but all will be forwarded. Please write to:

Morpheus Ravenna
℅ Llewellyn Worldwide
2143 Wooddale Drive
Woodbury, MN 55125-2989
Please enclose a self-addressed stamped envelope for reply, or $1.00 to cover costs. If outside the U.S.A., enclose an international postal reply coupon.

Many of Llewellyn's authors have websites with additional information and resources. For more information, please visit our website at
http://www.llewellyn.com